GW00726025

CHARTERED INSTITUTE FOR
SECURITIES & INVESTMENT

Certificate in Risk in Financial Services

Risk in Financial Services

Edition 7, May 2018

This learning manual relates to syllabus
version 7.0 and will cover examinations from
11 August 2018 to 10 August 2020

APPROVED WORKBOOK

Welcome to the Chartered Institute for Securities & Investment's Risk in Financial Services study material.

This manual has been written to prepare you for the Chartered Institute for Securities & Investment's Risk in Financial Services examination.

Published by:
Chartered Institute for Securities & Investment
© Chartered Institute for Securities & Investment 2018
20 Fenchurch Street
London
EC3M 3BY
Tel: +44 20 7645 0600
Fax: +44 20 7645 0601

Email: customersupport@cisi.org
www.cisi.org/qualifications

Author:
Andrew Brand BSc(Econ), MBA
Risk Consultant, Financial Risk Training Ltd

Reviewers:
Dr. Robert Webb
Yulia Sharipova, MCSI

A learning map, which contains the full syllabus, appears at the end of this manual. The syllabus can also be viewed on cisi.org and is also available by contacting the Customer Support Centre on +44 20 7645 0777. Please note that the examination is based upon the syllabus. Candidates are reminded to check the Candidate Update area details (cisi.org/candidateupdate) on a regular basis for updates as a result of industry change(s) that could affect their examination.

The questions contained in this manual are designed as an aid to revision of different areas of the syllabus and to help you consolidate your learning chapter by chapter.

Learning manual version: 7.1 (May 2018)

Learning and Professional Development with the CISI

The Chartered Institute for Securities & Investment is the leading professional body for those who work in, or aspire to work in, the investment sector, and we are passionately committed to enhancing knowledge, skills and integrity – the three pillars of professionalism at the heart of our Chartered body.

CISI examinations are used extensively by firms to meet the requirements of government regulators. Besides the regulators in the UK, where the CISI head office is based, CISI examinations are recognised by a wide range of governments and their regulators, from Singapore to Dubai and the US. Around 50,000 examinations are taken each year, and it is compulsory for candidates to use CISI workbooks to prepare for CISI examinations so that they have the best chance of success. Our workbooks are normally revised every year by experts who themselves work in the industry and also by our Accredited Training Partners, who offer training and elearning to help prepare candidates for the examinations. Information for candidates is also posted on a special area of our website: cisi.org/candidateupdate.

This workbook not only provides a thorough preparation for the examination it refers to, it is also a valuable desktop reference for practitioners, and studying from it counts towards your Continuing Professional Development (CPD). Mock examination papers, for most of our titles, will be made available on our website, as an additional revision tool.

CISI examination candidates are automatically registered, without additional charge, as student members for one year (should they not be members of the CISI already), and this enables you to use a vast range of online resources, including CISI TV, free of any additional charge. The CISI has more than 40,000 members, and nearly half of them have already completed relevant qualifications and transferred to a core membership grade. You will find more information about the next steps for this at the end of this workbook.

It is estimated that this manual will require approximately 100 hours of study time.

What next?
See the back of this book for details of CISI membership.

Need more support to pass your exam?
See our section on Accredited Training Partners and CISI elearning at the back of this book.

Want to leave feedback?
Please email your comments to learningresources@cisi.org

Chapter One
Principles of Risk Management

This syllabus area will provide approximately 12 of the 100 examination questions

Chapter Summary

Learning Objectives

1.1.1   Understand the processes typically used to identify, reduce and manage specific aspects of risk

This first chapter provides an introduction to **risk** and describes the specific risks that financial services firms face. Every business faces risks that present threats to its success. In its broadest sense, risk is defined as the possible harm associated with a situation – the product of impact and probability.

Risk management is the practice of using **processes**, methods and tools for quantifying and managing these risks and uncertainties.

An important aspect of the financial services sector is the management of **financial risk** on behalf of both customers and owners. To discuss the risks faced by a financial services firm is, therefore, to address one of the core reasons for its existence. For risk management practitioners, that is what gives the disciplines within risk management their importance – and their intellectual appeal.

The basic concepts are not difficult to grasp, as will be seen as we progress through this workbook, but understanding their interrelationship is sometimes less straightforward.

The diagram below shows a financial services firm – for example an asset manager, broker or bank – in the context of the risk environment within which it operates. Detailed definitions will be provided as we meet each element in its relevant chapter, but an initial overview will help to set the scene.

Risk in Financial Services

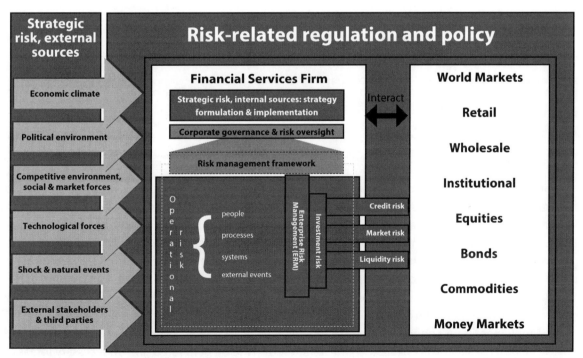

© Andrew Brand

1. **Credit, market and liquidity risks** – these are at the centre of the diagram because the management of these risks lies at the heart of the complex financial transactions performed by the industry. These transactions include:
    - increasing the long-term wealth of investors and entrepreneurs by making investors' assets available to those in the global economy who can put them to best, most productive, use
    - enabling long-term mortgages and corporate or sovereign financing using short-term sources of funding, such as retail deposits
    - providing the payment and safe-keeping mechanisms that underpin a modern wealth-creating economy.
2. **Investment risk** – the credit, market and liquidity risks referred to above are managed for the benefit of the firm – its owners and clients. Many of these clients are investors whose funds are managed by the firm. We refer to the combination of risks involved in providing the 'right' level of return to these investors as 'investment risk'.
3. **Operational risk** – the act of managing credit, market, liquidity and investment risk is itself subject to a different set of risks. These emerge from the people, processes, systems and external events that the firm needs to manage in running its business. These are four key factors that are collectively referred to as operational risk.
4. **Enterprise risk** – understanding the different risks to which a financial services firm is subject is key to its success and, therefore, risk information is regularly reported up the chain of command. Separate reporting mechanisms have traditionally been used for the separate risk types but, increasingly, firms find it useful to group the risk types together and report on them collectively. This provides the 'risk equivalent' of the firm's accounting tools, where the balance sheet, profit and loss account, and cash flow statement enable a focused view of the firm's finances. Enterprise risk management is a method of providing the firm with a succinct view of all its key risk information, thus enabling the senior team to make balanced, firm-wide risk decisions.
5. **Strategic risk (internal)** – the firm does not exist in isolation, and interacts not only with global financial markets, but also with the 'real' economy. These interactions with the real economy give rise to the sorts of strategic risks that every firm faces, regardless of its industry. Some of the more important internal drivers of strategic risk stem from:
    - a firm's chosen strategy
    - translation and execution of the firm's strategy into its business (or operational) model
    - its financial management
    - its internal compliance with externally imposed regulation and laws.
6. **Strategic risk (external)** – arises from unforeseen changes in:
    - the global economy
    - the political arena
    - the competitive environment
    - social and market forces
    - technological innovation.
7. **Corporate governance and risk oversight** – within the organisation there are both tactical and strategic risk-takers. The strategic risk-takers – chief executive officer (CEO), directors and senior managers – formulate a strategy for the firm that requires certain risks to be taken, and others expressly to be avoided. They communicate the strategy to the traders, asset managers and research analysts, whose job it is to manage the tactical risks involved in implementing it. For this communication process to function properly, and to enable the strategic risk-takers to monitor the subsequent progress in the strategy's implementation, there needs to be a set of robust processes for:
    - ensuring that the firm is properly governed to formulate and implement the strategy
    - implementing a coherent firm-wide risk framework to enable oversight of the strategic and tactical risks that will enable the anticipated returns to be generated and unnecessary losses or impairment of the company's value to be minimised.

Having gained an understanding of the broad spectrum of risks to which financial services firms are potentially exposed, and the underlying drivers of each type, a firm needs to address the various ways in which the actual risks it faces can be managed. A 'risk register' of risk types (eg, operational) and specific risks (eg, failure of the customer relationship management system) is compiled and used by firms so that the risks and the associated mitigating actions and controls can be understood, owned and monitored.

The firm then needs to decide how much risk it is willing to take, a concept known as risk appetite, and make sure that this appetite is not exceeded, through the use of formal controls and high-quality risk reporting. In addition to controls and risk reporting, the so-called risk culture of the firm also plays a key role in enabling the risk appetite set by the board to be understood and adhered to at all levels of the organisation.

1. Introduction to Risk in Business

1.1 Risk Management, Risk and Uncertainty

Learning Objectives

1.1.2 Understand the key elements of risk management and the differences between risk and uncertainty

Risk is generally discussed as if it were synonymous with uncertainty, but there is a technical distinction between the two. Variability that can be quantified in terms of probabilities is best thought of as risk; but variability that cannot be quantified at all is best thought of simply as 'uncertainty'.

However, to quantify an event's probability of occurring, we need large amounts of observable, repeating data that can be grouped and analysed. This sort of data is available for credit and market risk analysis, and information mining and other 'big data' techniques can be applied to it with useful consequences. However, strategic or operational risks, by their very nature, have much less 'repeatable' data because strategic and operational risk events are often unique.

Nevertheless, this technical difference between risk and uncertainty should not prevent firms from protecting themselves against the negative consequences of less quantifiable events.

Risk management focuses on identifying what could go wrong, evaluating which risks should be dealt with and implementing strategies to address those risks. Firms that have identified their risks 'in advance' and have formulated a response plan will be better prepared and have a more cost-effective way of dealing with them if they do occur.

A Simple Framework for Managing Risk

As shown in the following diagram, the key elements of a simple risk framework are:

- Risk policies and governance at board level (this is covered in chapter 9 on Risk Oversight and Corporate Governance).
- Risk oversight – often performed by a dedicated risk management function or functions, often organised by risk type and performing the following tasks:
  - identify risks
  - assess risks
  - ensure that risks are appropriately controlled
  - monitor and report on the risks and their associated controls.
- Day-to-day risk management – this activity is inseparable from good business management and must be owned by the business units, not the risk function.

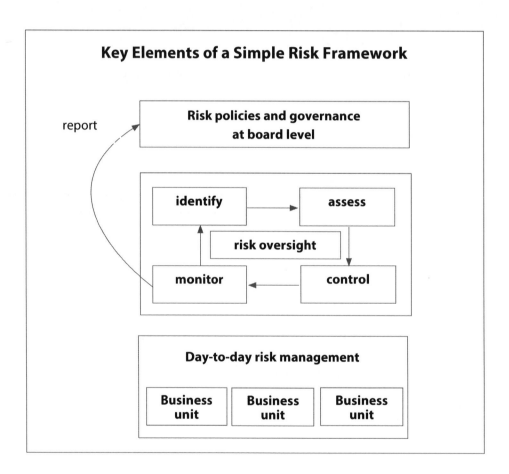

© Andrew Brand

1.2 External Sources of Risk

Learning Objective

1.1.3 Know the key external sources of risk and their potential impact on a business: economic; political; competitive environment, social and market forces; technological including cyber security; shocks and natural events; external stakeholders and third parties

As described in the chapter summary, external risks arise from unforeseen changes in:

- the global economy
- the political arena
- the competitive environment
- social and market forces, and
- technological and cyber security.

Further external risks are also posed by unexpected shocks and natural events, and by the actions of external stakeholders and third parties.

1.2.1 Economic Risk

The economy, in its simplest terms, consists of the interaction between individuals and firms, and the allocation of their limited resources to maximise their financial positions. In other words, the economy is shaped by human behaviour, whether as individual consumers or as collectively arranged organisations.

Therefore, a firm has to understand the current and potential future patterns of human behaviour that will affect the products or services it sells. For example, during an economic boom, a failure to anticipate an imminent downturn will result in firms continuing to increase their stocks using current input prices of raw materials. They will then find they need to reduce the prices of their finished goods to sell them in a recession. Equally, financial services firms with securitised mortgages on their books will find it difficult to sell them if there is a fall in house prices.

1.2.2 Political Risk

Wealth creation and its distribution tend to be viewed in different ways by different political parties. Therefore, a change in government will generally affect the financial services sector and may be the cause of a rise, or fall, in the markets. This will depend upon the economic strategies that commentators expect the new leadership to implement.

Other political events, such as changes in economic policy, or tax law, will also affect the financial services sector. Political changes, being so closely linked to the economy, can affect financial services firms in three main ways:

1. A rise or fall in the markets in which firms invest.
2. An increase or decrease in demand for the products which the industry sells.
3. Changes to the legislative and regulatory environment in which financial services firms operate.

1.2.3 Risks from the Competitive Environment, Social and Market Forces

Firms are affected by the performance of other companies, especially those operating in related industries and markets. For example, if a competitor gains a critical mass of market share, it may become too expensive for some of the other firms to continue servicing the remaining customers. This will force one or more of them to exit that part of the market. On the other hand, if a close competitor fails, there may be scope to buy parts of their business at below their market price.

Firms in the finance sector are also particularly susceptible to certain changes in social and market forces, such as:

* the propensity to save
* attitudes to living on credit
* house prices and their relationship to demographic changes.

1.2.4 Technological and Cyber Security Risk

The development of new technology is behind many of the increases in productivity that create economic growth.

The availability of fast and efficient telecommunications has enabled new ways of reaching customers and organising internal resources. In the past, workers may have had to relocate to where employers delivered their services. Now, a firm can 'outsource' customer communication functions to lower-cost overseas locations.

Information management has also changed – both in terms of firms making use of consumer data, and consumers gaining access to more information about products and services. Firms that do not anticipate or keep up with technological change run the risk of becoming obsolete.

These advances have also brought new threats that are collectively referred to as cyber risk. Cyber risk covers a broad range of risks that are related to the theft of, or damage to, information stored on (or exchanged between) computers, as well as the systems and websites that run on those computers. Whole new disciplines, such as information and cyber security, have emerged to counter these risks and the UK government has published a set of helpful guidelines on cyber threat management.

These guidelines make it clear that, just as with other corporate risks, cyber risks need to be managed proactively by the board, led by senior management and assured by corporate governance.

The following three-part model for managing cyber risk is suggested, and is set out in terms of simple questions which a board should consider:

1. **Make protecting the firm's information a board responsibility**
   * Has the board agreed what information assets are critical to the business?
   * Has the board decided its appetite for risk with regard to these assets?
   * Is the board proactively managing these risks?

2. **Implement an information risk management regime**
    - Has the board ensured that the firm's existing risk management regime encompasses information and cyber risk?
    - Has the board implemented appropriate security policies and controls?
    - Does the board maintain an up-to-date awareness of threats and vulnerabilities?
3. **Gain assurance that the information risk management regime is effective**
    - Has the board assured itself that the right information and cyber risks for its business are being managed?
    - Has the board implemented the right security controls at the right pace to meet these risks?
    - Is the board regularly testing, monitoring and reviewing the firm's security controls?

More detail on cyber defences is given in chapter 3, Operational Risk.

1.2.5   Shocks and Natural Events

Shocks or natural events in one part of a country have the potential to adversely affect the national, or even the global, economy. For example, in 2010, the eruption of the Eyjafjallajökull volcano in Iceland, caused enormous disruption to air travel across western and northern Europe. During April and May that year, approximately 10 million travellers were affected as many countries closed their airspace to commercial jet traffic. The International Air Transport Association stated that the total loss for the airline industry was around US$1.7 billion.

Industries beyond air transport were also affected. The car maker, BMW, had to suspend production at three of its German plants because of interruptions to its supply chain. There were also knock-on effects beyond Europe. For example, food exports from Africa were impacted, with farmers being forced to dump stocks of fresh food and flowers destined for European markets. Economic disruption was even felt in the US, 4,000 miles from Iceland. The Coachella Music Festival is one of the largest in the world and, in 2017, was attended by 250,000 people, grossing US$115 million. Ticket refunds were necessary in 2010 when British artist Gary Numan had to cancel because of the disruption to air travel caused by the volcano.

1.2.6   Risks from Stakeholders and Third Parties

External stakeholders that can present external risks typically include a firm's parent company, any major institutional investors and any particularly large or important customers.

1. **The parent company**
    - Where the parent owns more than one business it will take a 'global view' and this, at times, may cause it to question or alter the plans of its subsidiary firms.
    - Unless parent firm expectations are carefully managed during the formulation of the plans, this can cause great inconvenience to the subsidiary firm. Quite often, by the time the plans are ready to be shared with the parent, staff may have been hired and external research may have been commissioned. Key customers may even have been consulted as part of the planning process.
2. **Significant holdings by institutional investors**
    Institutional shareholders that own more than a certain percentage of a firm's shares gain influence through voting rights. If these stakeholders have different views on, for example, the competence of certain board members, then in some cases there may be little that the firm can do to prevent them pushing for change.

3. **Large customers**

    If a firm has an over-reliance on a particular customer, then that relationship clearly needs to be carefully managed. This is particularly important, as there are often other firms in the industry that could provide the same services to this customer. Over the longer term, the firm should aim to dilute this risk by increasing its customer base.

The key to managing stakeholder risk is to:

- build relationships at senior levels
- understand their agenda and how it may differ from the firm's own agenda
- manage expectations with any new developments.

Other third parties that can also be a source of external risk might include:

- regulators
- brokers
- solicitors
- IT and data suppliers
- outsourced back-office administrators
- advisors/industry consultants.

It will be important for the firm to ensure that, where possible, it can source equivalent goods and services from alternative suppliers. That way, if a third party defaults or delays delivery, there should be no service interruption to the firm's customers.

1.3 Assessing External Sources of Risk

Learning Objective

1.1.4   Understand how the key external sources of risk are typically assessed

A number of different techniques are used to arrive at an understanding of a firm's external risk profile. Here are some examples.

1.3.1 PESTLE Analysis

This is an analysis of the external macro environment in which a business operates. This environment will inevitably contain factors which are beyond the firm's control or influence, but which are, nevertheless, important to be aware of when developing new products, businesses or strategies. PESTLE analysis is often performed as a brainstorm with internal and external experts.

Risks are considered under the following headings:

- **P**olitical
- **E**conomic
- **S**ocial
- **T**echnological
- **L**egal
- **E**nvironmental.

1.3.2 Business Continuity Planning

This will be considered further in chapter 3 on Operational Risk, but the act of planning for disaster recovery and business continuity will itself uncover a number of external risk factors.

1.3.3 Business Process Analysis

This involves:

- examining each high-level business process
- describing both the internal low-level processes and external factors which can influence those processes.

1.4 Internal Drivers of Risk

Learning Objective

1.1.5   Know the key internal drivers of risk: strategic; operational; financial

1.4.1 Strategic Risk

The European Banking Authority (EBA) defines **strategic risk** as: *'the current or prospective risk to earnings and capital arising from changes in the business environment and from adverse business decisions, improper implementation of decisions or lack of responsiveness to changes in the business environment'.*

In simple terms then, strategic risk takes two forms:

1. Is the strategy right?
   - Producing the wrong strategy can be one of the most serious mistakes a board can make.
2. Is the strategy being properly implemented?
   - Failing to implement even the best of strategies may also lead a firm to extinction.
   - Does the board know whether, and how well, its strategy is being implemented?
   - If the strategy is not implemented, is this because the firm is being run by inexperienced or lax management? Or is the strategy so complex that it is simply not possible to implement it?

1.4.2 Operational Risk

There is a degree of overlap between general business risk and specific operational risk. The latter is defined by the Bank for International Settlements (BIS) as *'the risk of loss resulting from inadequate or failed internal processes, people and systems or from external events'* and will be dealt with in detail in Chapter 3 on Operational Risk.

1.4.3 Financial Risk

The main risk types – commonly referred to as 'financial risks' – are credit, market and liquidity risks.

Credit risk is the risk of loss caused by the failure of a counterparty or issuer to meet its obligation and is addressed in more detail in chapter 4.

Market risk is the risk of loss arising from changes in the value of financial instruments and is addressed in more detail in chapter 5.

Liquidity risk is the risk that a firm has insufficient cash to meet its cash obligations and will either become insolvent, or will suffer losses from borrowing, selling assets at below market price, or paying contractual penalties. This is dealt with in more detail in chapter 7.

1.5 Assessing Internal Drivers of Risk

Learning Objective

1.1.6   Understand how the key internal drivers of risk are typically assessed

The internal drivers of risk (strategic; operational; financial) are assessed through a combination of techniques. These will be met as we explore each risk type in its relevant chapter, but they typically include:

- **Risk assessment workshops** – going through the firm's corporate goals, processes or products to bring out the risk factors that could prevent their successful implementation or continuation.
- **Discussion with external auditors** – having audited this and other firms means that the external auditors are often well placed to give advice on potential areas of risk that their auditing activities would not require them to focus on.
- **Stress testing** – varying one input factor at a time; for example, observing the difference that variations in the costs of capital across different business units might make.
- **Scenario analysis** – constructing realistic scenarios, perhaps based on past extreme events, which can be used to ask questions of the current situation. For example, the assumptions of a business plan could be analysed by applying the conditions from a previous major IT failure, and observing the effect on the plan's break-even point if customer payments could not be made on time.

1.6 The Nature of External and Internal Risk

Learning Objective

1.1.7   Understand the overlapping and interactive nature of external and internal risk drivers

Although we have discussed **business risk** from internal and external angles, in reality there is often an overlap between the two. External forces very often give rise to internal risks, and so these interacting external and internal risk drivers will need to be addressed simultaneously.

A good example of this is the development and launch of new products. There are internal risks involved – strategic, operational, compliance (covered in chapter 9 on Risk Oversight and Corporate Governance) and financial – and also several external risks, especially the economic climate and the competitive environment.

The following methods are typically used to reduce the levels of business risk associated with developing and launching new products:

- a gap analysis of the firm's strategy
- market surveys to establish external demand for potential new products
- market research to understand any similar products already being sold by competitors
- research and development to design the new product
- liaison with external stakeholders, such as the regulator
- 'test marketing' to fine-tune the product and its launch.

1.7 Additional Risk Terminology

Learning Objective

1.1.8   Understand the following risk concepts: risk culture and conduct risk; risk appetite; inherent (gross) risk; residual (net) risk; risk profile; risk mitigation

1.7.1 Risk Culture and Conduct Risk

Risk culture can be defined as the system of values and behaviours present throughout an organisation that shape risk decisions. Risk culture influences the decisions of management and employees, even if they are not consciously weighing risks and benefits.

We will consider risk culture and its determining factors more fully in chapter 9 on Risk Oversight and Corporate Governance, but the key features of a healthy risk culture are:

- the attitude to risk and ethics of the board and senior team
- the effectiveness with which these attitudes and ethics are communicated throughout the firm
- the degree to which risk is formally considered during decision-making
- the extent to which incentive schemes reinforce good risk management.

One specific manifestation of a poor risk culture is a situation where the firm enriches itself at the expense of its customers, rather than in pursuit of good customer outcomes. This is known as **conduct risk** which is defined as *'the risk that the firm's behaviour will result in poor outcomes for customers'*. The concern is that, left to their own devices, a firm's structures, processes and management culture and incentives will move away from putting the customer first and towards putting profit first, even at the expense of sub-optimal customer outcomes. Firms need to be constantly vigilant in ensuring that they consider customer outcomes when designing management incentives.

As well as a poor risk culture there are also inherent market factors that can interact to produce poor choices and outcomes in financial markets and thus contribute to conduct risk. These inherent factors are driven by market failures, such as a lack of available decision-making information, and often exacerbated by low financial capability among consumers.

1.7.2   Risk Appetite

Risk appetite is the type and amount of risk that a firm is willing to accept in the pursuit of its business objectives.

In the 'risk versus uncertainty' discussion above, we considered the differences in the amount of data available for assessing the likelihood of credit and market risk losses compared to that which is available for assessing the likelihood of strategic and operational risk losses. Risk appetite will need to be expressed in different ways for different risk types, to reflect the relative ease of assigning probabilities to the losses caused by each type.

For example, for more easily quantifiable risks the risk policy might include:

- an appetite level for direct financial loss, or
- specific risk measures, such as credit or market Value-at-Risk (VaR) metrics (covered in chapters 4 and 5 on Credit Risk and Market Risk).

For less easily quantifiable risks, the policy might specify non-financial statements, such as:

Our business continuity plans ensure that, following the loss of our main premises, the firm will re-open for business within eight hours.

The firm has no appetite for misselling risk. All external communications must be approved by the head of marketing.

At the group level, the firm will need to tie its overall risk profile, which in effect is its current default risk appetite, to its level of available risk capital. This will be dealt with further in chapter 10 on Enterprise Risk Management (ERM).

Setting a risk appetite tends to be an iterative process, and often needs both a top-down and a bottom-up approach.

The top-down approach involves the board and senior management:

- identifying threats to the firm's objectives
- relating them to the 'coverage' available from the firm's capital/earnings/assets, and

- recognising that holding capital is not always the best mitigant for every risk, and using scenario analysis (covered in chapter 3 on Operational Risk) to enable appropriate responses to be devised for each threat.

The bottom-up approach requires line management to adopt:

- a set of departmental 'acceptable occurrence' levels for errors and losses
- an appropriate set of key risk indicators which can be tracked against pre-defined appetites (see chapter 3 on Operational Risk).

The escalation mechanism for appetite breaches also needs to be defined so that the bottom-up approach can be linked to the top-down approach.

1.7.3 Inherent (Gross) Risk

Inherent risk, also called gross risk, is an assessment of risk without considering the beneficial effects of mitigating controls. This is an important step in the assessment process because, when controls fail, the firm is exposed to the gross risk. The gross risk will not necessarily be the maximum possible risk; a control can fail but the efforts of staff, and their honesty, will often tend to 'keep the show on the road'.

An example that is sometimes used to illustrate this concept is of someone accidentally leaving a reasonable sum of money on a desk in the office. Despite there being no controls in place to prevent it from being stolen, it will not automatically be taken, because people do not always act dishonestly. Equally, staff will often work diligently around shortcomings or failings of their IT systems.

1.7.4 Residual (Net) Risk

Residual risk, also referred to as net risk, is the firm's exposure after having taken mitigating controls into account. The net risk may not be zero because getting to that point might be too expensive or, in some instances, not even possible.

1.7.5 Risk Profile

A firm's **risk profile** is made up of the type and intensity of the risks to which it is exposed. It consists of the nature of the threats faced by an organisation, the likelihood of adverse effects occurring, and the level of disruption and costs associated with each type of risk.

1.7.6 Risk Mitigation

Depending on the risk type, mitigation techniques may include:

- ensuring that appropriate insurance policies are in place
- upgrading processes and IT systems to control an operational risk better
- hedging against a market risk
- holding collateral against a credit risk when lending to a third party: an asset belonging to that party is held by the lender so that if the borrower cannot repay the loan, the lender can liquidate the asset. This asset is known as collateral.

In other words, risk mitigation refers to the efforts made to reduce either the impact or the likelihood of the risk, or both.

1.8   How Risk Management Protects and Adds Value

Learning Objective

1.1.9   Understand how risk management protects and adds value to an organisation and its stakeholders

When firms embark on new areas of business, or launch new products, they very often justify the strategy with a cost/benefit analysis. This analysis compares the estimated likely revenues with the actual costs. If the former outweigh the latter then the project is given the green light.

However, the potential risk that the firm will incur as a result of this new business or product is sometimes overlooked by the business sponsor. Certain risks, such as client litigation, can vastly overshadow the operational costs of supporting the venture.

If risk management staff are involved in the process from the start, they will be able to advise on the likelihood and impact of any risks. Ideally, this would take place at an early enough stage that mitigation can be built into the solution. Over time, this approach will protect and add value to the firm.

In addition to launching new initiatives, a commitment to good risk management will also reduce the likelihood of unexpected outcomes on a day-to-day basis. This in turn will tend to reduce earnings volatility and therefore enhance the firm's share price.

A reduction in the likelihood of unexpected outcomes also benefits the firm's stakeholders – customers receive a more consistent service, regulators view the firm as a more predictable entity, and the firm's reputation is not damaged in the marketplace through unwelcome bad publicity.

2.   Specific Risks in Financial Services

2.1   Risk in Financial Services

Learning Objective

1.2.1   Know the specific key risks in financial services as defined by the Bank for International Settlements

The Bank for International Settlements (BIS) defines the following specific key areas of risk within financial services.

2.1.1   Operational Risk

This is the risk of loss resulting from inadequate or failed internal processes, people and systems or from external events.

2.1.2   Credit Risk

This is the risk of loss caused by the failure of a counterparty or issuer to meet its obligations. This risk is present to some extent in all parts of the industry, although it is most important in banks because lending, where credit risk management is crucial, remains their core activity and loans make up the bulk of their assets.

2.1.3   Market and Asset Liquidity Risks

Market risk is the risk of loss arising from changes in the value of financial instruments. Asset liquidity risk is clearly allied with market risk and represents the risk that an entity will be unable to unwind a position in a particular financial instrument at, or near, its market value because of a lack of depth or disruption in the market for that instrument.

2.1.4   Funding Liquidity Risk

Funding liquidity risk is the risk that a firm cannot obtain the necessary funds to meet its obligations as they fall due.

2.1.5   Interest Rate Risk

Interest rate risk is the exposure of a firm's financial condition to adverse movements in interest rates. Interest rate risk arises through some specific products with fixed rates or, more generally, because the overall structure of the firm's **balance sheet** creates an interest rate exposure.

2.2   Identifying and Managing Systemic Risk within Financial Services

Learning Objective

1.2.2   Understand the nature of systemic risk and recovery and resolution planning within financial services

Because of the tight interactions between firms across the whole financial services sector, risks that affect one firm, or a group of firms, can affect the stability of the whole financial system. This is known as contagion and it causes systemic risk. Examples of this phenomenon include the widespread run on US banks in the early 1930s after the Wall Street Crash, and the liquidity crisis that started in 2007 and then developed into a global credit crisis in 2008–09.

If depositors ever fear that a bank might fail, then that fear, even if ill-founded, causes them to withdraw their deposits en masse. This can actually cause a bank to fail, leaving insufficient funds to repay other depositors who had not been as quick to withdraw their cash. We explain further in chapter 2 how this risk has been reduced through the introduction of **deposit insurance** schemes.

Despite belonging to the same industry, non-bank financial institutions, such as securities trading firms and investment managers, perform very different roles from banks. With the failure of an investment manager, there may be no client loss at all, and the value of money circulating in the system remains unchanged. On the other hand, a bank failure can have implications not only for client deposits, but also for the international payment systems.

Therefore, regulators treat banks differently from other firms, often working with national governments to keep a troubled bank operating but allowing a troubled securities firm or investment manager to fail. However, when national governments take on the debts and other obligations of their banks, a new risk is created called sovereign default risk. If a country assumes a commitment such as guaranteeing its banking system, but has insufficient funds itself to honour that commitment then, in extremis, that country may default on its government-issued bonds.

A key challenge for regulators in managing systemic risk is the fact that it may be highest when individual firms' measured risk is lowest, since low measured risk encourages behaviour which creates increased systemic risks.

In recognition of the systemic risk inherent within financial services, regulators, in jurisdictions such as the UK, require banks and larger investment firms to construct and maintain what are called recovery and resolution plans which lay out:

1. *'credible recovery actions that the firm could implement in the event of a severe stress to restore its business to a stable and sustainable condition'*, and
2. the mechanism by which any absolute failure within the firm can be enacted in an orderly fashion.

This means, from the regulator's point of view, that, in the event of failure, *'it will be feasible to resolve that firm without severe systemic disruption and without exposing taxpayers to loss, while protecting vital economic functions and imposing losses on bank creditors'*.

2.3 Comparing Risk in Financial Services With Other Industries

We began this chapter with a diagram showing the types of risks which affect financial services firms. Of these, strategic and operational risks affect most industries, not just the finance sector.

As shown in the following diagram, the remaining risks – liquidity, market, credit and investment – also affect other industries to a greater or lesser extent, but they are inherent to the business of firms in the financial services sector.

© Andrew Brand

The combination of the following characteristics of the financial services sector tends to set it apart from other industries:

- complexity
- no physical product
- product life span often measured in decades
- not an 'optional extra' but a necessity of modern economic systems.

So, although strategic and operational risks do indeed affect all industries, there are, nevertheless, some that affect the financial services sector in particular; we will consider these as we meet them throughout the rest of this workbook.

End of Chapter Questions

Think of an answer for each question and refer to the appropriate section for confirmation.

1.   What is the difference between risk and uncertainty?
     Answer reference: Section 1.1

2.   Within a simple risk framework, which key activities would normally be carried out at board level?
     Answer reference: Section 1.1

3.   What are the three main ways in which political change can affect the financial services sector?
     Answer reference: Section 1.2.2

4.   Risks can arise from external stakeholders, such as a parent company. Name two other external stakeholders that can also be a source of risk for a business.
     Answer reference: Section 1.2

5.   What is the difference between gross (ie, inherent) risk and net (ie, residual) risk?
     Answer reference: Section 1.7

6.   What is meant by a firm's risk appetite?
     Answer reference: Section 1.7.2

7.   Why should risk management staff be involved in product development projects from a very early stage?
     Answer reference: Section 1.8

8.   What sort of risk is associated with contagion?
     Answer reference: Section 2.2

9.   Why might regulators strive to keep a troubled bank operating but allow an investment management firm to fail?
     Answer reference: Section 2.2

10. Give two examples from the last 80 years where high levels of systemic financial risk materialised and led to widespread harm to the economy?
     Answer reference: Section 2.2

Chapter Two
International Risk Regulation

This syllabus area will provide approximately 7 of the 100 examination questions

Chapter Summary

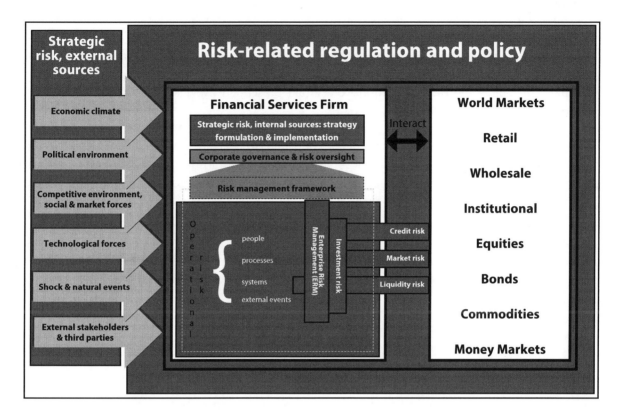

© Andrew Brand

In chapter 1 we used the diagram above to explore the risks faced by a financial services firm. The one area that was not addressed at the time was the border surrounding the firm itself and the markets with which it interacts. This is labelled 'risk-related regulation and policy' and is the subject of this chapter.

Individual countries, or groups of countries, impose a legal and regulatory regime on the firms operating within their jurisdiction; over recent years there have been increasing efforts to harmonise these regimes.

The Bank for International Settlements (BIS), based in Basel, Switzerland, is the main force behind this harmonisation, and so we will start by considering the international role it plays in financial regulation.

We will then look at the Basel Committee on Banking Supervision, which exists in order to enhance understanding of supervisory issues and improve the quality of banking supervision worldwide – a sort of 'regulators' regulator'. The Committee establishes standards on capital adequacy to ensure that banks have sufficient reserves to withstand specific levels of risk. A global standard helps to ensure a level playing field and prevents regulatory arbitrage at a national level – the amount of capital that a bank is required to hold has a major impact on the amount of credit which it can extend to customers and thus its level of profitability.

The capital adequacy requirements are grouped into three pillars:

- **Pillar 1** is a semi-formulaic approach to the calculation of the minimum level of capital which a firm should hold.
- **Pillar 2** enables the firm itself to offer its own view of the level of capital it should hold, and enables regulators to set the level which they think is most appropriate. In Europe and certain other countries, Pillar 2 is known as ICAAP (Internal Capital Adequacy Assessment Process).
- **Pillar 3** is simply the public disclosure of certain prescribed aspects of the firm's capital and approach to risk management.

The Basel Committee also establishes a set of core principles to which national regulators are expected to adhere in their interaction with financial services firms in their jurisdictions, including firms which operate in multiple jurisdictions. The core principles also extend to cover requirements for the governance and risk management of individual banks.

1.   The Bank for International Settlements (BIS)

1.1   Key Role of the Bank for International Settlements

Learning Objective

2.1.1   Understand the role of the Bank for International Settlements within the financial services industry

The Bank for International Settlements (BIS) is an organisation which serves as a bank for central banks, and fosters international monetary and financial cooperation. Its customers are central banks and international organisations; the BIS does not accept deposits from, or provide financial services to, private individuals or corporate entities.

Established in 1930, it is the world's oldest international financial organisation and provides a focal point for research and cooperation in international banking regulation – the 'regulators' regulator'. The headquarters of the BIS are in Basel, Switzerland.

The regulatory guidelines produced by the BIS do not have any force in national or international law, and countries around the world that choose to implement them do so by making changes to their own legal and regulatory processes.

1.2 Basel Committee

Learning Objective

2.1.2   Know the purposes for which the Basel Committee on Banking Supervision was established, and the drivers it introduced to calculate the capital adequacy of banks

The fundamental business of banking is to provide a safe means of storage for depositor funds, and to provide loans to businesses and individuals. The volume of cash deposits typically supports a larger volume of loans, which earn income for the banks. The reason why this method usually works is because depositors typically withdraw only a fraction of the total deposit at any given time. Capital adequacy is about having sufficient funds available to underpin the volume and quality of the loan portfolio and, more generally, any adverse movements in the value of the balance sheet.

Traditionally, the main risk for a bank was credit risk, through holding illiquid portfolios of loans supported by shorter-term deposits. In emergencies, loans could only be liquidated rapidly at discounted prices that would not provide enough capital to repay all depositors, and this placed banks at risk of runs – in other words, a situation where mass panic-driven demand to withdraw cash deposits cannot possibly be satisfied immediately. A run on a single bank can cause serious instability elsewhere in the financial system if depositors lose faith in banks in general, even healthy ones, and begin trying to withdraw their deposits from across the industry.

In other words, if depositors ever feared that a bank *might* fail, then that fear, even if ill-founded, would cause them to withdraw their deposits en masse, resulting in the bank *actually* failing because it would not have the funds to repay all its depositors, having lent their money elsewhere. This would leave insufficient funds to repay depositors who had not been as quick to withdraw their cash. The spread of this fear is called 'contagion'. It leads to a phenomenon known as 'systemic risk', which, if left unchecked, can bring down the entire banking industry.

After the 1929 Wall Street Crash in the US, deposit insurance and central bank '**lender-of-last-resort**' provisions were introduced, to reduce the risk of future bank runs. However, these provisions in turn caused a new problem: moral hazard (see chapter 9 on Risk Oversight and Corporate Governance). Depositors no longer had an incentive to consider a bank's financial viability before depositing funds and, without such market discipline, further regulation was required.

One solution was to require banks to hold a minimum level of capital. This, in simple terms, would prevent them from lending out every last penny, so that, even if certain loans were not repaid to the bank, it could still pay back its depositors.

Banks, therefore, need to consider two types of capital when running their businesses: economic and regulatory. Economic capital is a bank's best estimate of the capital it needs to manage its own risk profile. Regulatory capital is a mandatory level of capital which a regulator requires a bank to hold. Both types of capital require comprehensive measurement systems in order to calculate the level, but unless banks use standard measurement approaches, it is very difficult for regulators to compare levels across the global industry.

1.2.1 International Standards on Capital Adequacy

The Basel Committee on Banking Supervision (BCBS) is the primary global standard-setter for the **prudential regulation** of banks and provides a forum for cooperation on banking supervisory matters. Its mandate is to strengthen the regulation, supervision and practices of banks worldwide with the purpose of enhancing financial stability.

The Committee is concerned with banking regulation, but regulators in many jurisdictions, for example the UK, also apply a similar set of regulations to non-bank financial institutions such as investment management and securities firms. In other words, many of the banking regulations covered in the following sections may also apply, albeit in a modified form, to non-banks.

There was strong recognition within the Committee of the overriding need for a multinational accord to continually strengthen the stability of the international banking system and to remove a source of competitive inequality arising from differences in national capital requirements.

The Basel Accord stipulates the minimum capital ratios that should be maintained by banks in member countries. The minimum set of risks for which capital ratios are to be maintained are credit, market and operational risks. In other words, the greater the level of credit, market and operational risk within a firm, the more capital the firm should hold. In reality, as we will see below, other risk types are also subject to regulatory capital requirements but these tend to be firm-specific – whereas the assumption within the Basel Accord is that all firms in the financial sector are subject to credit, market and operational risks.

In recent years, enhancements to the Accord (now known as Basel III) have introduced several concepts beyond capital ratios, including:

- a countercyclical capital buffer, which places restrictions on participation by banks in system-wide credit booms with the aim of reducing their losses in credit busts
- a leverage ratio – a minimum amount of loss-absorbing capital relative to all of a bank's assets and off-balance sheet exposures regardless of risk weighting, and
- a set of liquidity requirements/ratios.

1.3 International Standards and Guidelines

Learning Objective

2.1.3 Understand the high level international guidelines and supervisory standards established by the Basel Committee

The Committee seeks to achieve its aims by setting minimum standards for the regulation and supervision of banks; by sharing supervisory issues, approaches and techniques to promote common understanding and to improve cross-border cooperation; and by exchanging information on developments in the banking sector and financial markets to help identify current or emerging risks for the global financial system.

1.3.1 Core Principles for Effective Banking Supervision

The Committee's Core Principles for Effective Banking Supervision define the minimum benchmark for assessing the quality of global supervisory systems. They enable countries who wish to sign up to the Basel Accord to identify any work necessary to achieve a baseline level of sound supervisory practices.

A series of national preconditions are also defined which provide a framework within which effective banking supervision can take place. The preconditions are:

1. Sound and sustainable macroeconomic policies.
2. A well-established framework for financial stability policy formulation.
3. A well-developed public infrastructure, including:
    - well-established private property laws and business laws
    - rules governing financial markets
    - well-regulated accounting, auditing and legal professions
    - efficient payment systems for the settlement of financial transactions to control counterparty risk
    - an efficient and independent judiciary.
4. A clear framework for financial crisis management, recovery and resolution.
5. Mechanisms for providing an appropriate level of systemic protection or public safety net.
6. Effective market discipline.

These preconditions, although mostly outside supervisors' direct control, do have a direct impact on the effectiveness of supervision in practice. This has become evident in recent years as regulators struggled to preserve financial stability after governments unwittingly violated the first of these preconditions by, for example, keeping interest rates unsustainably low in the early years of this century, thus encouraging banks to increase their lending. This, in turn, provided excess credit and liquidity that fuelled a series of asset prices bubbles. Once those bubbles burst, the resulting credit crunch of 2007 led to the global recession of 2008–09.

The 29 Core Principles for Effective Banking Supervision are categorised into seven groups, and have become the de facto global standard for sound regulation and supervision of banks:

Principles 1–13 address supervisory powers, responsibilities and functions, and Principles 14–29 cover supervisory expectations of banks, emphasising the importance of good corporate governance and risk management, as well as compliance with supervisory standards.

The 29 Core Principles are:

Supervisory powers, responsibilities and functions

Principle 1 – Responsibilities, objectives and powers:

- An effective system of banking supervision has clear responsibilities and objectives for each authority involved in the supervision of banks and banking groups.
- A suitable legal framework for banking supervision is in place to provide each responsible authority with the necessary legal powers to authorise banks, conduct ongoing supervision, address compliance with laws and undertake timely corrective actions to address safety and soundness concerns.

Principle 2 – Independence, accountability, resourcing and legal protection for supervisors:

- The supervisor possesses operational independence, transparent processes, sound governance, budgetary processes that do not undermine autonomy and adequate resources, and is accountable for the discharge of its duties and use of its resources.
- The legal framework for banking supervision includes legal protection for the supervisor.

Principle 3 – Cooperation and collaboration:

- Laws, regulations or other arrangements provide a framework for cooperation and collaboration with relevant domestic authorities and foreign supervisors.
- These arrangements reflect the need to protect confidential information.

Principle 4 – Permissible activities:

- The permissible activities of institutions that are licensed and subject to supervision as banks are clearly defined and the use of the word 'bank' in names is controlled.

Principle 5 – Licensing criteria:

- The licensing authority has the power to set criteria and reject applications for establishments that do not meet the criteria.
- At a minimum, the licensing process consists of an assessment of the ownership structure and governance (including the fitness and propriety of board members and senior management) of the bank and its wider group, and its strategic and operating plan, internal controls, risk management and projected financial condition (including capital base).
- Where the proposed owner or parent organisation is a foreign bank, the prior consent of its home supervisor is obtained.

Principle 6 – Transfer of significant ownership:

- The supervisor has the power to review, reject and impose prudential conditions on any proposals to transfer significant ownership or controlling interests held directly or indirectly in existing banks to other parties.

Principle 7 – Major acquisitions:

- The supervisor has the power to approve or reject (or recommend to the responsible authority the approval or rejection of), and impose prudential conditions on, major acquisitions or investments by a bank, against prescribed criteria, including the establishment of cross-border operations, and to determine that corporate affiliations or structures do not expose the bank to undue risks or hinder effective supervision.

Principle 8 – Supervisory approach:

- An effective system of banking supervision requires the supervisor to:
    - develop and maintain a forward-looking assessment of the risk profile of individual banks and banking groups, proportionate to their systemic importance
    - identify, assess and address risks emanating from banks and the banking system as a whole
    - have a framework in place for early intervention, and
    - have plans in place, in partnership with other relevant authorities, to take action to resolve banks in an orderly manner if they become non-viable.

Principle 9 – Supervisory techniques and tools:

- The supervisor uses an appropriate range of techniques and tools to implement the supervisory approach and deploys supervisory resources on a proportionate basis, taking into account the risk profile and systemic importance of banks.

Principle 10 – Supervisory reporting:

- The supervisor collects, reviews and analyses prudential reports and statistical returns from banks on both a solo and a consolidated basis, and independently verifies these reports through either on-site examinations or use of external experts.

Principle 11 – Corrective and sanctioning powers of supervisors:

- The supervisor acts at an early stage to address unsafe and unsound practices or activities that could pose risks to banks or to the banking system.
- The supervisor has at its disposal an adequate range of supervisory tools to bring about timely corrective actions.
- This includes the ability to revoke the banking licence or to recommend its revocation.

Principle 12 – Consolidated supervision:

- An essential element of banking supervision is that the supervisor supervises the banking group on a consolidated basis, adequately monitoring and, as appropriate, applying prudential standards to all aspects of the business conducted by the banking group worldwide.

Principle 13 – Home-host relationships:

- Home and host supervisors of cross-border banking groups share information and cooperate for effective supervision of the group and group entities, and effective handling of crisis situations.
- Supervisors require the local operations of foreign banks to be conducted to the same standards as those required of domestic banks.

Prudential regulations and requirements

Principle 14 – Corporate governance:

- The supervisor determines that banks and banking groups have robust corporate governance policies and processes covering, for example:
  - strategic direction, group and organisational structure
  - control environment
  - responsibilities of the banks' Boards and senior management, and compensation.
- These policies and processes are commensurate with the risk profile and systemic importance of the bank.

Principle 15 – Risk management process:

- The supervisor determines that banks have a comprehensive risk management process (including effective Board and senior management oversight) to identify, measure, evaluate, monitor, report and control or mitigate all material risks on a timely basis and to assess the adequacy of their capital and liquidity in relation to their risk profile and market and macroeconomic conditions.
- This extends to development and review of contingency arrangements (including robust and credible recovery plans where warranted) that take into account the specific circumstances of the bank.
- The risk management process is commensurate with the risk profile and systemic importance of the bank.

Principle 16 – Capital adequacy:

- The supervisor sets prudent and appropriate capital adequacy requirements for banks that reflect the risks undertaken by, and presented by, a bank in the context of the markets and macroeconomic conditions in which it operates.
- The supervisor defines the components of capital, bearing in mind their ability to absorb losses.
- At least for internationally active banks, capital requirements are not less than the applicable Basel standards.

Principle 17 – Credit risk:

- The supervisor determines that banks have an adequate credit risk management process that takes into account their risk appetite, risk profile and market and macroeconomic conditions.
- This includes prudent policies and processes to identify, measure, evaluate, monitor, report and control or mitigate credit risk (including counterparty credit risk) on a timely basis.
- The full credit lifecycle is covered including credit underwriting, credit evaluation, and the ongoing management of the bank's loan and investment portfolios.

Principle 18 – Problem assets, provisions and reserves:

- The supervisor determines that banks have adequate policies and processes for the early identification and management of problem assets, and the maintenance of adequate provisions and reserves.

Principle 19 – Concentration risk and large exposure limits:

- The supervisor determines that banks have adequate policies and processes to identify, measure, evaluate, monitor, report and control or mitigate concentrations of risk on a timely basis.
- Supervisors set prudential limits to restrict bank exposures to single counterparties or groups of connected counterparties.

Principle 20 – Transactions with related parties:

- In order to prevent abuses arising in transactions with related parties and to address the risk of conflict of interest, the supervisor requires banks:
  ◦ to enter into any transactions with related parties on an arm's length basis
  ◦ to monitor these transactions
  ◦ to take appropriate steps to control or mitigate the risks, and
  ◦ to write off exposures to related parties in accordance with standard policies and processes.

Principle 21 – Country and transfer risks:

- The supervisor determines that banks have adequate policies and processes to identify, measure, evaluate, monitor, report and control or mitigate country risk and transfer risk in their international lending and investment activities on a timely basis.

Principle 22 – Market risks:

- The supervisor determines that banks have an adequate market risk management process that takes into account their risk appetite, risk profile, and market and macroeconomic conditions and the risk of a significant deterioration in market liquidity.
- This includes prudent policies and processes to identify, measure, evaluate, monitor, report and control or mitigate market risks on a timely basis.

Principle 23 – Interest rate risk in the banking book:

- The supervisor determines that banks have adequate systems to identify, measure, evaluate, monitor, report and control or mitigate interest rate risk in the banking book on a timely basis.
- These systems take into account the bank's risk appetite, risk profile and market and macroeconomic conditions.

Principle 24 – Liquidity risk:

- The supervisor sets prudent and appropriate liquidity requirements (which can include either quantitative or qualitative requirements or both) for banks that reflect the liquidity needs of the bank.
- The supervisor determines that banks have a strategy that enables prudent management of liquidity risk and compliance with liquidity requirements.
- The strategy takes into account the bank's risk profile as well as market and macroeconomic conditions and includes prudent policies and processes, consistent with the bank's risk appetite, to identify, measure, evaluate, monitor, report and control or mitigate liquidity risk over an appropriate set of time horizons.
- At least for internationally active banks, liquidity requirements are not lower than the applicable Basel standards.

Principle 25 – Operational risk:

- The supervisor determines that banks have an adequate operational risk management framework that takes into account their risk appetite, risk profile and market and macroeconomic conditions.
- This includes prudent policies and processes to identify, assess, evaluate, monitor, report and control or mitigate operational risk on a timely basis.

Principle 26 – Internal control and audit:

- The supervisor determines that banks have adequate internal control frameworks to establish and maintain a properly controlled operating environment for the conduct of their business taking into account their risk profile.
- These include:
  - clear arrangements for delegating authority and responsibility
  - separation of the functions that involve committing the bank, paying away its funds, and accounting for its assets and liabilities
  - reconciliation of these processes
  - safeguarding the bank's assets, and
  - appropriate independent internal audit and compliance functions to test adherence to these controls as well as applicable laws and regulations.

Principle 27: Financial reporting and external audit:

- The supervisor determines that banks and banking groups maintain adequate and reliable records, prepare financial statements in accordance with accounting policies and practices that are widely accepted internationally and annually publish information that fairly reflects their financial condition and performance and bears an independent external auditor's opinion.
- The supervisor also determines that banks and parent companies of banking groups have adequate governance and oversight of the external audit function.

Principle 28 – Disclosure and transparency:

- The supervisor determines that banks and banking groups regularly publish information on a consolidated and, where appropriate, solo basis that is easily accessible and fairly reflects their financial condition, performance, risk exposures, risk management strategies and corporate governance policies and processes.

Principle 29 – Abuse of financial services:

- The supervisor determines that banks have adequate policies and processes, including strict customer due diligence rules to promote high ethical and professional standards in the financial sector and prevent the bank from being used, intentionally or unintentionally, for criminal activities.

2. Basel Regulatory Capital

2.1 The Basel Accord

Learning Objective

2.2.1 Know the purpose, key features and implementation implications of Basel: Pillars 1, 2 and 3; Sound practice principles; Internal Capital Adequacy Assessment Process (ICAAP)

2.1.1 Pillars 1, 2 and 3

The Basel Accord aims to encourage improved risk management through the use of three mutually reinforcing pillars. These three pillars are:

Pillar 1: Minimum regulatory capital requirements – this involves applying 'formulaic' methods for calculating the regulatory capital.

In simple terms, the basic Pillar 1 capital requirement for banks can be expressed as:

$$\frac{\text{capital}}{\text{credit risk} + \text{market risk} + \text{operational risk}} > 8\%$$

Pillar 2: Supervisory review process – this involves firms submitting information, in addition to that contained within Pillar 1, to enable the regulator to assess the amount of capital that should be held. Typically this 'extra' information would be concerned with:

- risks not covered under Pillar 1
- the way that risk is managed
- the quality of the controls infrastructure
- the way in which the calculated risk profile relates to the strategic and financial plans of the firm.

Pillar 3: Market discipline – firms are required to publish information about the way they manage the risks they face.

2.1.2 Sound Practice Principles

From time to time, the Basel Committee publishes 'sound practice' documents giving guidance on different aspects of risk management. These cover areas such as:

- operational risk
- credit risk
- interest rate risk
- liquidity risk.

These principles provide practical guidance for firms – and specific areas for regulators to address as part of their supervisory role. From both perspectives, practitioners will benefit from familiarity with their content.

2.1.3 Pillar 2 Assessment: The Internal Capital Adequacy Assessment Process (ICAAP)

UK banks, and banks in many other jurisdictions, are required to establish an Internal Capital Adequacy Assessment Process (ICAAP), which is a formalised process for meeting the Basel Pillar 2 requirements and requires a firm to:

- assess its risks and their mitigants
- subject the results to rigorous stress testing
- determine an appropriate level of capital for those risks.

It requires firms to submit risk and capital information, in addition to that contained within Pillar 1, to enable the regulator to assess the amount of capital that should be held.

The Key Elements of the ICAAP Framework

The resulting document would typically contain the following sections:

The Firm's Risk Exposure

This provides a clear articulation of the firm's risk appetite by risk category, and the quantification of any risks not included in Pillar 1. These will clearly differ from firm to firm, but may include:

- credit, market and operational risks, where the firm wishes to calculate them differently from Pillar 1
- liquidity risk
- insurance risk
- concentration risk
- residual risk
- securitisation risk
- business (strategic) risk
- interest rate risk
- pension obligation risk.

The Firm's View on the Adequacy of its Risk Management Processes

This enables the firm to justify holding less capital than the gross risks to which it is exposed. The better the quality of the risk and controls framework, the lower the net risk exposures and therefore, the lower the capital that would need to be held.

The Firm's Financial and Capital Plans

This would include a summary of the current and projected financial and capital positions, including the strategic position of the firm, its balance sheet strength, and future profitability.

Stress and Scenario Tests Applied by the Firm to its Risks and Financial Plans

In attempting to understand complex interactions between financial data and risk data, two techniques are often used to separate out the different influences of the various input factors:

- **Stress testing** – varying one input factor at a time; for example, observing the difference that an increase in interest rates might make.
- **Scenario analysis** – constructing realistic scenarios, perhaps based on past extreme events, which can be used to ask questions of the current situation described by the data. For example, the assumptions of a business plan could be analysed by applying the conditions from a previous prolonged market fall, and observing the effect on the plan's break-even point.

Regulators expect that a firm's risks and financial plans will be stressed individually, and that realistic combinations of each will be tested as scenarios. For example, a standard test which the UK regulator has required since ICAAP was introduced is the effect of a prolonged economic downturn on market levels. These tests then provide an upper loss limit against which the level of available capital can be assessed.

A description should also be given of any management actions that would be taken in response to the stresses and scenarios – especially any actions that would be taken to cope with an economic downturn.

The Firm's Capital Adequacy

The capital and dividend plan needs to be compared to the aggregated results of the various separate risk assessments. An overall view then needs to be given by the firm of its capital adequacy. At a technical level, this therefore requires a quantitative technique for combining risks, and any **correlations** used to derive diversification benefits need to be justified.

The 'Use Test' – the Extent to Which the ICAAP is Embedded within the Firm

Evidence to support the use test would include:

- Senior management or board challenge, review and sign-off procedures – including any relevant notes in minutes from board and risk committee meetings.
- The extent to which the ICAAP is part of the firm's capital management process, including the extent and use of capital modelling or scenario analysis and stress testing within the firm's capital management policy. For example, in setting pricing and charges and the level and nature of future business.

Setting the Regulatory Capital Level

The final stage in the supervisory review process is for the regulator to set the amount of capital which the firm must hold, based on the firm's ICAAP and the associated discussions between the regulator and the firm.

Within individual firms, the ICAAP process is designed to incentivise firms to increase the quality of their risk management. As well as being able to hold less Pillar 1 capital by pursuing more sophisticated approaches to market, credit and operational risks, regulators also expect to see Pillar 2 evidence of internal incentives for staff to adopt good risk behaviours. This evidence could include, for example, linking staff performance to good risk practice.

Over time, as the ICAAP process becomes more widely adopted within a firm, certain benefits should accrue to the organisation, for example:

1. **Business strategy** – once senior managers start to realise that new businesses and products will potentially cause extra regulatory capital to be required, they will be more diligent in their inclusion of risk factors earlier in the new business design process.
2. **Risk assessments** tend to be taken more seriously by senior managers when they realise that the regulator may ask them, personally, about the risks which the firm, or their part of it, faces.

Two of the main advantages of the ICAAP – an increased focus on risk within the firm, and senior management risk responsibility – also provide one of its key challenges. It is a reasonably intense process, requiring information from many different departments and committees. It requires senior management time at the design phase, during the risk and financial data collection phase, and for the sign-off phase – and senior management time is normally at a premium.

2.2   Home and Host State Regulation

Learning Objective

2.2.2   Understand the key principles of home-host state regulation

---

2.2.1   Basel Concordat on Cross-Border Banking Supervision

Because so many banks operate in more than one country, the Basel Concordat on Cross-Border Banking Supervision provides a framework for multi-jurisdiction supervision. It focuses on potential issues with international banks' solvency, liquidity, and foreign exchange positions, and requires the '*home or parent regulators to communicate closely with the host regulators in countries where the bank has branches, subsidiaries or joint ventures*'.

The main home/host principle is that parent banks and parent supervisory authorities should monitor the risk exposure of the banks or banking groups for which they are responsible, wherever their business is conducted. This principle does not imply any lessening of host authorities' responsibilities for supervising foreign bank establishments that operate in their territories, but it is recognised that the full implementation of the home/host principle may lead to some extension of parent responsibility.

The Concordat on Cross-Border Banking Supervision sets out certain principles which the Basel Committee believes should govern the supervision of banks' foreign establishments by parent and host authorities.

1. All international banks should be supervised by a home country authority that capably performs consolidated supervision.
2. The creation of a cross-border banking establishment should receive the prior consent of both the host country and the home country authority.
3. Home country authorities should possess the right to gather information from their cross-border banking establishments.
4. If the host country authority determines that any of these three standards is not being met, it could impose restrictive measures or prohibit the establishment of banking offices.

Banking supervisory authorities cannot be fully satisfied about the soundness of individual banks unless they can examine the totality of each bank's business worldwide – especially its solvency, liquidity, and foreign exchange positions. This requires the home or parent regulator to communicate closely with the host regulators in countries where the bank has branches, subsidiaries or joint ventures.

Likewise, host authorities should ensure that parent ('home') authorities are informed immediately of any serious problems which arise in a parent bank's foreign establishment.

3.   Principles-Based Regulation

3.1   Regulatory Risk

Learning Objective

2.3.1   Understand the main differences between statutory and principles-based approaches to financial regulation

There are two broad approaches to financial regulation.

1. One approach is based on specific legal rules which must be obeyed. This is known as the 'statutory approach' and is practised, for example, in the US by the Securities and Exchange Commission (SEC) which regulates non-banking financial activity.
2. The other approach is to set out in more general terms the types of behaviour that are expected of firms and individuals. This is known as the 'principles-based approach' and is practised by, for example, the UK regulatory authorities.

Neither approach is perfect, but adherents of principles-based regulation favour it because they believe that it is impossible to write a rule for every specific situation that a regulated firm might encounter. On the other hand, many practitioners operating in compliance or legal departments are more comfortable with a rules-based approach. When operating under a principles-based regime, they tend to seek detailed guidance on how to interpret principles in specific situations.

3.2   National Regulator Responsibility

Learning Objective

2.3.2   Understand the responsibility of the national regulator to implement supervision measures to address country-specific risks

3.2.1   Supervision Measures to Address Country-Specific Risks

'Supervision' is a term used to describe the day-to-day regulatory relationship with firms – the process of monitoring them to ensure they are complying with the regulatory requirements. Most national regulators are required not only to set the principles and rules for regulated firms, but also to monitor the regulated firms' subsequent compliance.

For example, the responsibility of the UK's **Financial Conduct Authority (FCA)** to implement principles-based supervision measures to address UK-specific risks stems from a piece of legislation called the **Financial Services Act**. This Act requires it to *'maintain arrangements to determine whether persons on whom requirements are imposed by this Act are complying with them'.*

The design of these arrangements is shaped by the FCA's three statutory objectives, which are to:

- protect consumers
- protect financial markets and enhance the integrity of the UK financial system
- promote effective competition in the interests of consumers.

The regulator in the UK, in common with other jurisdictions, has wide-ranging powers to reduce perceived risks to the UK's financial services sector, for example:

- Firms must permit representatives of the FCA, or persons appointed for the purpose by the FCA, to have access, with or without notice, during reasonable business hours to any of its business premises.
- The FCA is able to use 'mystery shoppers' to help it protect consumers. This is because one of the risks faced by consumers is being sold financial products which are inappropriate for them. A problem in protecting consumers from this risk is the difficulty in knowing, after the event, what a firm actually said to a genuine consumer. By recording what a firm says in discussions with a mystery shopper, the FCA can establish a firm's normal practices in a way which would not be possible by other means.

As a general principle, firms are supervised according to the risks they present to the regulator's statutory objectives. The risks are assessed in terms of their:

- impact (the effect on consumers and the market if they were to happen), and
- probability (the likelihood of the particular issue occurring).

The nature and extent of the supervisory relationship with an individual firm is then determined by how much risk it could pose to the regulator's statutory objectives.

In other words, it is important to understand that 'risk' in the context of the regulator's responsibility to address country-specific risks is not necessarily the same as a firm's own view of its risk profile.

For example, a bank may not consider that a certain aspect of its business is particularly risky. However, its regulator might take a different view, perhaps because of the fact that if all banks were to pursue the same objectives there would be unacceptable levels of systemic risk to the financial services sector.

An illustration of this can be seen (with hindsight) to have occurred at the height of the 2006 global credit boom. Banks were borrowing short-term to lend longer-term, assuming that if they ever ran into trouble to the extent that their depositors could not be repaid, banks would simply be able to borrow from other banks. All banks were acting on the same premise and so there was not enough 'emergency' liquidity in the system when all banks subsequently started experiencing difficulties.

3.3 Principles-Based Regulation for Risk Management and Control

Learning Objective

2.3.3   Understand the main features of the regulatory framework from the perspective of regulatory risk and implementation: consumer protection; business standards; regulatory standards

3.3.1 Consumer Protection

Consumer protection is an extremely important aspect of financial regulation. In a market whose products are conceptual and complex rather than physical and simple, and where the life of product is often measured in years or even decades, it is vital that consumers are properly protected.

Within the UK, the FCA is the regulator charged with protecting consumers. The FCA uses the term 'conduct risk' to describe the risk that a firm's behaviours or products may lead to sub-optimal outcomes for consumers. The firms selling these products know far more about them than most of their customers and so firms need to be intentional about putting customers first, over-compensating if necessary, to counter the asymmetrical nature of the information relationship between expert product providers and the consuming public.

This determination to protect consumers is reflected in the FCA's 11 'Principles for Businesses'. They set out the fundamental obligations of all firms regulated by the FCA.

The first five refer to behaviours and arrangements that indirectly affect customer outcomes:

A firm must:

1. Conduct its business with integrity.
2. Conduct its business with due skill, care and diligence.
3. Take reasonable care to organise and control its affairs responsibly and effectively, with adequate risk management systems.
4. Maintain adequate financial resources.
5. Observe proper standards of market conduct.

The next five refer to behaviours and arrangements that directly affect customer outcomes:

A firm must:

1. Pay due regard to the interests of its customers and treat them fairly.
2. Pay due regard to the information needs of its clients, and communicate information to them in a way which is clear, fair and not misleading.
3. Manage conflicts of interest fairly, both between itself and its customers and between a customer and another client.
4. Take reasonable care to ensure the suitability of its advice and discretionary decisions for any customer who is entitled to rely upon its judgment.
5. Arrange adequate protection for clients' assets when it is responsible for them.

The last one covers the relationship between a firm and its regulator(s):

A firm must:

• Deal with its regulators in an open cooperative way, and must disclose to the appropriate regulator anything relating to the firm of which that regulator would reasonably expect notice.

Because the FCA's first objective is the protection of consumers, even this last principle can be said to be about consumer protection.

These 11 principles set out the highest level outcomes that the FCA is seeking to achieve. They are underpinned by further rules for the firms which it regulates such as standards on the way that firms conduct business.

3.3.2 Business Standards

A regulator's 'conduct of business' standards address the way in which business is done, particularly the way that products are marketed, distributed, sold and managed.

Conduct of business standards set out the requirements that affect firms on a day-to-day basis, such as:

• guidelines on communicating with clients
• client asset guidance, including requirements for segregation of client money into separate accounts from those used for the company's own funds
• market conduct, setting out guidance for the wholesale and professional markets
• training and competence requirements for staff in financial services.

When regulators refer to 'conduct risk' they are describing the risk of a firm behaving in a way which delivers poor outcomes for customers. An example of a product which has not been beneficial to many customers that bought it is Payment Protection Insurance (PPI), which may accompany a loan. This insurance product, paid in addition to the loan repayments, is designed to protect customers from unexpected income reductions, for example caused by job losses or illness. In these situations the insurance would pay out to provide the cash to continue the loan repayments. However, in many cases customers who were already unemployed or ill were sold PPI, and indeed some were told by the selling firm that taking out PPI would enhance their chances of being approved for the loan. In the most extreme cases, customers simply had PPI premiums added onto their loan without their knowledge.

Regulators expect conduct risk to be considered at every stage of the product or service lifecycle. This means considering the outcomes for customers before, during and after the design and launch of products – and ensuring that product governance can demonstrate a clear emphasis on the benefits to consumers as well as the benefits to the firm of all product offerings.

3.3.3   The Senior Managers Regime

The FCA operates a set of targeted behavioural standards called the Senior Managers Regime (SMR). These standards focus on individuals who hold key roles and responsibilities in relevant firms. Such firms need to allocate and map out management responsibilities and prepare Statements of Responsibilities for individuals carrying out Senior Management Functions (SMFs).

Firms are also legally required to ensure that they have procedures in place to assess an individual's fitness and propriety before applying for approval and periodically thereafter.

The associated conduct rules set out a basic standard of behaviour that all those covered by the new regimes are expected to meet. It is the responsibility of firms who are subject to the SMR to ensure that affected staff are aware of the conduct rules and how they apply to them.

3.3.4   Regulatory Standards

The final piece of the jigsaw in a principles-based regulatory framework is the definition of the regulatory processes that define the regulator's supervisory and disciplinary functions.

Supervisory standards include:

- requirements on the provision of information that firms need to supply to the regulator
- rights of access that a regulator has to each firm that it regulates
- the frequency of regulatory reviews and risk assessment visits (see below).

In addition, regulatory standards also cover the disciplinary activities available to the regulator in the pursuit of its supervisory duties. These include:

- levying fines for misconduct
- forcing firms to compensate customers
- requiring firms to appoint a third-party expert at their own expense to investigate issues
- removing a firm's licence to operate.

3.4 Regulatory Reviews and Risk Assessment Visits

Learning Objective

2.3.4 Understand the purpose and process of risk-based regulatory reviews and risk assessment visits

The requirement for supervision measures to address country-specific risks (described previously), means that regulators need to get to know the firms which they supervise. The base level of supervisory intensity depends on the risk impact and probability scores assigned to a firm (or group of firms). The regulator uses these scores to determine the nature of the relationship with each firm.

For all firms, regardless of risk score, the regulator will typically apply a series of baseline monitoring activities. These involve analysing a firm's financial and other returns, and checking compliance with regulatory requirements.

This may take place remotely, through visits to the firm to interview staff and managers, or in some jurisdictions by the regulator having permanent desks in a firm's offices. Whichever method is used, the regulator needs to assess each authorised firm's:

- management, governance and culture
- control functions
- capital and liquidity.

In addition, for firms with significant retail or wholesale businesses, the following areas would typically also be assessed:

- customers
- products, and
- markets.

For firms with permission to hold or control client money, the arrangements for its safeguarding would also be assessed. Where shortfalls are identified, a risk mitigation programme would be agreed with the firm. Actions would then be followed up, typically with the firm's senior management and control functions.

4. Other Relevant Regulation

4.1 Considering other Legislation

Learning Objective

2.4.1 Understand the importance of considering other legislation within the processes of risk identification and management

If the law is broken by a firm or its staff, whether knowingly or unknowingly, there are harmful effects to the firm in the form of:

- reputational damage
- withdrawal of regulatory authorisation for certain profitable business activities
- fines/penalties
- criminal and civil liability
- loss of talented staff through dismissal or custodial sentence.

It is, therefore, extremely important that firms identify all legislation to which they are, or may be, subject. This is especially true for:

- new start-up firms
- existing firms launching new business lines
- existing firms that are setting up overseas offices.

The risk of inadvertently breaking the law can be mitigated through:

- obtaining professional legal advice
- formally communicating with the regulators
- participating in national and international industry groups.

End of Chapter Questions

Think of an answer for each question and refer to the appropriate section for confirmation.

1. What is the name given to a risk that could affect the whole financial services industry?
    Answer reference: Section 1.2

2. What example of moral hazard is regulatory capital a response to?
    Answer reference: Section 1.2

3. There are a number of national pre-conditions that must be met before a country can adopt the provisions of the Basel Accord. The first of these is the requirement that the country must adopt sound and sustainable macroeconomic policies. Why might this be?
    Answer reference: Section 1.3.1

4. Which of the Basel pillars deals with the supervisory review process?
    Answer reference: Section 2.1.1

5. What is the difference between stress testing and scenario analysis?
    Answer reference: Section 2.1.3

6. What is meant by the ICAAP 'use test'?
    Answer reference: Section 2.1.3

7   Why might a specific risk-type be included in both a firm's Pillar 1 and Pillar 2 returns?
    Answer reference: Section 2.1.3

8. What are the two differentiating factors between statutory and principles-based regulation?
    Answer reference: Section 3.1

9. What is meant by 'conduct risk'?
    Answer reference: Section 3.3.1

10. If a firm or its staff break the law, what are three potential harmful effects?
    Answer reference: Section 4.1

Chapter Three
Operational Risk

This syllabus area will provide approximately 15 of the 100 examination questions

Chapter Summary

As discussed in the first chapter, operational risks arise from the people, processes and systems in use within a firm, or from external events. This chapter introduces common examples of operational risk and discusses ways of managing them.

There is very little commonality between people or processes or IT systems or external events (such as bomb threats or power cuts). The techniques used to understand and manage operational risk are therefore very diverse.

As well as identifying, assessing and managing their operational risks, firms also need to remain vigilant to changes in their risk profile. The two common methods of achieving this are:

1. the creation of key risk indicators, and
2. the capture and analysis of loss data.

Firms also have choices to make on how to keep their operational risk exposure within their operational risk appetite. This can be achieved firstly by avoiding the risk altogether, for example by choosing to withdraw a product which has proved too complex to administer at an acceptable cost without repeated processing errors. A second method for reducing the risk profile to within appetite is to transfer the risk to a third party. This can take several forms including:

- outsourcing an area of the company, such as back-office administration, to another company who specialise in that type of business
- taking out insurance against certain events such as fraud or loss of premises through flooding.

In addition to managing expected operational risks, the Basel regulations also require firms to hold capital against unexpected operational losses.

1. Definition of Operational Risk

1.1 Basel Committee Definition

Learning Objective

3.1.1 Know the definition of operational risk according to the Basel Committee on Banking Supervision

The Bank for International Settlements (BIS) defines operational risk as *'The risk of loss resulting from inadequate or failed internal processes, people and systems or from external events'*.

This definition covers **legal risk** (including fines, penalties and punitive damage resulting from regulatory actions, as well as private settlements), but excludes reputation risk.

1.2   Basel Operational Risk Event Types

Learning Objective

3.1.2   Know the Basel operational risk event types and what forms they take: Internal Fraud; External Fraud; Employment Practices and Workplace Safety; Clients, Products & Business Practice; Damage to Physical Assets; Business Disruption & Systems Failures; Execution, Delivery & Process Management

3.1.3   Know where and how the Basel operational risk event types typically arise

The Basel Committee requires banks to hold capital for operational risk (see chapter 2), but the Committee recognised that the approach for operational risk management chosen by an individual firm would depend on a range of factors. These include its size and sophistication, and the nature and complexity of its activities.

At a high level, the BIS believes that for banks of all sizes, the following are crucial elements of an effective operational risk management framework:

- clear risk oversight by the board and senior management
- a strong operational risk culture
- a strong internal control culture, including:
  - clear lines of responsibility
  - segregation of duties
- effective internal reporting
- contingency planning.

Basel provides the following seven operational risk event types, with examples of where and how they might arise.

Event-type category	Examples
Internal fraud	Losses due to acts of a type intended to defraud, misappropriate property or circumvent regulations, the law or company policy, (excluding diversity/discrimination events), which involves at least one internal party
External fraud	Losses due to acts of a type intended to defraud, misappropriate property or circumvent the law by a third party
Employment practices and workplace safety	Losses arising from acts inconsistent with employment, health or safety laws or agreements, from payment of personal injury claims or from diversity and discrimination events
Clients, products and business practices	Losses arising from an unintentional or negligent failure to meet a professional obligation to specific clients (including fiduciary and suitability requirements), or from the nature or design of a product
Damage to physical assets	Losses arising from loss or damage to physical assets from natural disaster or other events
Business disruption and systems failures	Losses arising from disruption of business or system failures
Execution, delivery, and process management	Losses from failed transaction processing or process management, from relations with trade counterparties and vendors

1.3　Financial Crime Legislation

Learning Objective

3.1.4　Understand the implications of financial crime in terms of appropriate risk management, both internally and externally

The global financial services sector provides an essential role in the facilitation of international commerce. Unfortunately, it also has the potential to enable the financial proceeds of crime to be moved around the world quickly and easily. In addition, the nature of the industry means that there are sometimes opportunities for unscrupulous practitioners to make money through dishonest means, at the expense of clients or other market participants.

Therefore, in most jurisdictions there are strict rules in place, enforceable through national and international legal systems, to:

1. prohibit certain undesirable practitioner behaviours, collectively known as market abuse; these fall into two overlapping categories – insider information and market manipulation
2. oblige financial services firms to monitor financial transactions and report any that appear suspicious, to reduce the likelihood of criminal proceeds being moved around the system; these also fall into two related categories – money laundering and terrorist financing.

Examples of insider information market abuse include:

1. **Insider dealing** – when an insider (eg, a member of staff) deals on the basis of information which is not known to the market.
2. **Improper disclosure** – where an insider improperly discloses **inside information** to another person.
3. **Improper dissemination** – giving out information that conveys a false or misleading impression about an investment or the issuer of an investment where the person doing this knows the information to be false or misleading.

Money laundering is the process of turning 'dirty' money (money derived from criminal activities) into money which appears to be from legitimate origins. Dirty money is difficult to invest or spend, and carries the risk of being used as evidence of the initial crime. Laundered money can be invested and spent with less risk of incrimination.

There are three stages to a successful money laundering operation:

1. **Placement** – this is the introduction of dirty money into the financial system. Typically, this involves placing the criminally-derived cash into a bank or building society account, a bureau de change or any other type of enterprise which routinely accepts large amounts of cash.
2. **Layering** – this involves moving the placed money around the system in order to make it difficult for the authorities to link the placed funds with the ultimate beneficiary of the money. This might involve buying and selling foreign currencies, shares or bonds in rapid succession, investing in collective investment schemes, insurance-based investment products or moving the money from one country to another.
3. **Integration** – at this final stage, the layering has been successful and the ultimate beneficiary appears to be holding legitimate funds (ie, clean rather than dirty money). The money is regarded as 'integrated' into the legitimate financial system.

Broadly, the international anti-money laundering provisions are aimed at requiring firms to:

1. Identify customers and report suspicious transactions at the placement and layering stages.
2. Keep adequate records which should prevent the integration stage being reached.
3. Report suspicious activity or behaviour to the relevant regulatory or legislative authority.

Terrorist financing refers to activities that provide financial support to terrorists or terrorist groups. Many of the requirements of national and international anti-terrorism legislation on financial services firms are similar to the anti-money laundering provisions described above, and involve:

- customer identification
- record keeping

- reporting suspicious activity.

A person generally commits an offence if he enters into, or is linked with, an arrangement that facilitates the retention or control of terrorist funds.

The areas of financial crime considered above (market abuse, money laundering and financing of terrorism) require an appropriate set of risk management responses by firms, such as:

1. Educating staff on the risks to:
   - society, if financial crimes are committed
   - the firm, if placed under regulatory censure
   - the individual, of a custodial sentence or heavy fine.
2. Putting systems and controls in place to mitigate the risk of occurrence.
3. Monitoring staff compliance with the internal rules and the external legal and regulatory stipulations.
4. Escalating behavioural exceptions to a specific individual or committee for investigation.
5. Penalising contravention with the rules and if necessary informing the relevant authorities.

1.4 Distinguishing Operational Risk

Learning Objective

3.1.5 Be able to distinguish operational risk from: other forms of risk; further risks that arise as a consequence of operational risk

1.4.1 Operational Risk as a Distinct Risk Class

As described in chapter 1, it is relatively straightforward for an organisation to set and observe specific, measurable levels of market risk and credit risk. By contrast, it is relatively difficult to identify or numerically assess levels of operational risk and its many sources.

Historically, organisations had accepted operational risk as an unavoidable cost of doing business, and tended to consider any risk that was not market or credit risk to be operational.

However, the emergence of the modern global financial services sector has seen companies fail, not just because of market or credit risks, but also through operational risks such as malfunctioning internal processes, technology failure, undesirable staff behaviours or fraud, compliance issues and financial difficulties.

1.4.2 Operational Risk and its Consequential Effects

When an operational risk materialises, it often causes other risk issues too. These typically include:

- **Reputational risks** – if clients or the media become aware of the issue and it tarnishes the firm's reputation.

- **Compliance (or regulatory) risks** – certain process failures will result, for example, in customers not being treated fairly. This in turn is a regulatory breach and could result in fines or other sanctions being applied by the regulator.
- **Credit risks** – areas in the credit function where operational risk issues can lead to losses are:
  ○ data errors causing inadvertent credit limit breaches
  ○ lack of adequate monitoring and/or analysis or misinterpretation of a counterparty's financial statements due to a lack of training or incompetence
  ○ legal risk, including the inability to enforce contracts in credit-related areas such as the posting of collateral
  ○ failing to carry out suitable credit checks on counterparties, or wrongly assuming that credit rating agencies always get ratings right.
- **Market risks** – an undetected error in the portfolio management system might lead to a breach of a market risk limit.
- **Liquidity risks** – a process breakdown in the finance department could lead to the firm having insufficient liquidity to pay staff salaries.
- **Investment risks** – carelessness on the part of a fund manager, coupled with a process that contains no subsequent checking, could cause a mandate limit breach.

2.   Operational Risk Policy

A firm needs to have a written operational risk policy that defines a coherent, consistent approach to the firm's operational risk management. It provides a 'roadmap' to move the organisation from what might be a fragmented, non-strategic approach to operational risk management, to a comprehensive, firm-wide methodology that uses a common risk language throughout the organisation.

The policy defines the operational risk methodology, or framework, within which the firm will operate. Further detail is given below but, at a summary level, building this framework will involve, for example:

- defining the firm's operational risk appetite
- defining the methodology used to identify and categorise the operational risks that exist in the organisation
- defining the methodology used to measure and assess the significance of the identified risks
- assigning responsibility to line managers for owning the mitigating actions required to reduce risk exposures to within the risk appetite
- assigning responsibility for monitoring the effects of the mitigating actions
- establishing the reporting and escalating mechanisms for risk issues to all levels of the organisation in order to ensure transparency, and aid the decision-making process.

The process of developing an operational risk policy is cyclical and continuous, maturing in line with the firm's growing understanding of its operational risk profile.

A common operational policy and terminology, which exists globally and across all functions, allows:

- a balance to be struck between the need for global standardisation, and the need to recognise regional or divisional differences
- objectivity when risk prioritisation needs to be performed

- a sense of fairness when rewarding or penalising risk performance
- centralised control of the overall capital adequacy assessment performed across the organisation.

Because the risk policy takes a company-wide approach, and cuts across departmental boundaries, there should be a central risk management role responsible for its coordination and implementation. Depending on the size and type of organisation, this role may be set up as an independent department (see section 3.1).

2.1 Areas Addressed by An Operational Risk Policy

Learning Objective

3.2.1 Understand the following areas that are addressed by an operational risk policy and what they are designed to achieve: identification of key officers, define clear roles and responsibilities, segregation of duties, cross-functional involvement and agreement

The operational risk policy, then, is a document which outlines a firm's strategy and objectives for operational risk management. It is also where the boundary between other risk areas, such as market and credit risk, is clarified. To meet the prime objectives of operational risk management the risk policy and its associated standards should address the following areas:

1. identification of key officers
2. roles and responsibilities
3. segregation of duties
4. cross-functional involvement and agreement.

2.1.1 Identification of Key Officers

It is important for firms to identify and empower those individuals who are given key responsibilities in the management of operational risk. Key officers will include the following:

- Line managers within the independent operational risk management function, responsible for monitoring and reporting to the board.
- Senior business managers, responsible for operational risks within their areas of the business.
- The group risk management function, responsible for the firm's overall financial risk.
- Certain members of staff, sometimes called risk representatives or risk champions, may also be designated from within the business itself to monitor a department's operational risks on behalf of the owning manager. Risk representatives often have dual reporting lines into their own business area and also into the risk management function.

2.1.2 Roles and Responsibilities

The policy should provide clear responsibility and accountability for risk management at all levels. Staff throughout the organisation need to know precisely what is expected of them, and why. If they are accountable for managing risk, they also require the necessary control and authority to be able to take action and implement risk-reduction plans.

The risk policy should include clear lines of authority, identify key risk officers to carry out prescribed actions, and define their roles and responsibilities. The risk policy should also make clear the consequences of non-compliance for staff not observing the policy.

2.1.3 Segregation of Duties

To effectively manage and control its processes, the firm will need to ensure effective segregation of duties between the various key functions and processes, such as front-office, operations, accounting and risk monitoring. Barings Bank was ruined as a business because the head of its Singapore front-office was also head of the Singapore back-office and was able to cover up trading errors until they grew to a level that brought down the bank.

2.1.4 Cross-Functional Involvement and Agreement

The policy should promote collaboration between functions, departments and divisions, because many operational risks materialise as a result of ownerless or unnoticed boundary errors. Where possible, cross-functional teamwork should be encouraged (notwithstanding the need for segregation of duties) through effective reporting, incentives, education and a supportive organisational structure.

3. Operational Risk Framework

3.1 Key Aims

Learning Objective

3.3.1 Understand the key aims of the operational risk management function: identification and assessment of risks, management of risks, reduction of potential impact and likelihood of occurrence

Many operational risks are best managed within the departments in which they arise. So, for example, IT staff are best qualified to address systems-related risks, and back-office staff are best suited to address **settlement** issues.

However, overall planning, challenge and monitoring should be provided by a centralised operational risk management department which is independent from the business areas it serves. The role of the operational risk management function is to:

- work with managers and other risk owners to assess and quantify risks
- provide a dotted or solid reporting line for risk representatives within the business
- support and maintain the operational risk system used by the business to track their risks, controls, losses, actions and key indicators
- benchmark good industry practice
- provide risk oversight and monitoring
- ensure issues are properly escalated, and track the actions arising from operational risk incidents

- conduct qualitative operational risk analysis using, for example:
    ○ loss causal analysis, ie, establishing trends in the causes of the firm's losses
    ○ HR reports from exit interviews
    ○ internal audit reports, and the rate at which audit points are closed by the business
- conduct statistical modelling to quantify the firm's operational risk profile for regulatory and other purposes.

3.1.1 Identification and Assessment of Risks

A significant amount of time is required from managers and staff to ensure the compilation of a good quality, comprehensive operational risk register for each area of the business. There are a variety of methods used for the practical capture and identification of operational risk; the more common ones include:

- self-assessment
- key risk indicators (KRIs)
- risk and control assessment workshops
- loss data causal trend analysis
- external loss data (where available)
- audit reviews.

To capture the complete risk profile, all of these methods require the full involvement of the risk owners in the business, and support from the operational risk function. The latter will have experience of risks and mitigating controls elsewhere in the organisation. They will also be able to facilitate risk and control assessment workshops for the various business teams.

3.1.2 Management of Risk and Reduction of Potential Impact and Likelihood of Occurrence

Once risks have been identified and measured, the risk owner is in a position to address them where they fall outside of the firm's risk tolerance or appetite. Managing the risk involves taking steps to reduce both its likelihood and its impact, should it occur.

The key to reducing the likelihood of a risk materialising is to:

- clearly identify the risk before it occurs
- establish clear ownership for the risk, and ensure that the owner is able to put proper controls in place
- set up and monitor appropriate risk indicators, and act before they ever reach their predefined danger limits.

If the risk does materialise, its impact can be reduced by ensuring:

- speedy escalation to senior management if their help is necessary for resolution
- an owner has been assigned to fix the problem with the ability to draw in other resources if required
- if necessary, that appropriate insurance policies are in place.

3.2 Operational Risk Management

Learning Objective

3.3.2 Know the stages of an operational risk management framework: identification, measurement, management and control, management information, monitoring, escalation and remediation

Once the high level risk policy has been agreed, a risk management framework must be implemented to enable the risk management function to achieve its aims. The following figure describes a typical framework, which, starting and ending with the operational risk policy, includes the following stages:

A Risk Management Framework

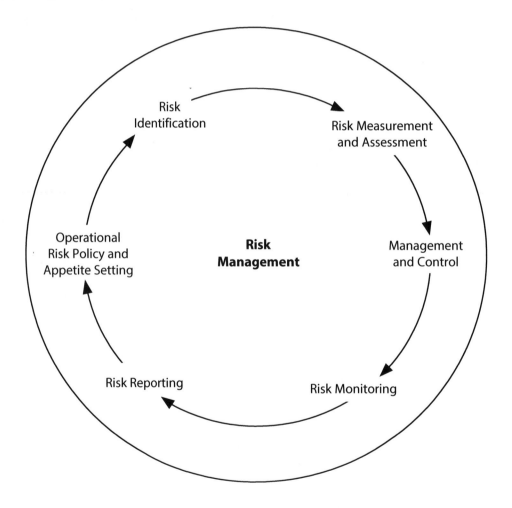

- **Risk Identification** – clearly identify the firm's risks using methods such as those described above.
- **Risk measurement and assessment** – score the impact and the likelihood of the risk against pre-defined criteria, as discussed below.
- **Management and control** – ensure that appropriate controls are in place to mitigate the risk. Put actions in place for under-controlled risks. Ensure that 'real-time' escalation mechanisms are set up, with pre-defined thresholds that define how high up the chain of command the limit breaches or loss incidents should be escalated. Ensure that remediation work is owned and tracked to completion.
- **Risk monitoring** – monitor the risk and control indicators and other risk management information (MI), and act before they ever reach their predefined danger limits.
- **Risk reporting** – reporting of risk MI should include indicators, the risks and controls to which they relate, and incidents – ideally both losses and near misses. Pre-defined danger limits should be defined by setting triggers and limits on the data – typically triggers signal an 'amber' status which requires management attention and limits signal a 'red' status which requires immediate management action.
- **Operational Risk Policy** – lessons learned during the operation of the risk framework are used to update the policy.

4. Operational Risk Identification

4.1 Operational Risk Identification and Categorisation

Learning Objective

3.4.1   Understand the purpose of identifying and categorising risks

Identifying and categorising operational risks helps firms to establish their risk profile and appetite for risk. A helpful starting point for defining a firm's operational risk categories might be to use the definition of operational risk itself, ie, process risks, people risks, system risks, external events. These can then be divided into further sub-categories.

Categorising the risks will enable:

- the provision of more succinct management risk information, grouped by risk category, rather than simply a list of individual risks
- a better understanding of where in particular the firm's operational weakness lie:
  ○ processes
  ○ systems
  ○ people, or
  ○ vulnerability to external events
- a sound basis for operational risk capital allocation across the different categories
- a common language for discussing, assessing and managing risk that allows clear and transparent communication and decision-making.

4.2　Self-Assessment Risk Identification

Learning Objective

3.4.2　Understand the self-assessment (self-certification) method of identifying operational risks

This typically involves a checklist of the risks that a particular area of the firm faces. Managers and staff in a department are required to score each risk, perhaps as part of a survey or questionnaire. The risks are usually scored by probability and impact.

Self-assessment as a single method of measurement has limitations because:

*   it is subjective, and is therefore open to abuse and manipulation by managers. For this reason it should be independently validated – for example by internal audit or a risk officer who does not report to the head of the department, and
*   combining the scores received from the participants for each risk into a single score for that risk can be difficult – it is not obvious whether an average score should be used, or some alternative approach that takes into account, and tries to understand the reasons for, any outlying scores.

Firms use a variety of approaches to overcome these weaknesses. A common approach is to assemble key staff in a workshop and brainstorm the risks to their departmental objectives. This enables a debate to occur and a consensus to emerge on the impacts and likelihoods assigned to each risk.

4.3　Application of Risk Categorisation

Learning Objective

3.4.3　Be able to apply risk categorisation to simple, practical examples of normal activity and change-related projects: people, processes, systems and external events

It was suggested earlier that categorising a firm's risks can be advantageous. A common approach to risk categorisation is the use of operational risk causes: process, people, systems and external events. The following table illustrates this approach with some examples of risks that fall under each of the causes.

People risks	Process risks	System risks	External event risks
Inadequately defined roles and responsibilities	Lack of written procedures	System unavailable during peak hours	Threat of terrorist action
Lack of succession plan for key staff	Absence of defined process	Data becomes subtly corrupted	Customer commits fraud against the firm
Staff not competent for role	Manual intervention causes pinch-points	Passwords being shared by staff	Outsource supplier delivers late
Improper staff conduct	Absence of escalation procedures	Denial of service attacks	

5. Operational Risk Assessment and Measurement

5.1 Operational Risk Assessment and Measurement

Learning Objective

3.5.1 Understand the main reasons for assessing and measuring operational risk, and the difficulties involved

Risk assessment and risk measurement are both concerned with understanding the likelihood of risks occurring and their potential impact on the business. Once an understanding of the size of a problem has been gained, appropriate action can be taken to address it. The reasons for measuring and assessing operational risk are to:

- establish a quantitative baseline for improving the control environment – knowing how much the firm might save by avoiding the risk is a useful input to the business case for upgrading processes and controls
- provide an incentive for risk management and the development of a strong risk culture
- improve management decision-making; by knowing the size of their risks, managers are in a better position to decide how much risk they wish to take
- satisfy regulators and shareholders that a firm is adopting a proactive and transparent approach to risk management, and
- make an assessment of the financial risk exposure that can be used for capital allocation purposes.

The main difficulty in measuring and assessing operational risk is the lack of relevant and objective data. Many firms do not have enough historic loss data of their own to predict objectively the likelihood and impact of new risks that have been identified.

The banking and insurance industries have attempted to solve this problem by anonymously sharing their losses with other firms in the same industry.

5.2   Basic Terminology

Learning Objective

3.5.2   Know the basic terms used in the assessment and measurement of operational risk

Risk measurement describes the use of quantitative techniques to understand the size of a firm's or business area's risk profile. These techniques include statistically modelling the frequency and impact of risk events and making statistical predictions of the future risk profile.

Risk assessment makes use of whatever objective data there is (such as the output of a measurement exercise), and uses human judgment to estimate the impact on the business. Where there is no objective data, subjective human experience alone is used.

For instance, a firm's risk indicators (a form of risk measurement) might show that the front office trading system is 98% reliable. A risk assessment could then be performed to establish whether or not this is acceptable for normal business performance.

5.3   Methods of Assessment

Learning Objective

3.5.3   Understand the following methods of assessing operational risk: impact and likelihood assessment, scenario analysis, bottom-up analysis

5.3.1   Impact and Likelihood Assessment

One of the simplest methods of assessing risk is the creation of an impact and likelihood assessment. This enables risks to be ranked in order of their severity.

The assessment may be subjective (using the experience of the professionals involved) or objective (being supported by historical data) – or both. In either event, the severity ranking decision depends on two criteria: the likelihood of the risk being realised and the magnitude of the impact.

Likelihood Probability Ratings

The likelihood of the risk can be represented as a range of probabilities that correspond to a rating. For example, depending on the business area being measured, the following ratings might be used:

Very low

- not likely to occur within the next ten years
- rating score = 1

Low

- likely to occur within the next three-ten years
- rating score = 2

Medium

- likely to occur within the next two-three years
- rating score = 3

High

- likely to occur within the next year
- rating score = 4

Impact Loss Ratings

The impact of the risk is the potential loss if the risk occurs. This can be represented as a monetary range, and also assigned a rating. For example:

Very low

- under £1,000
- rating score = 1

Low

- £1,000 to £10,000
- rating score = 2

Medium

- £10,000 to £50,000
- rating score = 3

High

- above £50,000
- rating score = 4

There is no 'correct' number of impact and likelihood scoring bands, although using four of each, as in the example above, is common. However, regardless of the number of bands, it is helpful to use an even number in order to prevent risks being scored 'medium' (ie, the middle value) by default.

The overall risk score is the product of the likelihood rating scores and the impact rating scores:

Risk score = likelihood score × impact score

The risks can then be ranked by their score. In addition, each risk can then be plotted on a heat map according to its score, as shown in the following figure. The heat map can be coloured red, amber, yellow and green to give an indication of which risks are inside or outside of risk tolerance.

Typical Heat Map

Likelihood score				
4	Yellow / Risk 1	Amber / Risk 2	Red	Red
3	Green	Yellow	Amber / Risk 3	Red
2	Green	Yellow	Yellow	Red / Etc
1	Green	Green	Yellow	Amber
	1	**2**	**3**	**4**

Impact score

© Andrew Brand

Firms will often score their risks separately on a gross and net basis. Gross risk assumes that there are no controls in place, or to put it another way, that all controls have failed. Net risk includes a consideration of the control environment. This gross/net approach allows the effectiveness of controls to be evaluated separately from the risks which they mitigate.

The advantages of an impact and likelihood assessment are the following:

- It provides a simple method for viewing the range of risks the business faces.
- It provides an evaluation of the effectiveness of the control environment if gross and net risk scores are plotted separately.
- It focuses management attention on the most important risks.
- It can be used with minimal hard data: if historical loss data is not available, a useful subjective view can still be obtained.
- It can capture a wide range of risk possibilities – from large, strategic risks to everyday, more detailed issues. For this reason it can be effective at all levels of an organisation.
- It encourages a risk-aware culture and a more transparent risk environment. In order to maintain the risk profiles, a culture of continuous assessment is needed. This encourages line staff and risk managers to work closely and allows good practice to be adopted more easily.

Its main disadvantages is that it may present an over-simplified, subjective view. As a matter of course, all subjective assessments should be validated by:

- real loss data, and/or
- an independent party, such as internal audit, a central risk function or peer review.

5.3.2 Scenario Analysis

Scenario analysis is a 'top-down' method of highlighting potential risk combinations in order to allow preventative action to be taken. It uses the experience of business professionals to capture possible scenarios that have occurred in the past, or may result in loss in the future. By investigating these scenarios, perhaps through stressing (ie, exaggerating) a particular aspect of each scenario, preventative measures can be taken to reduce their risk of occurrence. Methods for achieving this stress through statistical simulation are covered in chapter 8 on Model Risk.

5.3.3 Bottom-Up Analysis

The **bottom-up measurement** approach seeks to analyse the individual risks and adequacy of controls across business processes. It is called 'bottom-up' because it builds up a detailed profile of the risks that occur in each area, aggregating them to provide overall measures of exposure for departments, divisions or the firm as a whole. It uses the experience of line managers and staff, coupled with loss data as its source of information, so the resultant measures contain both qualitative and quantitative elements.

Its advantages are:

- It addresses risk and control issues at the process level.
- Accountability and responsibility for risk management can be clearly defined. The owner or manager of a process is usually made accountable for managing the risks it contains.
- It encourages a more transparent and risk aware culture.
- It encourages continuous improvement. As risks are identified and assessed, mitigation action can be taken immediately if necessary.
- It can improve the quality of management information.

Its disadvantages are:

- It takes time to implement. The assessment of process risks requires a detailed understanding of how a firm's processes work both within and across departmental boundaries. Documenting this can be a lengthy exercise.
- It can be subjectively influenced by managers if not properly managed.
- Aggregating risks 'upwards' is not straight-forward, although this can be facilitated by assigning individual risks to risk categories such as those described earlier.

5.4   Key Risk Indicators (KRIs)

Learning Objective

3.5.4   Understand the Key Risk Indicators (KRI) method of measuring operational risk

Having produced a list of risks, and having then ranked them in order of severity, the firm can designate the top 'x' risks as its key risks.

It is then possible to obtain data that describes the current status of those key risks, and to define upper and lower acceptable limits on the behaviour of this data. This approach provides indicators on the firm's key risks, or, in other words, it produces a series of '**key risk indicators**'.

For example, if one of the key risks is 'Loss of Key Staff', then it might be felt that certain factors will influence the likelihood of this risk occurring. These factors might include:

- General staff turnover as a proxy for key staff turnover
- Percentage of undocumented processes (ie, processes that are only known about by 'key' staff)
- Salary gaps identified by the annual salary benchmarking tests.

Warning thresholds can be established by defining limits of acceptability for each of these indicators. Some firms have found it useful to define a 'soft' amber limit so that action can be taken before reaching the 'hard' red limit. As well as defining appropriate escalation levels, these limits can also help firms to set their risk tolerance by adjusting the amber and red limits over time.

Plotting the indicator levels each month results in a graph such as the figure below:

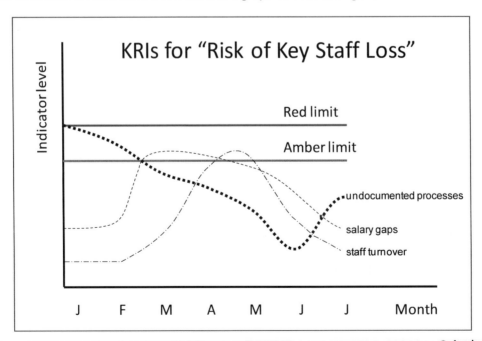

© Andrew Brand

The graph should be accompanied by a narrative such as:

'Good progress has been made in reducing the percentage of undocumented processes, although this is now starting to rise again. This increases the risk that key staff might leave without a proper hand-over being possible.

In February, when the results of the annual salary benchmarking became available it became evident that some staff were being paid below market levels. This was followed a few months later by an increase in staff turnover. The salary gaps have since been closed, and turnover has declined to within tolerance.

In summary, the three indicators together point to an overall reduction in the likelihood of key staff leaving.'

If we assume that the graph is published monthly, then back in February the narrative may have warned that, having identified gaps between current salaries and market benchmarks, a rise in staff turnover was becoming more likely.

The advantages of using KRIs are the following:

- They allow trends to be monitored and can therefore be used to anticipate problems.
- They allow limits of acceptability to be established.
- They can provide a basis for objective risk measurement.

Their main disadvantage, like any system of business measurement, is that they can cause skewed business performance if managers start 'managing to their KRIs' in an attempt to enhance their bonus ratings.

Case Study: Trade Confirmation Key Risk Indicators

Let us assume that 'Rising numbers of outstanding confirmations' has been identified as a key risk. In order to define key risk indicator(s) on this risk we need to know a little about the way in which the confirmations process works.

Financial transactions should be 'confirmed' with clients before they are settled. Confirmation ensures that the counterparty recognises the transaction and agrees with the legal, economic and settlement terms – thus allowing any discrepancies to be resolved before the trade is settled.

Confirmations can be made by telephone and in writing and their format is usually agreed through a legal agreement signed by the two parties involved as part of the set-up activity. For some products, such as listed instruments that use a central exchange or counterparty, the **confirmation process** can be standardised to such an extent that a high degree of computer automation is possible.

For products that are not dealt via an exchange, such as over-the-counter (OTC) derivatives, confirmations are performed as part of a bilateral agreement between the trading parties. They typically use hardcopy documents that follow certain pre-defined formats to help reduce the risk of error and legal ambiguity.

Operational risk exists in the trade confirmation process to the extent that transaction errors are not spotted, or because errors or delays are introduced into the settlement process.

Key risk indicators for the trade confirmation process might include:

- length of time taken to formalise a legal agreement
- number of confirmations not yet agreed with the counterparty
- number and type of confirmation errors found in the checking process
- time taken for counterparties to return confirmations.

The goal is to construct indicators on the drivers of the likelihood of key risks. Defining indicators on likelihood drivers means that the key risk indicators will be forward-looking and predictive – they will alert managers to changes in the likelihood of a key risk. If such drivers can be identified, then the key risk indicators will identify periods of increased operational risk before losses start occurring.

5.5   Historical Loss Data

Learning Objective

3.5.5   Understand how historical loss data can be used in measuring operational risk

Loss data evaluation is important in mapping the actual losses experienced by the firm back to a sensible categorisation system. Once the data has been collected (from either internal or external sources) it can be used in the measurement process, using benchmarking or statistical methods.

For instance, a 'loss distribution' curve may be created that records the value of all material (direct) losses in a particular risk category over a time period of, say, three years. By analysing this curve (using similar Value-at-Risk (VaR) techniques to those introduced in chapter 5 on Market Risk), some prediction of future losses can be made within specified confidence limits. The major difference will be the shape of the curve and, specifically, the 'fat tail' which reflects the fact that losses are not 'normally distributed' – extremely high impact losses occur only very rarely.

A typical loss distribution curve might look like the figure below:

Loss Distribution Curve

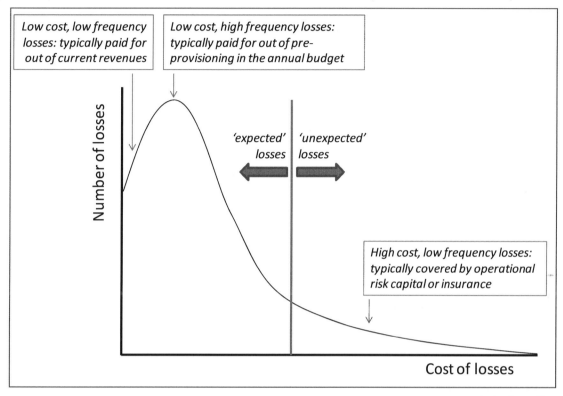

© Andrew Brand

Expected losses are those errors that occur with reasonable frequency. They represent known process weaknesses which perhaps would be prohibitively expensive to strengthen. The errors are paid for from current revenues or a general pre-provided budget item. This is equivalent to saying that these sorts of loss are within the firm's risk appetite or tolerance.

The unexpected losses are those low-frequency, high-impact events that can create serious problems. They are much more difficult to manage on a day-to-day level because they do not occur often enough to test the control environment. They are best managed using contingency planning, and their cost would be borne by the risk capital buffer.

5.6 Practical Constraints

Learning Objective

3.5.6 Understand the practical constraints of implementing an operational risk management framework

Some of the practical obstacles to implementing an operational risk management framework:

- **Data collection constraints** – in practice, it is very difficult to build a truly comprehensive data set. Apart from the general lack of data, system constraints and a lack of standardisation mean that the required data feeds from disparate sources cannot be easily developed. There is also relatively little availability of industry-wide data, as this depends on firms 'self reporting' and, by definition, it is not straightforward to gain an understanding of high impact, low-frequency events. Firms may also not be allowed to report for legal disclosure reasons.
- **Cultural constraints** – business heads need to be convinced of the value that operational risk management (ORM) will bring. If not implemented in a well-structured manner, it is often seen as a cost to the business, and even a nuisance, rather than a real asset. Consequently, many firms have rolled out risk management frameworks little by little – attempting to gain the confidence and support of one area before moving on to another.
- **Resource and cost constraints** – firms continually underestimate the amount of time and resources required to implement identification and measurement systems. In an era of tight cost control, resource constraints put a limit on how quickly or comprehensively implementation is carried out.
- **Indicator constraints** – it can be difficult to design risk indicators that monitor the full range of risks. There is a natural tendency to use indicators that are already available (such as existing management information), but these are often designed to monitor performance rather than risk. Time and effort needs to be spent designing and maintaining an appropriate set of risk indicators.

6. Managing Operational Risk

Risk management refers to activities and decisions that are intended to control, reduce, eliminate or optimise a risk. This section covers a variety of different operational risk management techniques.

6.1 A Risk Register and its Core Features

Learning Objective

3.6.1 Know the purpose of a risk register (risk log) and its core features: objectives, description of risk, risk ranking, lead person or department, action plan, target and completion dates, sources of assurance and oversight and mitigating controls

Having identified and then assessed the various operational risks facing the firm, and having then ranked the risks to decide the priority order for mitigation, the next stage in the process would be the construction of a risk register, also known as a risk log.

There is no widely accepted definition of what a risk register should look like, so the following discussion presents an illustrative example. The actual content and format of a risk register will depend on the level within the organisation for which it is being constructed, and the risk types to which it refers.

For the purposes of this example, a risk register could consist of a list of identified risks, linked to the business objectives, processes or products whose success would be threatened if the risk materialised. The overall risk score is used to sort the risks so that the list runs from the most significant to the least significant.

Each risk would be assigned to an owner or lead person – ideally a member of staff or perhaps a department – and then the mitigating actions would be listed, along with their deadlines for completion.

Finally, the sources of assurance and oversight would be given in order to allow periodic reassessment of the risk, and the status of the mitigating controls which the actions will have implemented. Both 'assurance', and 'oversight', refer to the mechanisms used by the firm to provide an objective view about the quality of each risk's management.

Mitigating controls are ways in which the likelihood and impact of a risk are reduced. They could include, for example, managerial sign-off of work before it leaves the department, or perhaps an IT system that requires a second member of staff to verify inputs for accuracy.

In summary then, the risk register's column headings would be:

- objectives, processes or products affected by this risk
- description of risk
- risk ranking
- lead person or department
- action plan
- target and completion dates
- sources of assurance and oversight (which may or may not be the lead person or department)
- mitigating controls, their effectiveness and owner(s).

6.2 Methods for Managing Operational Risk Exposure

Learning Objective

3.6.2 Understand and be able to distinguish between the following methods for reducing operational risk exposure: risk transfer, risk avoidance, risk mitigation, risk acceptance

Once risks have been identified and measured, the firm can take action to address those risks that fall outside of its risk appetite.

Different firms specialise in different areas of business and so certain third parties might be better equipped to deal with some types of operational risk. Therefore, it can make sense for these risk types to be contractually transferred to such a third party. Transferring risk can be achieved in a number of ways, such as **outsourcing** or insurance, and these are covered in subsequent sections.

If the level of a particular risk is unacceptable, and managing it to within acceptable levels would be too costly, then it may simply need to be avoided. In practical terms this could involve:

- withdrawing from a business
- changing a product offering
- deciding not to take on new business through planned mergers or acquisitions.

Many risks can be **mitigated** through a variety of management actions. The most common action to help manage risk is the introduction of key controls into the firm's processes. Controls are only required when a business has **accepted** the risk, as neither avoiding the risk nor transferring it to a third party would require the utilisation of controls. However, another method of accepting the risk could be to not expend resources to mitigate it, implying that controls are not required, thus simply accepting its possible consequences. This is commonly referred to as a 'risk acceptance'. The different types of available controls will be covered in the following section.

6.3 Operational Risk Mitigation

Learning Objective

3.6.3 Know the common methods for operational risk mitigation: controls, business continuity and contingency planning, outsourcing, insurance, information and cyber security, physical security, financial reserves, risk awareness training, data protection

6.3.1 Controls

All processes should have controls and check points designed into them to detect errors and prevent fraud and theft. For instance, firms have controls to ensure segregation of duties so that no single person has the end-to-end authority to process transactions (ie, one person may be able to book a payment into a system but another has to check it). This prevents fraudulent activities, such as assigning cash movements to personal bank accounts.

An example will help to show what controls are. This is the same trade confirmation example used previously, but this time we are using it to illustrate the possible controls in the process.

An Example of Operational Controls in the Trade Process

Transactions are confirmed with clients before they are settled. Confirmation ensures that the counterparty recognises the transaction and agrees with the legal, economic and settlement terms – thus allowing any discrepancies to be resolved before the trade is settled.

Confirmations can be made by telephone and in writing and their format is usually agreed through a legal agreement signed by the two parties involved as part of the set-up activity. For some products, such as listed derivatives that use a central exchange or counterparty, the confirmation process can be standardised to such an extent that a high degree of computer automation is possible.

For products that are not dealt via an exchange, such as over-the-counter (OTC) derivatives, confirmations are performed as part of a bilateral agreement between the trading parties. They typically use hardcopy documents that follow certain pre-defined formats to help reduce the risk of error and legal ambiguity.

Operational risk exists in the trade confirmation process to the extent that transaction errors are not spotted, or because errors or delays are introduced.

Key controls in the trade confirmation process therefore might include:

- ensuring that a legal agreement covering confirmation protocol is in place before trading
- front-office sign-off of the economic terms of each trade
- a back-office confirmation check
- daily follow-up actions to counterparties which have not returned written confirmations.

In general, controls fall into certain broad categories, the most common of which are 'preventative' and 'detective'.

Preventative controls are those that prevent errors occurring in the first place. They attempt to tackle the root causes of risk and are most effective when incorporated within processes at the outset by anticipating a risky outcome. Technology solutions are often used as a key means of implementing preventative controls.

For example, a key preventative control is the provision of individual IT passwords and system access control for all staff. Without it, firms would lose the ability to audit which system actions had been performed by which members of staff. System data security would also be compromised if there was no way of stopping people logging on to whichever systems they were interested in.

Other examples of preventative controls are:

- the setting up and ongoing maintenance of procedures to prevent unauthorised actions and errors
- the use of training to reduce the likelihood of human error arising from a lack of expertise
- the use of systems to automate processes that eliminate risks caused by human error.

Detective controls detect errors once they have occurred, and quality assurance checks fall under this category.

It is important to remember that processes frequently change. If the control structure is not reviewed and assessed as part of this change, it is possible that potential risks are introduced that are not covered by adequate controls. The identification of these control gaps is a key objective of the Operational Risk Management function.

6.3.2 Business Continuity Planning (BCP) and Disaster Recovery (DR)

In order to ensure that businesses can continue after a disaster, such as a terrorist event, two key pieces of planning need to be in place:

- A **business continuity plan (BCP)** which deals with the premises and people aspects – where will staff work if their main site is out of action?
- **Disaster recovery (DR)** procedures which deal with the IT and other infrastructure required to keep the business running.

In order to construct a robust BCP and DR solution, a thorough analysis of the causes of potential disruption is required, ranging from minor mishaps to major catastrophes. Typical risks whose materialisation could require staff to use temporary alternative working accommodation are:

- fire
- power failure
- civil unrest and strikes
- terrorism.

The BCP and DR solutions must be subject to regular testing and any shortcomings brought to the required standard.

As well as thoroughly testing the BCP and DR arrangements, firms also need to define crisis management teams (CMTs), and the methods to be used for both crisis management and business resumption. CMTs also benefit from periodic rehearsals of potential disasters so that they can practice how to respond to them.

6.3.3 Outsourcing

A firm may choose to outsource some aspects of its business to a third party with specific expertise in managing certain risks. This option of risk management is gaining popularity with financial institutions. However, it is important to remember that a firm only transforms the risk from, say, direct process management, to managing the quality of the outsourced process.

6.3.4 Insurance

Another common method of transferring risk is to purchase insurance cover. Insurance policies can be constructed to cover losses due to fire, theft and losses caused by human error. When taking out insurance, a firm needs to be very clear what the insurance will pay out for and when it will pay out. Insurance policies often cover litigation risk but because the legal process can be complex, and therefore slow, a policy that pays out only after judgment has been made may be too late to save the firm if it has already suffered substantial losses.

6.3.5 Information and Cyber Security

Information and cyber security continues to be high on most corporate agendas in response to the increasing threat from cyber criminals.

Information and cyber security are both associated with IT risks but information can of course also be held on paper. A firm should categorise the types of information which it receives and processes so that appropriate steps can be taken to protect it regardless of the medium. For example, personal staff or customer information needs greater care than a report downloaded from the internet which is already in the public domain.

Guidelines must be developed to enable staff to know what they are allowed to do with different types of information – for example, information categorised as 'personal' might only be allowed to be emailed if it's been password protected.

Important information should be locked away at night, and many companies operate a clear desk policy. This not only protects against theft but also mitigates against information loss if, for example, the windows of the building are damaged. Firms whose buildings have been affected by terrorist bombs have often found that important documents have been blown onto the street outside. Locking paperwork away also helps to prevent damage in the event of burst water pipes or other internal incidents. Important information that exists only on paper should be held in a fire-proof safe.

Information held on IT systems is at risk of cyber theft. The UK government has published on its website an extremely useful and user-friendly guide called '*10 Steps To Cyber Security*'. It provides the following comprehensive guidance on information and cyber security.

Information Risk Management Regime – assess the risks to your organisation's information assets with the same vigour as you would for any other risk.

Secure IT systems – remove or disable unnecessary functionality from IT systems, and keep them patched against known vulnerabilities. Patching refers to the periodic updates which software vendors release to close any security weaknesses that have been discovered in their systems.

Network security – connecting to untrusted networks (such as the internet) can expose your organisation to cyber attacks. Filter all traffic at the network perimeter so that only traffic required to support your business is allowed, and monitor traffic for unusual or malicious incoming and outgoing activity that could indicate an attack (or attempted attack). Assess the effectiveness of the perimeter filters by conducting regular penetration tests.

Managing user privileges – users of your IT systems should only be provided with the user privileges that they need to do their job. Control the number of privileged accounts for roles such as system or database administrators, and ensure this type of account is not used for high risk or day-to-day user activities.

User education and awareness – produce user security policies that describe acceptable and secure use of your organisation's IT systems. These should be formally acknowledged in employment terms and conditions. All users should receive regular training on the cyber risks they face as employees and individuals. Security related roles (such as system administrators, incident management team members and forensic investigators) will require specialist training.

Incident management – establish an incident response and disaster recovery capability that addresses the full range of incidents that can occur. All incident management plans (including disaster recovery and business continuity) should be regularly tested. Report online crimes to the relevant law enforcement agency to help build a clear view of the national threat and deliver an appropriate response.

Malware prevention – viruses and other malicious software are known as malware. Produce policies that directly address the business processes (such as email, web browsing, removable media and personally owned devices) that are vulnerable to malware. Scan for malware across your organisation and protect all host and client machines with antivirus solutions that will actively scan for malware. All information supplied to or from your organisation should be scanned for malicious content.

Monitoring – continuously monitor inbound and outbound network traffic to identify unusual activity or trends that could indicate attacks and the compromise of data.

Removable media controls – where the use of removable media is unavoidable (for example USB keys or external hard drives), limit the types of media that can be used together with the users, systems, and types of information that can be transferred. Scan all media for malware using a standalone media scanner before any data is imported into your organisation's system.

Home and mobile working – assess the risks to all types of mobile working where the device connects to the corporate network infrastructure. Train mobile users on the secure use of their mobile devices for locations they will be working from. Protect data using encryption if the device supports it.

6.3.6 Physical Security

The operational risks associated with physical security can be reduced by firms making often quite simple arrangements, including, for example:

- vetting all staff and contractors for previous criminal records
- visible ID cards for all staff
- sign-in for all visitors to the building
- remaining vigilant and preparing for external threats such as protests or marches, especially those aimed at financial services firms.

6.3.7 Risk Awareness Training

Risk awareness training for all relevant staff should be given by the firm to help staff understand the principle of reducing the likelihood of risk occurring, and the key role which they play in achieving this. Details of the training being given, and attendance, should be recorded and tracked by the operational risk function.

6.3.8 Data Protection

Firms are legally obliged to take the greatest care with data relating to their customers. Under the European Union's General Data Protection Regulation (GDPR), very large fines can be levied – up to €20 million or 4% of global revenue, whichever is higher – for any company with European customers that mishandles their data. Customers must be able to give and retract their consent on how their data is used and stored, including having the right to be 'forgotten' through having all their data deleted. These requirements are not straightforward to meet, and they require firms to control and track data both internally and across inter-firm boundaries. Organisations processing personal data on a large scale need to appoint an independent, adequately qualified data protection officer charged with overseeing the firm's data protection strategy and implementation to ensure compliance with GDPR requirements.

6.4 Operational Loss Data

Learning Objective

3.6.4   Understand how historical loss data can be used in managing operational risk

We saw above that historical loss data can be used to measure operational risk. Another use for the same data is the management of operational risk. There are two main ways in which this data is used.

1. **Escalation thresholds** – these can be defined so that losses of various amounts are escalated to pre-defined levels within the organisation. This enables the relevant governance bodies to monitor losses across the firm and to direct resources to areas that move outside their risk appetite or tolerance.
2. **Loss causal analysis** – if the underlying cause(s) of a loss can be understood then there is a greater chance of preventing a similar occurrence of the same issue elsewhere in the firm. The temptation is to focus on fixing the immediate, visible effects of an incident, and while this is clearly important,

the incident will probably recur unless the root causes of the loss are also be tackled. Over time, as losses are captured, perhaps within an operational risk database, causal trends can be monitored. For example, it might be seen that the majority of losses are caused by IT system issues. Alternatively it might be a lack of process documentation which seems to be the most common cause. Causal trend analysis requires standard causal categories to be pre-defined. Without these predefined categories, each loss will be assigned a differently worded cause which will make trend analysis very difficult. Many firms have found that the Basel event categories provide an insufficient taxonomy, and have extended them using their own loss causal categories. The category list can grow over time, and its successful compilation depends largely on a combination of common sense and the ability to look back over previous losses to examine the in-house set of 'typical' causes.

End of Chapter Questions

Think of an answer for each question and refer to the appropriate section for confirmation.

1.   What is the Basel definition of operational risk?
     Answer Reference: Section 1.1

2.   What are the four areas an operational risk policy should address?
     Answer Reference: Section 2.1

3.   Name six stages of a risk management framework.
     Answer Reference: Section 3.2

4.   Give an example of a risk for each of the four operational risk causes.
     Answer Reference: Section 4.3

5.   Why is it difficult to measure operational risk quantitatively?
     Answer Reference: Section 5.1

6.   Is it more useful to construct Key Risk Indicators on the likelihood or the impact of a risk?
     Answer Reference: Section 5.4

7.   Give an example of each of the two main control types.
     Answer Reference: Section 6.3.1

8.   What are the two main aspects to business continuity planning?
     Answer Reference: Section 6.3.2

9.   Give examples of three possible defences against cyber theft.
     Answer Reference: Section 6.3.5

10. Give three examples of ways to reduce the operational risks associated with information and physical security.
     Answer Reference: Section 6.3.6

Chapter Four
Credit Risk

This syllabus area will provide approximately 15 of the 100 examination questions

Chapter Summary

The original Basel Accord focused on credit risk in recognition of its primary importance in the risk profile of many financial institutions. This chapter introduces the basic methods of credit risk measurement and presents some common mitigation techniques.

At the most basic level, credit risk is simply the risk that, having extended a loan to another party, it is not repaid as agreed. Therefore, this chapter introduces techniques that can be used to assess the probability that third parties default (ie, fail to repay). These techniques can be applied to individual third parties (known as counterparties) or the industry within which they operate, or even the country within which they are based. This is because the likelihood of a counterparty defaulting is strongly correlated with the success of their industry, and the economic state of their home country.

Larger counterparties are credit-rated by firms known as ratings agencies: the higher the rating the better the credit risk – or to put it another way, the lower the likelihood of default. Smaller firms are not rated by an agency, and so lending institutions have to perform their own assessment of the likelihood of default. This is also true for retail customers.

Another important consideration when assessing credit risk is the quality of any assets that have been used as security in the event of default. The higher the quality, the less concerned is the lending institution about default because the underlying security (perhaps the house of one of the borrowing company's directors) can be sold to recoup the loss.

1. Identification of Credit Risk

1.1 Key Components of Credit Risk

Learning Objective

4.1.1   Understand the key components of credit risk and how they arise: counterparty risk, issuer risk and concentration risk

Credit risk is the risk of loss caused by the failure of a counterparty or issuer to meet its obligations. The party that has the financial obligation is called the **obligor**. The goal of credit risk management is to maximise a firm's risk-adjusted rates of return by maintaining credit risk exposure within acceptable parameters.

* Credit risk exists in two broad forms: counterparty risk and **issuer risk**. Counterparty risk is the risk that a counterparty fails to fulfil its contractual obligations. A counterparty is one of the parties to a transaction – either the buyer or the seller. Examples of counterparty credit risk from a bank's perspective would include:
    ◦ the risk that a customer fails to pay back a loan
    ◦ the risk that a company with whom the bank does business declares bankruptcy before having paid for goods or services supplied by the bank
    ◦ the risk that a broker from whom the bank has purchased a bond fails to deliver – or delivers late.

In the third of the above examples, the bond itself also carries issuer risk. This is the risk that the issuer of the bond could default on its obligations to pay **coupons** or repay the principal on the bond.

Concentration risk arises through an uneven distribution of exposures to individual issuers or counterparties (single-name concentration) or within industry sectors and geographical regions (sectorial concentration).

For example, if a bank is overly-dependent on a small number of counterparties – single-name concentration risk – then, if any of those counterparties default, the bank's revenues could drop by a significant amount. Over-concentration at the country, sector or industry levels also holds risk for a bank – if, for example, the country in which it is overly concentrated suffers an economic downturn, then its revenues will again be adversely affected compared to competitors who are better diversified.

1.2   Counterparty and Issuer Risk Exposures

Learning Objective

4.1.2   Know the main areas of exposure of counterparty, systemic and issuer risk within banking, securities and investment functions

It can be seen then that credit risk consists of counterparty and issuer risk, and that the following differences exist between them.

1. A broker could fail to deliver a bond issued by a good quality company that is currently paying its coupons and redeeming its bonds. This is counterparty risk.
2. The same broker could deliver the bond exactly as required, but the issuing company, previously assessed as being of high quality, runs into trouble. It declares bankruptcy and stops paying its interest on bonds. This is issuer risk.

Some examples of different firms and combinations of credit risk will help to illustrate the main areas of exposure of counterparty and issuer risk within banking, securities and investment functions.

1. A fixed income fund is exposed to issuer credit risk in its holdings of financial instruments whose values are based on the continuation of the commitments made by the original issuers. So, for example, if a fund holds bonds or other forms of corporate debt, and the issuers of any of the bonds should default, the coupon payments would cease. This would reduce the overall returns of the fund.
2. A broker takes on counterparty credit risk when, for example, it agrees to buy shares from a long-standing client. The money is credited to the client's account but the client declares bankruptcy before delivering the shares.
3. A bank is exposed to counterparty credit risk when it issues mortgages to retail customers, a portion of whom will default on their mortgage.

For most banks, loans are the largest and most obvious source of credit risk; however, other sources of credit risk exist throughout the activities of a bank, including in the banking book and in the trading book, and both on and off the balance sheet. These sources include:

- the extension of commitments and guarantees
- interbank transactions
- financial instruments such as futures, options, swaps and bonds
- the settlement of these and other transactions.

Transaction settlement is a key source of counterparty risk. This is the point at which the buyer and seller exchange the instrument and the cash to pay for it. There is a risk that one party delivers, but the other fails to do so.

Ideally, the transfer of the purchased item and the transfer of cash would occur at exactly the same time, and there are electronic settlement systems to ensure that this happens. However, this is not always possible – and even when it is, there is always the chance that the mechanism may fail and one party to the agreement is still owed what they were due.

Another example of **settlement risk** is when an investment company has a **forward** contract to exchange euros for US dollars with a foreign bank. On the contract's maturity date, the investment company makes its euro payment but, because of time differences, there is a delay in the foreign bank making its corresponding dollar payment. Because it is possible that the firm will fail to make its payment, the investment company faces settlement credit risk.

Certain financial instruments also carry '**pre-settlement risk**'. This is the risk that an institution defaults before the settlement of the transaction, where the traded instrument has a positive economic value to the other party. This can occur during an interest rate swap. This is an agreement between two counterparties where one stream of future interest payments is exchanged for another based on a specified principal amount. Interest rate swaps often exchange a fixed payment for a floating payment that is linked to a well-known published interest rate. A company will typically use interest rate swaps to limit or manage exposure to fluctuations in interest rates, or to obtain a marginally lower interest rate than it would have been able to get without the swap. However, if interest rates then move in favour of counterparty A, the other counterparty B will owe a net obligation. Failure to perform on this obligation creates pre-settlement risk for counterparty A.

Systemic Risk

Systemic risk refers to a possible breakdown of the entire financial system rather than simply the failure of an individual firm. Systemic risk exists because of the close interlinkages between the different parts of the financial system. These interlinkages create feedback loops that can turn relatively minor events into major crises.

For example, the credit crisis that started in the US housing market caused banks around the world to withdraw from the interbank lending markets as trust in the resilience of other banks evaporated. Northern Rock, a UK bank, had built its business model on borrowing cheaply on the short-term interbank markets, and turning those loans into long term mortgages. A slowdown in the US and global financial system directly impacted the UK when Northern Rock failed in 2007–08 – the first banking failure in the UK caused by deposit withdrawals for 140 years.

On the other hand, when Barings Bank failed in 1995 as a result of losses caused by a rogue trader, the bank went into bankruptcy, but this did not lead to a wider crisis. This is because the causes of its failure were unique to that institution rather than being a set of circumstances common to all banks and so there were no contagion effects.

In chapter 1 we looked at recovery and resolution as a regulatory response to systemic risk, and systemic risk mitigation is a key question for regulators and policymakers. However, individual firms need to formulate their own strategies in light of the existence of systemic risk rather than relying on governments to prevent systemic failure.

1.3   Credit Risk Boundary Issues

Learning Objective

4.1.3   Understand credit risk boundary issues as identified within Basel

In chapter 3 we defined operational risk as *'The risk of loss resulting from inadequate or failed internal processes, people and systems or from external events'*. Basel describes the following key operational ('boundary') risks to be considered when banks are developing their credit administration areas.

- **Internal processes** – the efficiency and effectiveness of the credit administration operations, including:
    - prescribed management policies and procedures monitoring documentation
    - adequacy of controls over all back-office procedures
    - contractual requirements
    - legal covenants
    - collateral management.
- **Systems** – the accuracy and timeliness of credit risk information provided to management information systems.
- **People** – adequate segregation of duties.

2.   Credit Risk Measurement

2.1   Credit Risk Measurement Techniques

Learning Objective

4.2.1   Understand the following techniques for measuring credit risk and what they are designed to achieve: credit exposure; credit risk premium; credit ratings

This section explains the following basic techniques for measuring credit risk:

- credit exposure

- credit risk premium
- credit ratings.

2.1.1 Credit Exposure

Credit exposure is the amount that can potentially be lost if a debtor defaults on its obligations. It is used to quantitatively assess the severity of credit risk from:

- counterparties, and
- portfolios.

Credit exposure consists of two parts:

1. current exposure
2. potential future exposure.

The **current exposure** is the current obligation outstanding which is normally fairly straightforward to calculate. Potential future exposure is an estimate of the likely loss at some point in the future and this is harder to calculate because of uncertainty arising from:

- credit facilities which banks make available to companies – and, by their nature, these are often not actually drawn down until the company is in financial trouble
- financial instruments which have different future economic values according to circumstances which have not yet arisen, such as changes in interest rates.

The potential future exposure calculation is usually performed using statistical techniques, such as Value-at-Risk (VaR) modelling, which is explained below.

2.1.2 Credit Risk Premium

A **credit risk premium** is the difference between the interest rate a firm pays when it borrows and the interest rate on a default-free security, such as a government bond. The premium is the extra compensation the market or financial institution requires for lending to a firm that has a risk of defaulting.

As an obligor's credit risk increases, lenders demand a higher credit risk premium through an increase in the amount of interest paid. This increase is necessary to offset the heightened probability that the loan will not be repaid in accordance with its terms.

2.1.3 Credit Ratings

There is a strong relationship between credit risk premium and **credit rating** (see next section). In theory, the higher the rating is, the more creditworthy the obligor is and the lower the obligor's risk premium. This means that the cost of borrowing will be less for a higher rated firm as a reflection of its lower likelihood to default. Conversely, downgrades in a company's credit rating can (and, typically, do) significantly increase its borrowing costs.

From the perspective of potential investors and lenders, one measure of a firm's credit risk is its credit rating. A credit rating is an expression of a firm's creditworthiness and financial health. An independent credit rating agency will assign a credit rating to companies based on 'numeric' factors, such as the analysis of the company's financial statements.

The ratings agency will also consider softer factors such as the quality of a firm's management, its competitiveness within its industry and the expected growth trajectory of its industry.

As well as rating the issuers, agencies also rate individual issues, and these latter ratings usually carry a short-term and long-term outlook.

2.2   Role and Influence of Credit Rating Agencies

Learning Objective

4.2.2   Understand the role and influence of credit rating agencies

There are more than 75 ratings agencies around the world, many of whom specialise in certain geographic regions or areas of credit finance.

The Basel Accord (see chapter 2 on International Risk Regulation) introduced a ratings-based method to the calculation of credit risk for the standardised approach, and the Basel Committee defined a set of guidelines that national regulators could use for recommending permissible rating agencies.

In the UK, the regulators nominated:

* Fitch Ratings
* Moody's
* Standard & Poor's (S&P).

Elsewhere in Europe, the Bundesbank in Germany nominated the same three plus another two, Dominion Bond Rating Service (DBRS) and Japan Credit Rating Agency (JCRA).

This official recognition added great influence to an already influential set of market players, and investors came to rely heavily on their ratings.

Moody's, S&P and Fitch all use similar, but not identical, terminologies for their bond ratings. They are based on letters of the alphabet, with, for example, 'AAA' being the highest S&P rating. The terms 'investment grade' and 'speculative grade' have emerged to describe the categories 'AAA' to 'BBB' (investment grade) and 'BB' to 'D' (speculative grade), but these terms are simply market conventions, and do not imply any recommendation or endorsement of a specific security for investment purposes.

2.3 Merits and Limitations of Credit Ratings

Learning Objective

4.2.3   Understand the merits and limitations of using credit ratings to assess creditworthiness of companies and financial instruments

Credit ratings are a useful method for lenders to assess the creditworthiness of a borrower.

Sovereign credit ratings take into account the overall economic conditions of a country, including the volume of foreign, public and private investment, capital market transparency and foreign currency reserves. Sovereign ratings also assess political conditions, such as overall political stability and the level of economic stability a country will maintain during times of political transition.

Institutional investors rely on sovereign ratings to qualify and quantify the general investment atmosphere of a particular country. The sovereign rating is often the prerequisite information that institutional investors and banks use to determine whether they will further consider specific companies, industries and classes of securities issued in a specific country.

Credit ratings, debt ratings or bond ratings are also issued to individual companies and to specific financial instruments. Long-term ratings analyse and assess a company's ability to meet its responsibilities with respect to all of its securities issued. Short-term ratings focus on the specific securities' ability to perform, given the company's current financial condition and general industry performance conditions.

In theory, the ratings agencies play a useful part in helping firms assess the credit risks of worldwide companies. However, in the run-up to the recent credit crunch, many investors had started to rely more on the ratings supplied by the credit rating agencies than on their own credit risk analysis.

Many investors misunderstood the fact that ratings only measure credit quality and do not capture the risk of a decline in market value or the liquidity prospects of an instrument. It seemed that investors were treating the credit rating as if it were also a measure of the market or even liquidity risk of the instrument.

In addition, the fact that a rating is just an opinion – albeit an 'expert' opinion – was often forgotten. *The Oxford English Dictionary* defines an 'opinion' as a *'view or standpoint not necessarily based upon facts or knowledge'*, hence investors ought to be cautious when they are making their investment decisions purely based on the opinion of a credit rating agency. When the ratings agencies started downgrading instruments in the summer of 2007, many investors lost faith in ratings and stopped buying complex instruments altogether.

Specific criticisms of the rating agencies include the following:

*   Companies have not been downgraded fast enough. For example, the major US firm Enron's rating remained at investment grade up until four days before the company went bankrupt, despite the fact that the credit rating agencies had been aware of the company's problems for some months. This is a balancing act though, and the agencies' ratings would lose their stability if they moved up and down in line with every market movement.

- Rating agencies have been criticised for having too familiar a relationship with company management, possibly opening themselves to undue influence or the vulnerability of being misled. In addition, any business model that allows the receiver of a rating to pay for it, and not the user, may encourage conflicts of interest on the part of the rating agency.

- Certain credit rating agencies have made errors in rating some structured products, particularly in assigning AAA ratings to structured debt instruments, which in a large number of cases have subsequently been downgraded or defaulted. The three agencies mentioned above (Fitch, Moody's and S&P) all subsequently made public statements admitting that they had not anticipated the credit crunch and, therefore, had needed to downgrade firms and instruments.

- During the liquidity and credit crisis of 2008–09, rating agencies came under immense public scrutiny and, as a result of this pressure, revised their rating criteria. This particularly affected the whole array of structured finance products. This led to investment grade ratings being downgraded straight to speculative grades on a scale that had never before been seen. However, many of those bonds that suffered severe downgrades have not actually experienced defaults. Subsequently, rating agencies were accused of becoming too conservative in their rating methodologies as banks, who were holding large originally AAA-rated portfolios, suddenly experienced massive surges in related capital charges. This is because the capital requirements for holding such instruments depend upon the instruments' credit rating.

2.4 Counterparty Credit Risk and Applications in Practice

Learning Objective

4.2.4   Understand the key issues relating to counterparty credit risk and applications in practice: probability of default (PD), loss given default (LGD), exposure at default (EAD), recovery rates (RR), credit events, maturity, wrong way risk, non-performing assets

For credit risks associated with loan defaults, we can say that:

Expected loss (EL) = PD x EAD x LGD

where:

PD = Probability of Default (%)
EAD = Exposure at Default (Amount)
LGD = Loss Given Default (%)

These terms will be explained in more detail, as will the following related credit risk concepts:

- credit events
- maturity.

When a counterparty defaults on payment, the loss to the bank is not necessarily the total of what the counterparty owes. For example, if Newbank lent ABC Co. £500 million, and ABC then defaulted, how much would Newbank lose?

Newbank may have a guarantee in place with ABC and may be able to reclaim some of that amount through the legal process. In addition, ABC may have placed collateral with Newbank which would offset some of loss to the bank.

If the actual loss is £300 million then the **loss given default (LGD)** would be 60% (LGD is expressed as a percentage). Newbank might then use 60% as a factor to apply to its other outstanding loans in recognition of the fact that its loss in this particular case was 60% of what it could have been.

The **probability of default (PD)** of a borrower or group of borrowers is a measure of the likelihood of their failing to pay what they owe. The bank will estimate the probability of default using historical experience and empirical evidence. The higher the default probability estimate, the higher the interest rate the lender will charge the borrower to compensate for the higher default risk.

The exposure at default (EAD) is the amount which a bank will be exposed to in the future at the point of a potential default. This amount may not be the amount they are exposed to 'now'. In many cases it will be the same, but for certain facilities (eg, those with undrawn commitments), the EAD will include an estimate of future lending before default.

2.4.1 EAD and Maturity

EAD will also depend on the maturity, or 'time to completion', of the loan arrangements. The longer the time to maturity, the larger is the probability that the credit quality will decrease, as the obligor has both an increased opportunity and perhaps an increased need to draw down the remaining credit line.

When a bank's counterparty defaults, the bank may lose all the market value of the position, but often a certain 'recovery value' is to be found through bankruptcy proceedings or other agreed settlement.

The amount it is likely to recover is called the 'recovery value', or, expressed as a percentage, the recovery rate (RR). RR is the 'other side' of LGD described above.

$$\text{RR} = 100\% - \text{LGD}$$

2.4.2 Credit Events

It is important for firms to know when a credit risk has materialised because that will trigger certain actions on the part of the bank and other creditors of the bankrupt firm.

Although the term 'credit event' is a recognised industry trigger point, it does not have a precise definition. It is commonly understood to include bankruptcy, insolvency, receivership, or simply a failure to meet payment obligations when due. A **credit event** can also be simply a credit-rating downgrade.

2.4.3 Wrong Way Risk

Wrong way risk (which is often referred to as wrong way exposure) is defined by the International Swaps and Derivatives Association (ISDA) as the risk that occurs when *'exposure to a counterparty is adversely correlated with the credit quality of that counterparty'*. If the creditworthiness of a counterparty and the exposure of a transaction with that same counterparty are measured and modelled independently then this correlation will be missed.

An example of wrong way risk is the situation where securities issued by a counterparty or its related entities are accepted as collateral against the risk of that counterparty defaulting. This is because the nearer to default the counterparty moves, the lower the value of its equities and hence the less they provide the required cover against default.

2.4.4 Non-Performing Assets

Non-performing assets are loans whose repayments are not being made on time. If payments are late for a short time, a loan is classified as past due. Once a payment becomes really late (usually 90 days), the loan is classified as non-performing.

A high level of non-performing assets compared to similar lenders may be a sign of problems, as may a sudden increase in the level of non-performing assets. However, this needs to be seen in the context of the type of lending being done. Some banks lend to higher-risk customers than others and therefore tend to have a higher proportion of non-performing debt, but will compensate for this by charging borrowers higher interest rates.

Equally, where the loan is backed by security, a default will be less of a concern than in the case of an unsecured loan. This is because, after a default, any security underlying the loan can be sold by the bank to recover the loss from the unpaid loan.

2.5 Credit Limits for Trade Book and Loan Product Risk Management

Learning Objective

4.2.5 Know the basic principles of setting credit limits for trade book and loan product risk management

Credit limits are maximum limits for all aspects of credit exposure set by financial institutions. Firms need to establish overall credit limits at the level of:

- individual borrowers
- counterparties, and
- groups of connected counterparties.

The better quality the counterparty, the higher the lending limit would be, and such limits are frequently based in part on the internal risk rating assigned to the borrower or counterparty.

Every financial institution will set credit limits, whether it be a bank making corporate loans, a derivative dealer transacting with counterparties, a fund manager buying bonds for a **portfolio** or a credit card company providing credit to cardholders. These limits help to ensure that the firm's credit-granting activities are adequately diversified.

As mentioned earlier, much of the credit exposure faced by some banks comes from activities and instruments in the trading book and off the balance sheet. Limits on such transactions are particularly effective in managing the overall credit risk profile or counterparty risk of a bank, and linking it into the overall risk appetite (see chapter 1).

Limits should also be established for particular industries or economic sectors, geographic regions and specific products. A bank might also set a total exposure credit limit for all its corporate lending activities. To be effective, credit limits should be binding and not driven by customer demand.

2.6 Limitations of Credit Risk Measurement

Learning Objective

4.2.6 Understand the main limitations of credit risk measurement

Although the science of measuring credit risk has been developing rapidly in recent years, there are some common assumptions used by both firms and regulators that can introduce errors into the risk models and produce inaccurate credit risk calculations.

Some of the main issues are:

- **Using simplified calculations of potential exposure** – generally, the **potential exposure** of a portfolio is greater than its current exposure. Institutions may apply charges to account for potential exposure based on broad categories that oversimplify the different levels of risk. These charges are stated as percentages of **notional amounts** but notionals are not always true measures of the underlying credit risks.
- **A lack of recognition of the time period of credit risk** – default risk increases as the time of exposure increases. This is sometimes not accounted for.
- **A lack of recognition of portfolio diversification** – overall credit risk is significantly reduced by diversification but measurement calculations may not take this into account.
- **Financial institutions use probabilities which are a best 'guestimate' of the future**. Such calculations are based upon past information and so financial institutions can and do miscalculate the probability of default.

3. Credit Risk Management

3.1 Examples of Credit Risk Protection and Mitigation

Learning Objective

4.3.1 Understand the following examples of credit risk mitigation, and how they may be typically applied: underwriting standards; guarantees; credit limits; netting; collateral; diversification; insurance/credit derivatives; credit default swaps; collateralised debt obligations, loan sales and securitisation; central counterparties

3.1.1 Underwriting Standards

Underwriting standards are the standards that financial institutions apply to borrowers in order to evaluate their creditworthiness and, therefore, manage the risk of default.

Evaluation requires specific knowledge of their business and includes:

- a review of the borrower's cash flow and financial statements
- the consideration of earnings, profit margin and outstanding debt
- analysis of industry variables such as competitive pressures, product cycles and future growth potential
- controlling the terms of the loan, eg, limiting loan size, establishing a repayment schedule and requiring additional collateral for higher risk loans.

3.1.2 Guarantees

To make their bond issues more attractive to investors, many issuers arrange for another organisation, generally one with very strong finances, to guarantee the debt. This means that if the issuer cannot pay the interest or capital from its own resources, the guarantor will make the repayments. The investor therefore relies on the creditworthiness of the guarantor, as opposed to that of the issuer, for security. This exposes the investor to the counterparty risk associated with the guarantor.

In the same way, smaller companies also make use of guarantees from third parties in order to more easily obtain loans from banks.

For the borrower there is a cost associated with obtaining a guarantee, but this would be offset by the ability to gain access to lower-cost funding.

3.1.3 Credit Limits

Refer back to section 2.5.

3.1.4 Netting Agreements

A **netting** agreement allows two parties that exchange multiple cash flows during a given day to agree bilaterally to net those cash flows to one payment per currency. This reduces each party's settlement risk, and also reduces transaction costs and communication expenses. To actually reduce risk, such agreements need to be sound and legally enforceable.

Examples of Cash Netting

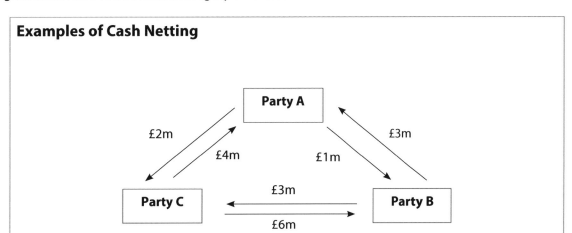

The diagram above shows the end-of-day commitments between parties A, B and C. No netting agreement is in place. If, for instance, party C defaulted on its commitments, the replacement costs would be £4 million for party A and £6 million for party B.

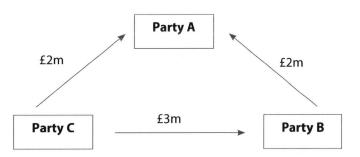

The diagram above shows the same commitments but this time a netting agreement exists between each party. The cash flows shown above reflect the net obligation between each party. Now if party C defaults, the replacements costs would be only £2 million for party A and £3 million for party B.

3.1.5 Collateral

Collateral is an asset held by a lender on behalf of an obligor, under certain agreed conditions, as security for a loan. It can be a physical asset (such as a house that secures a mortgage loan), or can be in the form of cash or securities, and is used by the lender as a form of insurance to reduce credit exposure to a counterparty. In the event that the obligor defaults, the lender may retain the collateral.

Collateral is used to mitigate credit risk for a variety of transactions, such as foreign exchange forwards, securities lending and **derivatives**. A collateral arrangement can be:

* A **unilateral arrangement** means that one party gives collateral to the other.
* A **bilateral arrangement** allows for two-sided obligations, such as a swap or foreign exchange forward. In this situation, both parties may post collateral for the value of their total obligation to the other.
* A netted arrangement means that the net obligation may be collateralised so that, at any point in time, the party which is the net obligor posts collateral for just the value of the net obligation.
* In a typical arrangement, the collateral is periodically marked-to-market (ie, its present value is calculated using current market prices/rates), and the amount adjusted to reflect changes in value.

3.1.6 Diversification

Diversification can be used as a means of reducing portfolio credit risk by ensuring that the portfolio is spread across borrowers in different, negatively correlated industry sectors that have an inverse economic relationship to each other.

This approach enables institutions to avoid unacceptable concentrations of credit risk because when one industry sector enters a downturn and its borrowers start to default, the other sector might be booming. The earnings of some of the loans in the portfolio will therefore offset the losses of others, making it less likely that the portfolio will lose money overall. The portfolio 'highs' will not be as high, but neither will the 'lows' be as low, and so the volatility of returns will be lower.

3.1.7 Insurance and Credit Derivatives

In addition to loan-based instruments such as bonds, a range of 'secondary' instruments exist which derive their value from an underlying loan or series of loans. These are called **credit derivatives**, and the two most common types are the **credit default swap** (CDS) and the collateralised debt obligation (CDO).

In the simplest form of CDS, the bank making a loan pays a premium to a third party that, in turn, agrees to make the bank whole in the event of a default on the underlying loan or bond. This transaction resembles an insurance contract, where the insured pays a premium to a third party (an insurance company) in return for a promise to make the insured whole in the event of a loss.

The other type of basic credit derivative is a CDO. As in a CDS, the parties to a CDO contract are shifting the risk of an underlying debt instrument from lender to investor, but, instead of doing so for a corporate loan or bond from a single borrower, they do so for a series of loans or bonds from many borrowers. In this way diversification is achieved, since the risk for an investor of any one loan defaulting is absorbed by gains on other debtors that do not default. CDSs and CDOs are explained in more detail in the following sections.

Credit Default Swaps (CDSs)

As with other credit derivatives, institutions can use CDSs to increase or decrease their credit exposure to a particular counterparty, for a particular period of time. They are attractive because they allow financial institutions to:

- buy (or sell) a form of insurance to mitigate their (or the other party's) credit risk
- improve their portfolio diversification by reducing undesirable credit risk concentrations
- customise their credit exposure to another party without having a direct relationship with them
- transfer credit risk without adversely affecting the customer relationship.

CDS contracts are an important innovation in credit risk mitigation, but they can also expose the user to other types of risk such as operational, counterparty, liquidity and legal risks.

Example of a Credit Default Swap (CDS)

As we have seen, a CDS is a form of insurance against counterparty default. It is a bilateral financial contract in which one counterparty (the protection buyer) pays a periodic or one-off fee (typically expressed in basis points on the notional amount). This is in return for a payment by the other counterparty (the protection seller) if a credit event (see above) ever occurs to some other party, called the reference entity or asset.

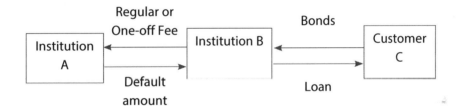

In the diagram above, Institution B purchases bonds (the reference asset) from Customer C (the reference entity). B then enters into a CDS with Institution A, whereby B pays A a fixed periodic coupon, or one-off fee, for the life of the swap. In return, if Customer C defaults due to a credit event, A pays B the default amount and the swap then terminates.

This provides B with protection against the possibility of C defaulting on its payments, as A assumes the credit risk. Institution B is exposed instead to the counterparty risk associated with Institution A.

Collateralised Debt Obligations (CDOs), Loan Sales and Securitisation

Lenders with loans on their balance sheets can create an income stream from those loans, assuming that they continue to perform. Instead of simply relying on the underlying income stream as a source of revenue running for the length of the loan agreement, the lender can choose to sell the loans to another institution in order to receive an immediate 'lump sum' payment. This is a **loan sale**.

Another form of loan sale is **securitisation**, and the process involves a number of participants. The 'originator' is the firm whose assets are being securitised. The most common process involves an 'issuer' acquiring the assets from the originator and issuing bonds to finance the purchase of the securitised loans. The income stream from the underlying loans is then used to repay the bondholders.

The issuer is often a company that has been specially set up for the purpose of the securitisation, which is known as a special purpose vehicle (SPV). The creation of an SPV ensures that the underlying asset pool (for example, mortgages or other loans) is held separately from the other assets of the originator. This means that, if the originator is ever declared bankrupt, the assets that have been transferred to the SPV will not be affected.

The securitised loans are often rated by a ratings agency in order to facilitate the sale of the issuer's bonds. An advantage for originators of this sort of arrangement is that a lower-rated entity can access cheaper debt capital markets that would otherwise be the preserve of higher-rated institutions. This is because a specific pool of assets can attract a higher credit rating than the originating firm itself.

Although securitisation can have many advantages to both sides of the transaction, over-complexity can become a disadvantage if underlying loans start to default. In the run-up to the 2008 financial crisis, pools of sub-prime mortgages were mixed with higher-rated mortgages in complex CDOs which attracted higher overall ratings than the sum of the parts might have warranted. These CDOs were then often re-cut with other securitisations and sold on to different institutions.

However, in 2007, as interest rates started to rise, the underlying sub-prime mortgages began to default.

At that point it became impossible to determine the quality of securitisations and so demand for them tailed off. However, many institutions had become reliant on securitisation processes to maintain their funding, and these institutions were some of the early casualties of the resulting credit crunch which spread as inter-bank trust evaporated.

Central Counterparties (CCPs)

The use of a **central counterparty**, or clearing house, is a method used by many exchanges to reduce credit risk. The clearing house acts as the guarantor of all transactions, limiting the exposure of its clearing members by protecting them from defaults.

Rather than two members of an exchange being involved in a direct counterparty-to-counterparty contract (and so assuming each other's credit risk), the clearing house acts as a simultaneous counterparty to each. If one clearing member defaults, the clearing house will guarantee the performance of the contract to the other member. CCPs also boost the scope for netting among the members of an exchange.

For clearing houses to be able to reduce credit risk, they need to have significant resources to cope with any potential defaults. They obtain these resources through capital supplied by:

*   their members
*   fees generated by the exchange, or
*   other parties that do not have a direct relationship with their market.

3.2   Making Calculations

Learning Objective

4.3.2   Be able to calculate a simple margin or collateral adequacy calculation

Many investment management firms lend their stock to institutions that wish to take **short positions** (see chapter 6). To protect against losing the stock if the borrowing firm becomes insolvent, the borrower places collateral with the lender. This often takes the form of government bonds, or other high-quality liquid assets.

The value of the collateral could be set to equal the value of the lent stock, but if its price drops during the period the stock is lent out, then the lending firm will not be able to realise the full value of the stock if the borrower defaults. To overcome this potential loss in value, an extra amount, called a haircut, is added to the collateral's value. The haircut will depend on the **volatility** of the asset serving as collateral; for government bonds it might be, say 3%.

If £100 million IBM shares are lent, and government bonds are offered as collateral, how much collateral should be lodged with the lending firm?

$$£100m + (£100m \times 3\%) = £103m$$

3.3   Credit Risk Management

Learning Objective

4.3.3   Understand the role and sound practice features of an effective credit risk management function

The credit risk management function is responsible for ensuring that the firm's credit risk is properly managed, although it will not own any risk itself. This means implementing a sound credit risk management policy to manage credit risk in a company-wide context and includes:

- owning the credit policy and ensuring that it is adhered to
- setting, monitoring and reviewing credit limits
- assessing potential credit risk events
- ensuring decisions on granting credit are made independently of the trading areas
- measuring and monitoring daily credit exposure. This will also involve providing information for the assessment of capital adequacy
- performing credit analysis by counterparty, country, sector and instrument or financial product (this could include the performance of regulatory 'know your customer' checks, as well as simply assessing the customer's creditworthiness).

The actual role of the credit risk function will vary according to the type of firm, because credit risk management requires a different approach for a bank than for an investment manager, for example. For a bank trading on its own account, certain limits can be applied 'across the board', whereas each fund in an investment management firm could have a different risk appetite for market, credit and other risk types.

3.4 Reporting and Escalation Tools

Learning Objective

4.3.4 Understand the role of reporting and escalation tools of credit risk management

Firms need to develop and implement comprehensive procedures and information systems to monitor the condition of individual and grouped counterparties across the bank's various portfolios. These procedures need to define criteria for identifying and escalating potential counterparty credit issues to senior management, to enable them to resolve issues, to minimise loss to the firm. Problem areas will need more frequent monitoring, as well as possible corrective action, classification and/or provisioning.

3.5 Basel Key Stages

Learning Objective

4.3.5 Know the Basel key stages of credit risk policy development, modelling and control: development, validation, approval, implementation, review and post-implementation monitoring

Basel states that the board of directors should have responsibility for approving and periodically reviewing (at least annually) the firm's credit risk strategy and significant credit risk policies. The strategy should reflect the bank's tolerance for risk and the level of profitability the bank expects to achieve for incurring various credit risks.

Senior management should have responsibility for implementing the credit risk strategy approved by the board of directors and for developing policies and procedures for identifying, measuring, monitoring and controlling credit risk. Such policies and procedures should address credit risk in all of the bank's activities.

To be effective, credit policies must be communicated throughout the organisation, implemented through appropriate procedures, monitored and periodically revised to take into account changing internal and external circumstances. Banks should have methodologies/models that enable them to quantify the risk involved in exposures to individual borrowers or counterparties. Banks should also be able to analyse credit risk at the product and portfolio level in order to identify any particular sensitivities or concentrations. The measurement of credit risk should take account of:

1. the specific nature of the credit (loan, derivative, facility, etc.) and its contractual and financial conditions (maturity, reference rate)

2. the exposure profile until maturity in relation to potential market movements
3. the existence of collateral or guarantees (and any additional counterparty risks associated with these arrangements), and
4. the potential for default based on the internal risk rating. The analysis of credit risk data should be undertaken at an appropriate frequency with the results reviewed against relevant limits.

Banks should use measurement techniques that are appropriate to the complexity and level of the risks involved in their activities, based on robust data, and subject to periodic validation, such as:

- data quality assurance
- model validation review
- reviews of the underlying model assumptions.

3.6 Managing and Measuring Credit Risk

Learning Objective

4.3.6 Understand the methods used to manage credit risk: credit scoring systems; factor inputs: financial, non-financial and extraordinary; stress testing; segmentation; external ratings; setting limits or caps; internal credit rating; provisioning and impairment; key statistics and key performance indicators

3.6.1 Credit Scoring Systems

For retail customers, credit scoring systems include using questionnaires and standard credit request application forms which are subsequently scored. The questions are chosen to enable standardised credit profiles to be applied to new applicants, and would include:

- age
- credit history
- occupation
- years in current job
- home owner or renting.

Credit scoring for firms would include the factor inputs described below. Banks should also consider the results of stress testing as part of their overall credit risk limit setting and monitoring processes.

3.6.2 Factor Inputs

In applying credit scores to firms, banks will use financial, non-financial and other inputs:

- **financial inputs** will include an assessment of each firm's earnings, cash flow, asset values, liquidity, leverage, financial size and debt capacity
- **non-financial inputs** will include a view of each firm's:
  - management quality
  - governance structure

- ◦ industry characteristics
- ◦ country risk
- ◦ credit rating

- **extraordinary inputs** might include:
  - ◦ court actions
  - ◦ other one-off factors that emerge from time to time and which could impact the firm's ability to honour its commitments.

3.6.3   Stress Testing

Stress testing involves identifying possible events or future changes in economic conditions that could have unfavourable effects on a bank's credit exposures, and assessing the bank's ability to withstand such changes.

Areas for stress testing which the BIS recommends that banks could 'usefully examine' are:

- economic or industry downturns
- interest rate and other market movements
- market-risk events, and
- liquidity conditions.

Stress testing can range from relatively simple alterations in assumptions about one or more factor inputs, to the use of highly sophisticated financial models. Typically, the latter are used by large, internationally active banks.

Whatever the method of stress testing used, the output of the tests should be reviewed periodically and appropriate action taken in cases where the results exceed agreed tolerances. The outputs should also be incorporated into the process for assigning and updating policies and limits.

Finally, the results of the stress tests can be used to form action plans that management could use, for example, to hedge against the outcome, or reduce the size of the exposure.

3.6.4   Segmentation

Under Basel, retail banking attracts less capital compared to commercial banking, and banks have to provide regulators with PD, LGD, and EAD statistics for clearly differentiated segments of their portfolios. Segmentation should be based (i) on credit scores (or some equivalent measure), and (ii) on the time that the transaction has been on the bank's books.

3.6.5   External Ratings

Although the information provided by external rating agencies can be useful, it is of limited value to the needs of a sophisticated credit risk management function. This is because it is often too historic and credit rating agencies have, to date, been slow in their response to adverse events. In addition, the output from the credit rating agencies may not be detailed enough to fully meet the firm's requirements and is not as sensitive to changes as the firm's own analysis.

3.6.6 Credit Limits

As discussed in section 2.5, limits need to be set for all counterparties whether single or part of a group. It can be tempting only to limit the firm's exposure to lower rated firms, and lend with no limit to higher rated ones – but that will lead to increased concentration risk.

3.6.7 Internal Credit Rating

One of the aims of the Basel Accord is to incentivise banks to improve their risk management, and as part of this improvement, banks are encouraged to develop their own internal credit rating systems.

A well-structured internal risk rating system is a good means of differentiating the degree of credit risk in the different credit exposures of a bank. This allows more accurate determination of the overall characteristics of the credit portfolio, concentrations, problem credits and the adequacy of **loan loss reserves**.

More detailed and sophisticated internal risk rating systems, used primarily at larger banks, can also be used to determine internal capital allocation, pricing of credits, and profitability of transactions and relationships. In addition, it avoids the issue of 'split ratings', when a counterparty or financial instrument attracts different external ratings (sometimes differing by several notches) by different rating agencies. This raises the question of which ratings system is the most appropriate.

Typically, an internal risk rating system categorises credits into various classes designed to take into account gradations in risk. Simpler systems might be based on several categories ranging from satisfactory to unsatisfactory; however, more meaningful systems will have numerous gradations for credits considered satisfactory to truly differentiate the relative credit risk they pose. In developing their systems, banks must decide whether to rate the riskiness of the borrower, the risks associated with a specific transaction, or both.

Internal ratings assigned to individual borrowers or counterparties at the time the credit is granted must be reviewed on a periodic basis and individual credits should be assigned a new rating when conditions either improve or deteriorate. Because of the importance of ensuring that internal ratings are consistent and accurately reflect the quality of individual credits, responsibility for setting or confirming such ratings should rest with a credit review function independent of that which originated the credit concerned. It is also important that the consistency and accuracy of ratings is examined periodically by a function such as an independent credit review group.

To ensure that impairment in loans is identified in a timely manner, loans should be regularly reviewed for deterioration in credit quality.

3.6.8 Impairment

Evidence of impairment includes:

- information about significant financial difficulties of the borrower (eg, as indicated by liquidity or cash flow projections)
- an actual breach of contract (eg, delay in the borrower making principal or interest payments)

- a high probability of bankruptcy or other financial reorganisation of the borrower (eg, as indicated by a downgrading of credit status by a credit rating agency)
- the granting by the lender to the borrower, for economic or legal reasons relating to the borrower's financial difficulties, of a concession that the lender would not otherwise consider.

3.6.9 Provisioning

Loan impairment will result in a loss for the lending firm, and the firm therefore needs to set aside an allowance for this loss in its accounts. This is the equivalent of a manufacturing company's allowance for returns on goods sold, and is known as provisioning.

3.6.10 Key Statistics and Key Performance Indicators (KPIs)

A management dashboard should be defined to cover all the factors discussed above. It would display key statistics and **key performance indicators (KPIs)** such as:

- number of debtors past due date
- clients breaching covenants
- credit downgrades.

3.7   Controlling Concentration Risk

Learning Objective

4.3.7   Understand the purpose and methods of controlling concentration risk: single name entity; country, sector and industry risk

As we saw above, concentration risk in credit portfolios arises through an uneven distribution of exposures to individual borrowers (single-name concentration) or within industry sectors and geographical regions (sectoral concentration).

If a bank is overly dependent on a small number of counterparties – single-name concentration risk – then, if any of those counterparties default, the bank's revenues could drop by a significant amount.

This problem needs monitoring centrally via the use of lending limits per counterparty. However, there are further challenges:

1. A bank needs to make sure it knows the relationships between the various counterparties it deals with to ensure that they are not part of a wider corporate group, despite having different names.
2. The loan exposure to these counterparties may only be half the picture – the bank could hold equities in the firms, have lent stock to them, be managing assets on their behalf and so on.

Over-concentration at the country or industry level also holds risk for a bank – if, for example, the country in which it is overly concentrated suffers an economic downturn, then its revenues will again be adversely affected compared to competitors who are better diversified. Again, limits need to be set that govern the extent to which loans can be extended across specific countries and industry sectors.

3.8 Controlling Trading Book Risk

Learning Objective

4.3.8 Understand the purpose and principles of controlling trading book risk: Value-at-Risk (VaR) and confidence levels

There are a number of sophisticated approaches to modelling credit risk in the trading book, both at the individual bond level, and at the portfolio level. VaR is a concept that will be further developed in chapter 5, where we consider the concept of **probability distributions**. Before explaining how VaR can be used to estimate future bond values, we will first illustrate the general idea by using a non-financial example.

Let us assume that we want to build a beach hut. We want to position it not too far from the water's edge, but not so close that it is frequently flooded by high tides. How can we work out the best place to build it?

What we would like to know is how high the tide generally comes up the beach, and then get an idea of how often it comes up significantly further.

- For any variable quantity, in this case the height of the tide, we measure its value over a time period.
- We then rank the measurements, listing them from highest value to lowest. This enables the values over a certain point to be examined. For example, if we took 100 measurements then we could say that for the fifth highest measurement, there is only a five in one hundred, or 5%, probability of the tide exceeding this value.
- For further sophistication we can plot the distribution of our measurements, and using the concept of standard deviation (see chapter 5), we can read off the values at various probabilities.

So, in the case of the VaR for a bond, we need to establish which variable we want to measure. A frequently used measurement is the value of the bond in one year's time, according to its probability of moving from one credit rating to another.

The rating agencies publish these 'credit migration' probabilities, so, knowing what the rating in one year might be, we can work out the corresponding value of the bond at that point. Because the credit migration is only a probability, the standard deviation is also published (see chapter 5). It is this that enables us to plot a distribution and read off the value at the required probability.

For a portfolio of bonds, a similar approach is used, although the correlations between the bonds also need to be taken into account to define any diversification benefit (these concepts are explained in chapter 5).

The probabilities are referred to as confidence intervals and are expressed as a percentage that a given value will not be exceeded. So we might say that the credit VaR of a portfolio over a one-year time horizon is £5 million at the 95% confidence level. This means that there is only a 5% chance that we will lose more than £5 million on this portfolio in that time frame.

End of Chapter Questions

Think of an answer for each question and refer to the appropriate section for confirmation.

1.   What is the definition of credit risk?
     Answer Reference: Section 1.1

2.   What are examples of pre-settlement and settlement risks?
     Answer Reference: Section 1.2

3.   Name three credit rating agencies.
     Answer Reference: Section 2.2

4.   What are the three components of Expected Loss (EL)?
     Answer Reference: Section 2.4

5.   Give three occurrences that could be counted as credit events.
     Answer Reference: Section 2.4.2

6.   What are three assumptions that can produce inaccurate credit risk calculations?
     Answer Reference: Section 2.6

7.   What is collateral?
     Answer Reference: Section 3.1.5

8.   Give four examples of a credit risk function's duties.
     Answer Reference: Section 3.3

9.   Give an example of a non-financial input to a credit scoring model.
     Answer Reference: Section 3.6.2

10. What is concentration risk?
     Answer Reference: Section 3.7

Chapter Five
Market Risk

This syllabus area will provide approximately 15 of the 100 examination questions

Chapter Summary

One of the major aims of many financial institutions is the generation of profits through investment in global financial markets. This business, by its nature, is based on **price uncertainty** – the uncertainty of knowing whether market prices will move in a favourable or adverse direction.

Price uncertainty is the mechanism that allows profits or losses to be made and the risk of loss associated with it is known as market risk. This risk reflects the uncertainty of an asset's future price. The factors affecting market risk are complex. For instance, when investing in a company's shares there are direct and **indirect market risk factors** to consider.

Direct market risk factors are those that directly reflect the performance of a company, such as the health of its balance sheet, its vision and strength of its management team. Indirect factors are those that indirectly affect the performance of a company, such as interest rate levels, economic events, political, sector sentiment and environmental effects.

The financial services sector takes advantage of the existence of market risk to make a profit. The aim of managing this risk is not to eradicate it but to understand and quantify it. If this is done accurately an informed decision can be made on how acceptable the risk is and, hence, whether it is a worthwhile investment. As there are vast profits to be made in getting this right, financial institutions have invested heavily in research, tools and expertise to try to predict the future performance of their investments.

The need to understand this market risk is also important in the pricing of some financial products, such as **futures** and options. For these reasons, the methods and tools used for measuring market risk have become very advanced, involving cutting-edge mathematical theory and computer processing technology. This chapter provides a basic understanding of these methods and tools, and explains how they fit into an overall risk management strategy.

Market risk can be defined as: *'The risk of loss arising from changes in the value of financial instruments'*.

1. Identification of Market Risk

1.1 Identifying Market Risks

Learning Objective

5.1.1 Know and be able to identify the different types of market risk: volatility risk, market liquidity risk, currency risk, basis risk, interest rate risk, commodity risk, equity risk

Market risk can be sub-divided into the following types:

1.1.1 Volatility Risk

Volatility risk is the risk of price movements that are more uncertain than usual affecting the pricing of products. All priced instruments suffer from this form of volatility. This particularly affects options pricing because if the market is volatile then the pricing of an option is more difficult and options will become more expensive.

1.1.2 Market Liquidity Risk

In the context of market risk, this is the risk of loss through not being able to trade in a market or obtain a price on a desired product when required. **Market liquidity risk** can occur in a market due to either a lack of supply or demand or a shortage of market makers (liquidity risk is explained in more detail in chapter 7).

1.1.3 Currency Risk

This is caused by adverse movements in exchange rates. It affects any portfolio or instrument with cash flows denominated in a currency other than the firm's base currency. Currency risk is also inherent when trading cryptocurrencies. These are digital currencies in which encryption techniques are used to regulate the generation of units of currency and verify the transfer of funds, operating independently of a central bank. Cryptocurrencies often display far higher volatility than so-called fiat currencies.

1.1.4 Basis Risk

This occurs when one risk exposure is hedged with an offsetting exposure in another instrument that behaves in a similar, but not identical, manner. If the two positions were truly 'equal and opposite' then there would be no risk in the combined position. **Basis risk** exists to the extent that the two positions do not exactly mirror each other.

1.1.5 Interest Rate Risk

This is caused by adverse movements in interest rates and will directly affect fixed income securities, futures, options and forwards. It may also indirectly affect other instruments.

1.1.6 Commodity Price Risk

This is the risk of an adverse price movement in the value of a commodity. The price risk of commodities differs considerably from other market risk drivers because most commodities are traded in markets where the concentration of supply in the hands of a few suppliers can magnify price volatility.

Fluctuations in the depth of trading in the market (ie, market liquidity) often accompany and exacerbate high levels of price volatility. Other fundamentals affecting a commodity's price include the ease and cost of storage, which varies considerably across the commodity markets (eg, from gold, to electricity, to wheat). As a result of these factors, commodity prices generally have higher volatilities and larger price discontinuities (ie, moments when prices leap from one level to another) than most traded financial securities.

1.1.7 Equity Price Risk

The returns from investing in equities come from:

- **capital growth** – if a company does well, the price of its shares should go up
- **income** – through the distribution by the company of its profits as dividends.

Therefore, investing in equities carries risks that can affect:

- **the capital** – the share price may fall, or fail to rise in line with inflation or with the performance of other, less risky investments
- **the income** – if the company is not as profitable as hoped, the dividends it pays may not keep pace with inflation; indeed they may fall or even not be paid at all. Unlike bond coupons, dividend payments are not compulsory.

1.2 Boundary Issues

Learning Objective

5.1.2 Understand the boundary issues that can arise between different types of market risk

Many of the constituent market risk elements described above are related to each other. For example:

- liquidity risk could be caused by a lack of supply or demand – which also causes **price level risk**
- an increase in volatility risk will exacerbate price level risk for investors wishing to buy or sell
- interest rate risk will indirectly affect the real economy and therefore the markets.

These boundary issues mean that it is not straightforward to analyse exactly which factors are causing which movements.

1.3 Market Risk Examples

Learning Objective

5.1.3 Be able to apply an understanding of market risk to simple, practical situations

As discussed above, three key drivers of market risk are currency, interest rate and liquidity risks. Some concrete examples will help to apply the concepts to the real world.

1.3.1 Currency Risk

A UK investor purchases an **equity** portfolio in the US. The investment itself, in dollars, provides a positive return of 10% but because the dollar loses 8% of its value against the pound, the investor's return is only 2%.

1.3.2 Interest Rate Risk

An investor purchases a long-term bond in the UK hoping to sell it at a profit in the future. Bond prices move inversely to interest rate moves, so if interest rates increase, the price of bonds will fall. For short-term bonds (less than three years) the change in prices will be relatively minor compared to the change in price for a long-term bond (more than ten years). This is because longer-term bonds are generally more volatile because the distant future is unknown and therefore riskier.

1.3.3 Liquidity Risk

An investor purchases a commercial property to rent out. Because of liquidity issues in the property market, it takes much longer to sell again – even reducing the price may not help if no-one else wants to own the property, or if it becomes difficult to obtain credit for a mortgage.

2. Market Risk Management

2.1 Techniques and their Application

Learning Objective

5.2.1 Understand the following techniques and their application in managing market risk: hedging; market risk limits; diversification; high-frequency trading (HFT)

2.1.1 Hedging

Hedging is a means of reducing the risk of adverse price movements by taking an offsetting position in a related product. It is a means of insuring against market risk.

The main financial instruments used in hedging are derivatives, in particular futures and options. For instance, an investor who has bought an equity is at risk of losing money if the market declines. This risk could be hedged by buying a put option, costing a fraction of the price of the equity investment. This option gives the investor the right, but not the obligation, to sell the stock at a set price (the strike price) within a particular time in the future. The investor is now protected against adverse market movements.

The decision to hedge is a trade-off between the risk of adverse market movements and the cost of the hedge – in this case the purchase price of the option. However, it is difficult to achieve perfect offsetting of the risk and the use of hedging introduces, or exacerbates, other risks such as basis risk (described earlier), credit risk and operational risk.

2.1.2 Market Risk Limits

Market risk limits are used as a tool for managing market risk in the same way that credit limits are applied to protect firms from credit risk (see chapter 4). When an organisation takes a risk, it will often specify the maximum loss that it is prepared to make on a portfolio or transaction. This is called the market risk limit or **stop-loss limit** and may be expressed in terms of VaR (see section 2.7), or as an absolute number of the instrument being traded.

The effectiveness of risk limits to manage market risk is dependent upon the accuracy of the risk measurement used to set the limits. The potential problems of using over-simplified risk measurement are:

- risk limits usually have to be inflated in order to accommodate the errors and uncertainty in the measurement. This adversely affects the potential profit of the firm
- traders or other investment professionals may exploit the inaccuracy of risk measurement and take risks that they know the measurement does not account for.

Provided that high quality risk data is used, risk limits can be very effective. While investment professionals sometimes see them as restrictive, they can also be viewed as empowering because they set the risk appetite of the firm and represent explicit authority to take specified levels of risk. For electronic trading, position limits are an extremely effective mitigant against market risk because machines can trade up to, but not beyond, the limit with great speed and accuracy.

2.1.3 Diversification

The market risk of holding two securities in isolation is given by their respective standard deviation of returns. However, by combining these assets in varying proportions to create a two stock portfolio, the portfolio's standard deviation of return will, in almost all cases, be lower than the weighted average of the standard deviations of these two individual securities.

The weightings are given by the proportion of the portfolio held in each security. This reduction in risk for a given level of expected return is due to the effects of diversification. A very simple example of diversification would be to combine shares in a sun cream factory with shares in an umbrella business. The sun cream factory does well when the summers are hot, while the umbrella business does well on rainy days. Although the earnings of each individual business can be volatile, the combined earnings will be less so because of the inverse relationship, or **negative correlation** between their earnings.

Of course, most portfolios hold many more than two stocks, so to quantify the diversification potential of various multi-stock combinations, a concept called correlation is used, which is explained in section 2.6. Diversification is achieved by combining securities whose returns ideally move in the opposite direction to one another or, if in the same direction, at least not to the same degree.

2.1.4 High-Frequency Trading (HFT)

In recent years, a new kind of trading has emerged that uses mathematical models to predict the market price of securities over the next few minutes or hours. These models are run on extremely fast computers that are co-located within a market's data centre; and this gives a speed advantage that enables liquid positions to be unwound at short notice. This allows such firms to offer tight **spreads**, to the advantage of other participants. It also enables high-frequency trading firms to turn over very high volumes of trades throughout the day, with the result that they only need to earn a small amount per trade – which in turn enables small position limits to be employed. This combination of small position limits and fast liquidation time drastically reduces the level of market risk that needs to be taken, which in turn means that such firms can act as market makers, committing to transacting a minimum volume of trades throughout the day.

Other HFT firms pursue speed above all else, rather than developing economic price prediction models. Such firms need to invest heavily in infrastructure, such as microwave links, in order to outperform the fibre networks used by most other market participants. However, speed alone is not a sustainable advantage because it can be replicated by competitor firms with the ability to invest in the necessary computer and telecoms hardware. In addition, price prediction models allow HFT firms to hold positions for minutes or even hours whereas pure-speed HFT firms hardly hold their positions for any time at all. Flash crashes are sometimes blamed on general HFT activity in the popular media because the distinction between the two types of HFT firm is not always well understood.

2.2 The Market Risk Management Function

Learning Objective

5.2.2 Understand the role and sound practice features of an effective market risk management function

In the same way that institutions use a credit risk management function to manage credit risk, it is also essential that they develop and implement an independent market risk management function to manage market risk in a company-wide context.

An effective market risk function will include the following features:

* ownership of the firm's market risk management policy
* proactive management involvement in market risk issues
* defined escalation procedures to deal with rising levels of trading loss, and market risk limit breaches
* independent validation of market pricing and adequacy of VaR models
* ensuring that VaR is not used alone, but is combined with stress testing and scenario analysis
* independent daily monitoring of risk utilisation through the daily production of profit and loss (P&L) accounts and review of front-office closing prices (independent means a separately accountable function reporting directly to senior management).

The role of the market risk function varies according to the type of firm because market risk management requires a different approach in a bank than in a securities trading firm or an investment management firm. For example, a bank trading on its own account has limits applied 'across the board', whereas each fund in an investment management firm could have a different risk appetite for market, credit and other risk types.

2.3 Calculating Dispersion and Variance

Learning Objective

5.2.3 Be able to calculate the key measures of dispersion and variance: mean, median, mode; range, inter-quartile range and quartile deviation; variance; standard deviation

The aim of market risk analysis is not to eliminate risk, but to be able to predict which market risks will yield the greatest returns. We have seen that there are many causal factors within market risk, factors such as liquidity, currency and interest rates.

In addition, unlike operational risk, market risk analysis is able to draw on large amounts of data. However, having a large amount of available data is a mixed blessing because the larger the dataset, the harder it can be to distinguish which data items represent 'expected' behaviours (which will be replicated in the future with a high level of certainty), from those data items that are outliers (and therefore may or may not recur from time to time).

Often market datasets become so large and cumbersome that using and making inferences from samples is the only viable and cost-effective means of analysing the whole population.

We need to know three things about the **sample**:

1. What is its 'typical' value? It would be useful to derive a single number that captures the 'essence' of the distribution. This is referred to as the central tendency.
2. Do the other values stray very far on either side of this 'typical' value? This is referred to as the dispersion.
3. How closely do the characteristics of our sample mirror that of the whole population? This is factored into the formulae for standard deviation shown below.

To illustrate these concepts, the following diagram shows a typical 'distribution' of values from naturally occurring data sets, such as people's IQ or the age of staff in a company.

On the horizontal X axis are the different values which the data item could have. On the vertical Y axis are the number of times each value of the data item appears in our sample. The curve is this shape because there are lots of similar values in the dataset, with fewer small values and fewer large values. The concepts of central tendency and dispersion are illustrated on the graph.

Illustrating Normal Distribution (1)

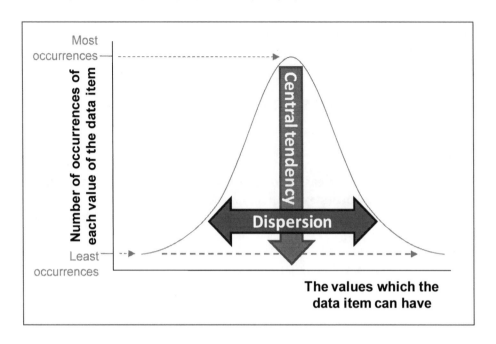

© Andrew Brand

Many naturally occurring datasets actually form this shape when they are plotted as a graph – for example, adult human height. In the graph of people's heights (below) it can be seen that the dispersion is smaller than in the previous graph, reflecting the fact that people's heights tend to cluster around a central range with very few extreme values.

Illustrating Normal Distribution (2)

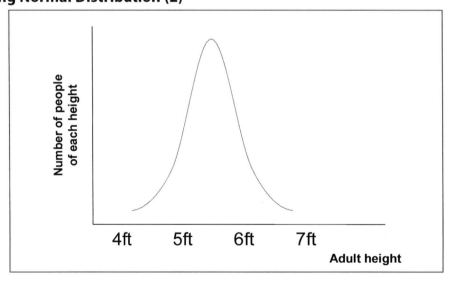

© Andrew Brand

This shape is called a normal or Gaussian distribution and it has certain properties which are very useful for predicting things about which we may not be aware. This is explained further below.

Plotting human height does not reveal anything that we do not already intuitively know simply from the people that we meet. However, if it could be shown that this 'special' shape also fitted other distributions for data about which we know far less (such as historic market returns), then we could use its predictive properties to make assertions about market returns in the future.

2.3.1 Measures of Central Tendency

The idea of 'central tendency' is that it gives us a single number that is typical of the data. So for people we might estimate that the average height across male and female adults in the UK is 5ft 7in.

Three common measures of central tendency and the way in which each is calculated are:

- **mean** – the average value of all the data
- **median** – the middle item(s), with exactly half the data above and half below
- **mode** – the most frequently occurring value in the data.

Mean

The **mean** is the central tendency measure that is most commonly referred to as the 'average'. It is calculated by adding together all of the values in a data set and then dividing that sum by the number of observations in that set to provide the average value of all the data.

So, for example, if you have six investment funds in your portfolio that produce returns of 7%, 8%, 9%, 10%, 11% and 12%, then the average or mean return is:

$$(7\%+8\%+9\%+10\%+11\%+12\%) \div 6 = 9.5\%$$

Therefore, the mean = the sum of all of the observed values ÷ the number of observations

The mean is expressed as the following formula:

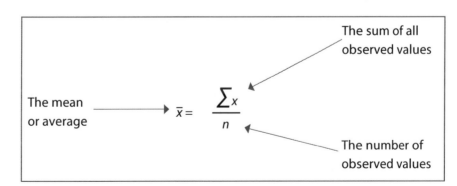

The mean or average → $\bar{x} = \dfrac{\sum x}{n}$

The sum of all observed values

The number of observed values

115

Median

The **median** is the value of the middle item in a set of data arranged in ascending order. It is established by sorting the data from lowest to highest and taking the data point in the middle of the sequence. So, for example, with a range of data, as below, the median can clearly be seen. There is an equal series of numbers both below and above it:

2	5	8	9	12	13	15	16	18
Four numbers				Median	Four numbers			

If the data has an even set of numbers then the median is equal to the average of the two middle items as shown below:

2	5	8	9	12	13	15	16	18	19
				Median = 12.5 $\frac{(12+13)}{2}$					

Mode

The third method of calculating the central tendency is to use the **mode** – which is the most frequently occurring number in a set of data. There can be no mode if no value appears more than any other. There may also be two modes (bimodal), three modes (trimodal), or four or more modes (multimodal). For example, the mode of the following classic car values is £100k:

£100k, £125k, £100k, £115k, £135k, £95k, £100k

2.3.2 Which Measure to Use

The mean is what people often refer to as the average and is the most commonly used measure of central tendency. However, it needs to be recognised that any outliers at the extremes of the data will influence the result.

The median is not influenced in the same way and is often used where there are extreme outliers or where there is skewed data that is not normally distributed. In technical terms it is a more robust measure of central tendency.

With non-normal distributions, for example people's weekly income, the presence of a few millionaires in the data pushes the average salary up above the median. This is shown in the following graph:

Income Distribution

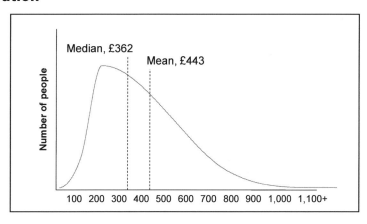

As can be seen, the distribution is skewed, with around 60% of individuals having household incomes below the national average or mean. Because of the potential differences between mean and median, it is generally useful to consider both.

On the other hand, the mode can clearly only be used where there is a 'most commonly occurring value'. It is useful when working with qualitative not quantitative data. For example, the following graph shows the results of the textual analysis performed by Samuel Morse (to establish the patterns for his eponymous code). The data has a mode of 8,000 because five letters (a, i, n, o and s) all appear about 8,000 times in the set of letters he examined to establish 'normal usage'.

The Number of Letters Occurring in the Sample Used by Samuel Morse to Establish the Patterns for Morse Code

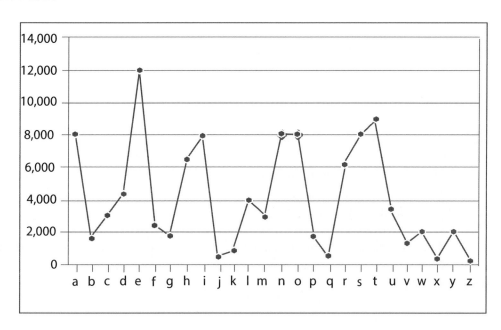

2.3.3   Measures of Dispersion

Having established a typical value for the data, we also need to see how widely spread, or dispersed, around this typical value the data is. We can quantify how dispersed the data is through the use of dispersion measures, and the following techniques are used:

- range and inter-quartile range (used to establish the distribution of values around the median)
- quartile deviation (used to establish the distribution of values around the median)
- variance (used to establish the distribution of values around the mean)
- standard deviation (used to establish the distribution of values around the mean).

Understanding the dispersion of investment returns is the basis of many hedging techniques, as well as being an important indicator of portfolio returns.

Range

The simplest measure of dispersion is the range, which is the difference between the highest and lowest values in a set of data.

Let us assume that the following numbers represent the returns from an investment fund over ten years. Using the range measure would indicate that the average returns from the fund had a range of 11 (13–2).

Year	2006	2007	2008	2009	2010	2011	2012	2013	2014	2015
Return	7	6	5	2	3	3	6	9	11	13

The main drawback in using range as a measure of dispersion is that it is distorted by extreme values and ignores the numbers in between.

Inter-Quartile Range

We saw above that the median is a value that subdivides the ordered data into two halves. Further subdivisions are also commonly used:

- the quartiles subdivide the data into quarters
- the deciles subdivide the data into tenths
- the percentiles subdivide the data into hundredths.

The inter-quartile range provides another measure of dispersion. It ranks data (such as performance returns from different funds), against each other and presents the data as a series of quartiles. It then measures the difference from the lowest rank quartile to the highest.

Let us assume that the following figures represent the returns from a number of comparable investment funds. The data is first ranked in order of lowest to highest, the median is identified and the set is then divided into a series of quartiles.

E	F	G	H	I	J	K	L
5%	5.75%	6%	6.5%	7%	7.5%	8%	9%

| Median | | | | | | | |
| 5.875% | | | | | | | |

nd quartile	3rd quartile	4th quartile
Inter-quartile range		

would, therefore, rank in the top half of fund performances, ave delivered returns that have been exceeded by 75% of the

in returns between the 25th percentile ranked fund and the the range, the less difference there is in the funds being

dispersion through the middle half of a distribution. It is the culated as half the difference between the upper and lower because it is not influenced by extremely high or extremely

e deviation = ½ (Q3 – Q1)

with a dataset of values listed in order from smallest to largest, we can compute the quartile deviation as follows:

Step one

- Find the median of the data set and call this median Q2 (Q2 is also called the second quartile value).

Step two

- Use Q2 to divide the original data set into two parts.
- The lower 50% consists of those values less than Q2.
- The upper 50% consists of values greater than Q2.

If the number of items in the dataset is odd, then include Q2 in both the lower and upper data sets.

Step three

- Calculate Q1 as the median of the lower data set (Q1 is called the first quartile position).
- Calculate Q3 as the median of the upper data set (Q3 is called the third quartile position).

Step four

- (Q3 – Q1)/2 is the quartile deviation.

Example: Quartile Deviation Calculation

Assume that the following numbers represent investment returns:

49; 54; 59; 60; 62; 65; 65; 68; 77; 83; 84; 89; 90

The number of returns is n = 13

Q2 is the median of the data set, ie, the seventh data point, 65

49; 54; 59; 60; 62; 65; **65**; 68; 77; 83; 84; 89; 90

The lower data set is therefore 49; 54; 59; 60; 62; 65; **65**

- Q1 is the median of the lower data set, ie the fourth data point, 60

The upper data set is **65**; 68; 77; 83; 84; 89; 90

- Q3 is the median of the upper data set, ie, the fourth data point, 83

Quartile deviation = (Q3 − Q1)/2, ie, (83 − 60)/2 = 11.5

Variance and Standard Deviation

Variance is a measure of dispersion and shows the spread of data around the mean.

The mean for the average fund returns used in the range example above is as follows:

$$(13\%+11\%+2\%+6\%+5\%+8\%+7\%+9\%+7\%+6\%) \div 10 = 7.4\%$$

The variance calculates the difference between each return from the mean and then squares it. These are then totalled and their average then represents the variance.

This is shown in the table below. Row two shows the difference in the return each year from the mean (7.4%, calculated above) and row three shows this difference squared. Row four shows the average variance for the data.

An Example of Variance

	Year	2009	2010	2011	2012	2013	2014	2015	2016	2017	2018	Total
1	Return	13	11	2	6	5	8	7	9	7	6	
2	Difference from the mean	5.6	3.6	−5.4	−1.4	−2.4	0.6	-0.4	1.6	−0.4	−1.4	
3	Difference squared	31.36	12.96	29.16	1.96	5.76	0.36	0.16	2.56	0.16	1.96	86.4
4	Average variance (86.4/10)											8.64

The **standard deviation** of a set of data is simply the square root of the variance and is the most commonly used measure of dispersion.

Although the variances and standard deviations of both ordered and raw **frequency distribution** data can be calculated quickly and easily by using the relevant function on a scientific calculator, it is useful to understand how to work through the calculations manually. In summary, the steps you should take in making these calculations manually are as follows:

- obtain the mean
- obtain the set of deviations from the mean
- square each deviation
- divide the sum of the squared deviations by the number of observations to obtain the population variance
- take the square root of the variance to obtain the standard deviation.

To ensure precision in the calculation of the variance and standard deviation, statistical rules require a slight change to the formula if measuring a sample rather than the whole population. A small data set might not provide a representative picture of the population as a whole and so sampling error may arise. As a result, a slight adjustment to the standard deviation formula is made by reducing the number of observations by one.

Population standard deviation =

$$\sqrt{\frac{\Sigma (x - \bar{x})^2}{n}}$$

Sample standard deviation =

$$\sqrt{\frac{\Sigma (x - \bar{x})^2}{n - 1}}$$

In effect, by taking the square root of the variance, the standard deviation represents the average amount by which the values in the distribution deviate from the mean.

2.4 Relevance and Application of Dispersion and Variance Measures

Learning Objective

5.2.4 Understand the relevance and application of measures of dispersion and variance within risk analysis

The variance of a set of stock returns provides a measure of the returns' dispersion and is used to calculate the beta of the stock – a measure of how closely its movement mirrors that of the general market (see below). However, it results in a value with different units from the original values, whereas it is easier to conceptualise the dispersion of a set of values when its value is expressed in the same units as the returns themselves. To do this, we use the standard deviation.

The variability of returns generated by an asset or portfolio – its volatility – is a measure of its risk. The volatility of an investment's returns is expressed mathematically by the standard deviation of their values – because, as we have seen, standard deviation measures how widely the values are dispersed, or fluctuate, around their mean position.

The more volatile an investment's return is, the greater is the standard deviation. Low standard deviation implies low risk; high standard deviation implies high risk. Knowing the standard deviation can help us to know the range of different values of return we might expect from an investment. Experience shows that for about two-thirds of the time, we can expect the return to be within one standard deviation above or below the average return.

This concept is developed further in chapter 6.

2.5 Understanding the Terminology

Learning Objective

5.2.5 Understand the terms distribution analysis, confidence intervals, normal distribution and fat-tailed distribution, and how they are used within risk analysis

2.5.1 Distribution Analysis

Distribution analysis is a statistical means of using historical data to predict future events and relies on an understanding of probability distributions – of which one such distribution is the '**normal distribution**', which we discussed in section 2.3. The distribution of weekly incomes was another example; it was positively skewed – unlike the normal, which is symmetrical about its mean.

A **normal distribution curve** has the following attributes:

- it is symmetrical about its mean
- it is defined by its mean and its standard deviation (represented by the Greek letter sigma, σ).

Statistical analysis shows that for a normal distribution:

- two thirds or 68.3% of the data will be within one standard deviation either side of the mean
- 95.5% of the data will be within two standard deviations either side of the mean
- 99.75% of the data will be within three standard deviations of the mean.

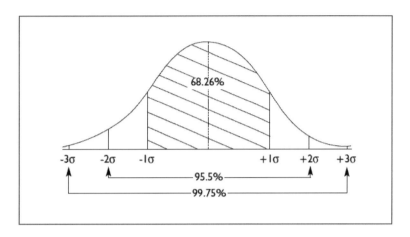

2.5.2   Confidence Intervals

Investment returns from primary instruments (but not derivatives), based on market factors, are often assumed to be normally distributed. By making this assumption, it is possible to create a model that will predict the future performance of the instrument to a given level of probability, which is linked to the number of standard deviations away from the mean at which we 'read off' our answer from the graph.

This probability is also known as the confidence interval.

So, using these twin distribution concepts of central tendency value, and confidence interval, we can start to include a measure of confidence in our reported measure of returns.

Instead of using simply the median or mean value, we can describe it by saying *'there is a 95.5% chance that the return will be within two standard deviations of the mean'* – where we will have calculated the value of 'two standard deviations'.

2.5.3   Fat-Tailed Distribution

It can be seen from the graph above, that after three, four, or perhaps five standard deviations, the edges of the graph, or its 'tails' will have touched the horizontal x axis.

However, this is one of the aspects of using normal distribution as a simplifying assumption that is often not true in 'real life'. Many probability distributions have what are known as fat tails, as illustrated by the weekly income graph in section 2.3. This means that using a normal distribution for simplicity when in fact the distribution is fat-tailed will result in periodically very large deviations from our expected returns.

2.6 Risk Measurement and Control Concepts

Learning Objective

5.2.6 Understand the following concepts used in risk measurement and control: probability, volatility, regression, correlation coefficients alpha and beta, optimisation

---

2.6.1 Probability

Probability is the measure of how likely an event is. In order to measure probabilities, mathematicians have devised the following formula for finding the probability of an event:

$$\frac{\text{The number of ways the event can occur}}{\text{The total number of possible outcomes}}$$

So as a simple example, if a single six-sided die is rolled, the probability of rolling a six would be:

$$\frac{\text{The number of ways to roll a six}}{\text{The total number of sides}} = 1/6$$

The probability of rolling an even number would be:

$$\frac{\text{The number of ways to roll an even number}}{\text{The total number of sides}} = 3/6 = 1/2$$

2.6.2 Volatility

When discussing market prices, the volatility is a description of how variable they are. So, typically, bond prices would be less volatile than equities.

Technically, volatility is a measure of the standard deviation of the returns of a financial instrument within a specific time horizon. It is often used to quantify the risk of the instrument over that time expressed in annualised terms, and it may either be an absolute number (£5) or a fraction of the mean return (5%).

2.6.3 Regression

Regression analysis is a statistical tool for the investigation of relationships between variables. It is used to ascertain the effect of one variable upon another – the effect of a price increase upon demand, for example, or the effect of changes in the money supply upon the inflation rate.

To explore such issues, data is gathered and regression analysis is employed to estimate the quantitative effect of one variable upon another. The statistical significance of the estimated relationships is also assessed, that is, the degree of confidence that the true relationship is close to the estimated relationship.

The simplest way of determining potential relationships between two variables is to measure their differing values over time, and then to plot a scatter-gram. The example below shows that there is a clear relationship between the variables plotted on the x and y axes. What it will not show is which variable is causing the change, and that will need to be determined using other methods.

Regression Line

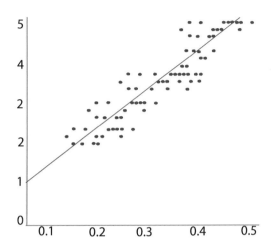

2.6.4   The Correlation Coefficients Alpha and Beta

The correlation coefficient measures the strength of the relationship between two variables, such as share prices, and has a value ranging from −1 (negatively correlated), through 0 (not correlated), to 1 (positively correlated).

- A **positive correlation** describes a relationship where an increase in the price of one share is associated with an increase in another.
- A **negative correlation** is a relationship where an increase in one share price is associated with a decrease in another.

The graph above shows a positively correlated relationship between the two variables.

As explained above, diversification is achieved by combining assets whose returns do not move in perfect synchronisation – are not perfectly positively correlated – with one another.

Only when security returns are perfectly negatively correlated, in that they move in the opposite direction to one another at all times and in the same proportion, can they be combined to produce a risk-free return.

However, even with zero or imperfect correlations, there are still diversification benefits to be gained from combining securities in a portfolio. A perfectly positive correlation, when security returns move in the same direction and in perfect synchronisation with each other, is the only instance when diversification benefits cannot be achieved.

In terms of correlation with the market, a measure called the **beta** of a stock, or portfolio, is used to describe the relationship of its returns with that of the financial market as a whole.

An asset with a beta of 0 means that its price is not at all correlated with the market. A positive beta means that the asset generally follows the market. A negative beta shows that the asset inversely follows the market; the asset generally decreases in value if the market goes up and vice versa.

Alpha is another measure used when looking at the performance of a fund or portfolio and refers to the extent of any outperformance against its benchmark, ie, the difference between a fund's expected returns, based on its beta, and its actual returns.

2.6.5 Optimisation

As we saw above, the behaviour of a portfolio can be quite different from the behaviour of individual components of the portfolio. The risk of a 'properly' constructed portfolio can display much lower risk characteristics than the average of the risks of its individual assets.

Optimisation refers to portfolio construction techniques that obtain the best expected returns from the right mix of correlations and variances.

Portfolio optimisation is often called mean-variance (MV) optimisation. The term mean refers to the mean or the expected return of the investment and the variance is the measure of the risk associated with the portfolio. The mathematical problem can be formulated in many ways as permutations of either:

- minimising the risk for a given return, or
- maximising the expected return for a given risk.

2.7 Value-at-Risk (VaR) Approach

Learning Objective

5.2.7 Understand the Value-at-Risk (VaR) approach to managing market risk: VaR limit setting and monitoring for bank trading positions, VaR as a portfolio measure of risk, validation and back testing

Value-at-Risk (VaR) is a widely used measure that, in simple terms, expresses the maximum loss that can occur with a specified confidence over a specified period.

Because there is uncertainty about how much could be lost over the specified time horizon, the VaR measure includes the level of confidence that the specified loss will not be exceeded. For example, if a portfolio's one-week VaR is stated as £1 million in 95 weeks out of 100, then the portfolio is predicted to lose less than £1 million at the 95% confidence level.

2.7.1 VaR Limit Setting and Monitoring

VaR is widely used by banks, securities firms and investment managers to estimate portfolio market risk.

The market risk function will set VaR limits. It will then monitor them to ensure that traders or fund managers do not exceed them. Where they are exceeded, escalation will take place to the head of trading, the relevant desk head or a risk committee.

The advantages of using VaR for measuring portfolio risk are:

- it provides a statistical probability of potential loss
- it can be readily understood by non-risk managers
- it translates all risks in a portfolio into a common standard, allowing a comparison of risks between asset classes and, hence, the quantification of firm-wide, cross-product exposures.

Its main disadvantage is that it does not specify how bad the situation could get. Losing no more than £10 million on 95 days out of 100 says nothing about the other five days – except that the loss will be a minimum of £10 million.

2.7.2 Validation and Back Testing

Like any mathematical model, VaR models can break down if the assumptions that they are based upon are violated or are simply found to be untrue. This risk is called model risk and is covered further in chapter 8 on Model Risk.

It is important with any model to validate its assumptions and test its output accuracy as far as possible. This is achieved by back testing.

Back testing is the practice of comparing the actual daily trading exposure to the previously predicted VaR figure. It is a test of reliability of the VaR methodology and ensures that the approach is of sufficient quality. It is usually performed on a daily basis by the financial reporting function and if unsatisfactory differences between reality and estimation are found, the VaR model must be revised.

2.7.3 The Three Different Approaches to VaR

Learning Objective

5.2.8   Know the three different approaches to Value-at-Risk (VaR): historical simulation, parametric, Monte Carlo

---

VaR can be calculated in three main ways:

1. **Historical simulation** – this involves looking back at what actually happened in the past and basing our view of the future on that analysis.
2. **The parametric (or analytical) approach** – this assumes that the distribution of possible returns can be plotted, based on a small number of factors, so that the required confidence level can be 'read off' the graph.

3. **Monte Carlo simulation** – this involves generating a random set of results based on the actual underlying risk factors and again 'reading off' the graph.

Historical Simulation

This method uses historic analysis of the portfolio's **risk factor** values to estimate its risk exposure in the future. The steps are as follows:

1. Identify the risk factors that affect the returns of the portfolio, such as:
   - individual stock prices
   - individual stock volatilities
   - the correlations between the stocks (described above).
2. Select a sample of actual historic risk factor changes over a given period of time – say, the last 500 trading days.
3. Systematically apply each of those daily changes to the current value of each risk factor, revaluing the current portfolio as many times as the number of days in the historical sample.
4. List out all the resulting portfolio values, ordered by value and, assuming the required VaR is at the 95% confidence level, identify the value that represents the fifth percentile of the distribution in the left-hand tail.

VaR: The Historical Simulation Approach

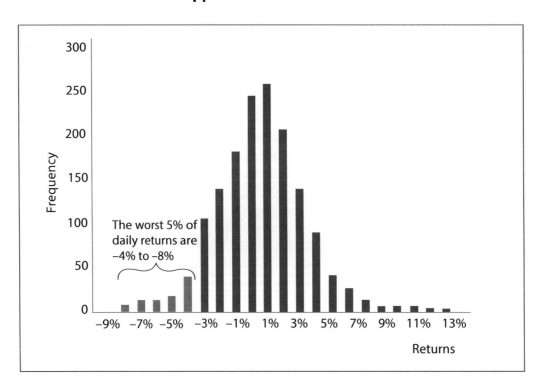

© Andrew Brand

Advantages and Disadvantages of the Historical Simulation Approach

The **historical simulation** approach reconstructs the actual historical returns, and ranks them from worst to best. An advantage of this method is that it is conceptually simple enough to communicate easily to non-specialists. In addition, unlike the next two methods, there is no need to make any assumption about the distribution of the portfolio's returns. There is also no need to estimate the volatilities and correlations between the various assets in the portfolio. This is because the distribution, the volatilities and the correlations are implicitly captured by the actual daily values of the portfolio's assets over time.

The main disadvantage is that it assumes that history will repeat itself, which is clearly often not the case. For a predictive tool this is a drawback: at the point when it could be most valuable, for example just before a market crash, its output could still be suggesting that future returns will remain in line with those experienced during the previous period.

The Parametric (also called 'Analytical') Approach

This approach assumes that portfolio returns are normally distributed, and uses the standard deviation (volatility) of the returns to 'plot the graph' and hence derive the VaR figure at the required **confidence level**. The approach is called 'parametric VaR' because of the assumption that the returns are normally distributed: the normal distribution is an example of a 'parametric' distribution.

VaR: The Parametric or Analytical Approach

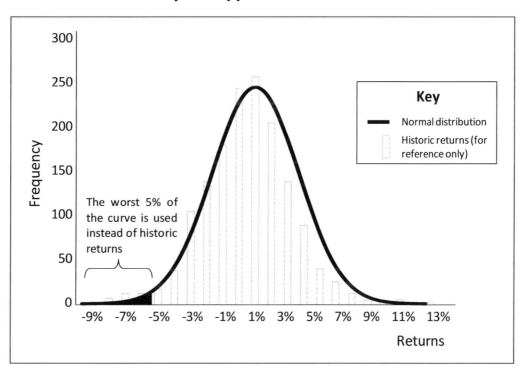

© Andrew Brand

Advantages and Disadvantages of the Parametric Approach

The parametric approach is the simplest methodology used to compute VaR. A limited amount of input data is required, and, since there are no simulations involved, minimal computation time is required.

However, its simplicity is also its main drawback. Firstly, if the actual returns are not actually normally distributed, as is assumed, then clearly the results will be inaccurate.

Secondly, it cannot be used with securities such as options, because returns from these instruments do not follow a normal distribution.

Monte Carlo Simulation Methods

The third method involves developing a model (ie, a set of equations) for future stock price returns and then running multiple hypothetical values through the model to obtain a distribution of return values. The process of generating hypothetical trials involves producing random numbers in a 'controlled' fashion, dictated by whichever distribution is felt to be most representative for the portfolio. This process of producing random numbers in a controlled fashion and iteratively using them as values in an equation is known as Monte Carlo simulation.

Computing VaR using Monte Carlo simulation follows a similar algorithm to the one used for historical simulations. The main difference lies in the first step of the algorithm – instead of picking a return from the historical series of the asset and assuming that this return can recur in the next time interval, we generate a random number that will be used to estimate the return of the asset.

Repeating this procedure over a large number of iterations (typically 10,000 or more) produces a set of values (ie, hypothetical portfolio returns) which, as with the historical simulation approach, are then ranked from worst to best in order to arrive at the desired percentile confidence level, for example 95%.

VaR: Monte Carlo Simulation Approach

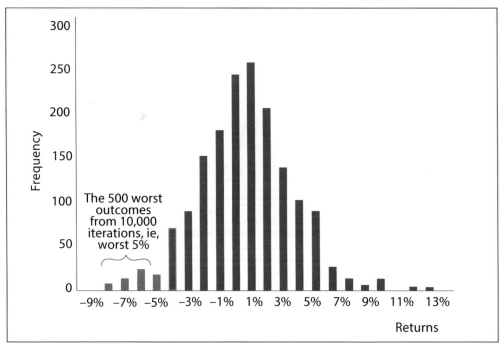

© Andrew Brand

130

Advantages and Disadvantages of Monte Carlo Simulation Approach

Monte Carlo simulation has one major advantage over the parametric method – it can be used to produce VaR for non-normally distributed instruments such as options. A large number of simulations are made of the price of the instrument underlying the option, and then the option is re-priced for each simulation. The VaR is then the result of the appropriate simulation drawn from a ranked list of outcomes.

The main disadvantage of Monte Carlo simulation for VaR is the computing power that is required to perform all the simulations, and thus the time it takes to run the simulations. A portfolio of 1,000 assets requiring 10,000 simulations on each asset will need ten million simulations (without accounting for any sub-simulations that may be required to price assets such as options).

2.8   Scenario and Stress Testing

Learning Objective

5.2.9   Understand the underlying purposes, principles and application of the main types of scenario and stress testing: extreme event, risk factor, external factors

We said above that VaR does not specify how bad the situation could get, simply that in, say, 95 days out of 100 not more than a certain amount will be lost.

That is why scenario analysis and stress testing is so important.

The difference between a stress test and a scenario is the number of variables that are altered. A stress test alters one variable at a time to analyse its effect on the rest of the portfolio. Scenario analysis looks at how the portfolio behaves under conditions of multiple changes.

The portfolio must be subjected to 'extreme' market event scenarios, in order to bring out particular risks that may, or may not, have been captured by the VaR calculation.

Stress tests should alter each relevant risk factor in exceptional, but plausible, ways.

Risk factors will include:

- general interest rates
- individual stock prices
- individual stock volatilities
- the correlation coefficients that describe the relationships between the instruments in the portfolio.

Scenarios can either be invented – say, a doubling of volatility combined with a sharp increase in interest rates – or they can be based on previous external factors, such as large one-day stock market falls.

The market risk management process itself should include regular scenario analysis and stress tests. An institution may choose scenarios based either on analysing historical data or on empirical models of changes in market risk factors.

The objective should be to allow the firm to assess the effects of sizeable changes in market risk factors on its holdings and financial condition. Therefore the chosen scenarios should include low-probability adverse stresses that could result in extraordinary losses. Scenario analysis and stress tests should be both quantitative and qualitative.

Scenario analysis and stress testing should, as far as possible, be conducted on an institution-wide basis, taking into account the effects of unusual changes in market and non-market risk factors. Such factors include prices, volatilities, market liquidity, historical correlations and assumptions in stressed market conditions, and the institution's vulnerability to worst-case scenarios such as the default of a large counterparty.

Scenario analysis and stress testing would enable the board and senior management to better assess the potential impact of various market-related changes on the institution's earnings and capital position. The board and senior management should regularly review the results of scenario analyses and stress testing, including the major assumptions that underpin them. The results should be considered during the establishment and review of policies and limits.

End of Chapter Questions

Think of an answer for each question and refer to the appropriate section for confirmation.

1. What is the definition of market risk?
    Answer reference: Chapter Summary

2. Volatility risk is one type of market risk; name three more.
    Answer reference: Section 1.1

3. What is hedging?
    Answer reference: Section 2.1.1

4. What is a stop-loss limit?
    Answer reference: Section 2.1.2

5. Give three of the six features of an effective market risk function.
    Answer reference: Section 2.2

6. What is the relationship between the variance and the standard deviation?
    Answer reference: Section 2.3.3

7. Is an increase in volatility of returns reflected in a higher or a lower standard deviation?
    Answer reference: Section 2.4

8. What are the two attributes of a normal distribution (bell) curve?
    Answer reference: Section 2.5.1

9. What is back testing?
    Answer reference: Section 2.7.2

10. What is the difference between a stress test and scenario testing?
    Answer reference: Section 2.8

Chapter Six
Investment Risk

This syllabus area will provide approximately 10 of the 100 examination questions

6

Chapter Summary

The credit and market risks referred to in the two previous chapters are managed for the benefit of the firm's owners and clients. Many of these clients are investors whose funds are managed by the firm, and we refer to the combination of risks involved in providing the 'right' level of return to these investors as 'investment risk'.

Investment is the decision to forgo the use of current resources, in the belief that they can instead be used to create future benefits which are greater than their current value. Investment risk is the risk that these future benefits do not materialise or are less than required.

Savers and investors pass their funds over to an investment management firm in the belief that such a firm can grow the value of their funds beyond the levels possible through simply depositing funds in a savings account. This is especially true in times of low interest rates, or high inflation.

Investment management firms, therefore, need to employ staff and develop systems that can understand and manage the best investment opportunities to create the returns expected by investors. This requires a detailed knowledge of the available investment asset classes such as equities, bonds, currencies and commodities. Each asset class displays different risk and return characteristics – so for example, equities may return much more than bonds in good years, but bonds produce a steadier flow of returns compared to the higher volatility displayed by equities. Different asset classes are also correlated in different ways to the performance of the economy. For all assets though the aim is the same – to minimise the risk while maximising the return. This is generally achieved through applying different mixtures of asset types to achieve diversification.

In order to track the returns being generated per unit of risk taken, investment managers require the ability to apply certain key ratios to their portfolios. These include tracking error, the information ratio and the Sharpe ratio.

Where possible, funds are measured against a benchmark which is typically an index such as FTSE 100, or a peer group of similar funds.

1. The Measurement of Investment Returns

1.1 Basic Concepts and the Measurement of Investment Returns

Learning Objective

6.1.1 Understand the basic concepts and measurement of investment related returns: nominal returns; real returns; total returns; holding period return

Inflation is defined as an overall general upward price movement of goods and services in an economy. Another way of looking at the same phenomenon is to consider inflation as the reduction in what can be bought over time with a fixed quantity of currency.

Because inflation tends to erode a currency's value slowly, it is not immediately obvious why it can be such a problem for investors – especially for those receiving the majority of their returns from fixed income products such as bonds.

The graph shows the value of a 1974 pound in each year from 1974 to 1998. It can be seen that for an investor with an annual fixed income in 1974, each pound received would be worth only 17p by 1998.

Value of the £, 1974–1998

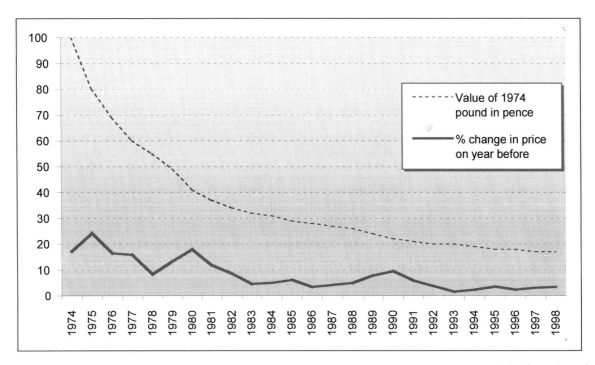

© Andrew Brand

138

1.1.1 Nominal Returns

The nominal return on an investment is simply the return it gives, unadjusted for inflation. Thus, a bank account paying 12% interest annually has a nominal return of 12%.

1.1.2 Real Returns

The real return is the return the investment provides an investor after stripping out the effects of inflation. If inflation is running at say 8%, then in real terms the value of the cash in a 12% bank account is actually growing by just 4% a year.

This rough calculation is useful for giving an approximation of the investment's real rate of return – but if we need an exact measure, it is a little more complicated. To get a completely accurate figure, the relationship between the rate of inflation, the real rate of return and the nominal rate of return is as follows, with rates expressed as a decimal (eg, 4% would be expressed as 0.04):

(1+ real rate of return) × (1+ inflation rate) = 1+ nominal rate of return

If the nominal rate of return is 12% per annum and the annual rate of inflation is 8% per annum, the real rate of return is the return earned after allowing for the return needed just to keep pace with inflation.

We may rearrange the equation above to find the real rate of return:

$$\frac{1 + \text{nominal rate}}{1 + \text{inflation rate}} = 1 + \text{real rate}$$

$$\frac{1.12}{1.08} = 1 + \text{real rate}$$

Therefore:

$$1.037 = 1 + \text{real rate}$$

Therefore:

$$\text{Real rate} = 3.7\%$$

It is possible for a real return to be negative; in the example above, if inflation were to run at 6% per annum but a bank account continued to pay 4% per annum, then the real return on it would be around –2%. Put another way, the purchasing power of a deposit held in that bank account would be falling at 2% a year.

1.1.3 Total Returns

Total returns mean the returns on an investment both from its income production, and any capital gains (or losses) it generates.

1.1.4 Holding Period Returns

Holding period return is the total return on an asset or portfolio over the period during which it was held. It is one of the simplest measures of investment performance.

It is calculated as the percentage by which the value of a portfolio (or asset) has grown for a particular period. It is the sum of income and capital gains over the period, divided by the initial period value.

1.2 Effects of Compound Interest and the Time Value of Money

Learning Objective

6.1.2   Understand the effects of compound interest and the time value of money

The term compound interest describes what happens when an investor leaves his interest invested with the main deposit (the principal), instead of withdrawing it to spend. Interest is earned on that interest (compounded), and the investment increases in value all the faster for it.

Example: Compound interest

Suppose that £2,000 is invested at 10% interest for two years.

Year 1	£
Original capital investment	2,000
Interest on investment of £2,000 at 10% per annum	200
Total capital + interest at the end of Year 1	2,200
Year 2	
Total capital + interest brought forward from end of Year 1	2,200
Interest on investment of £2,200 at 10% per annum	220
Total capital + interest at the end of Year 2	2,420

Instead of performing the calculations shown above, we can calculate compound interest using a standard formula, as follows: $S = X(1 + r)^n$, where X = the original sum invested, r = the interest rate (5% is written as 0.05), n = the number of periods over which we are compounding and S = the sum invested after n periods.

Compounding effects may appear to be minimal over one or two periods, but over a longer time they make a considerable difference to the growth of an investment. In the previous examples, interest has been calculated annually, but this is not always the case. Interest may be compounded daily, weekly, monthly or quarterly.

When considering the passage of time, understanding the compounding effects we have just considered is critical. The principle of discounting is rather like compounding in reverse, as it allows us to calculate, among other things, what rate of interest or return will produce a specific sum at a future date.

If someone has a choice between (a) £1,000 now, and (b) £1,000 in one year's time then they will have a preference for (a). If you have £1,000 now, you could invest it and earn interest, or simply spend it.

This example shows that money has a 'time value'. The option of having money now is of more value than the option of having money at a future date because we can make it work for us from an earlier point. Interest can be seen partly as the return required by the lender to compensate for the time value of money that the lender is supplying to the borrower.

The formula we use to calculate the effects of compounding is that if we invest £X now for n years at r% interest per annum we should obtain $£X(1 + r)^n$ in n years.

Thus if we invest £10,000 now for four years at 10% interest per annum, we will have a total investment worth £10,000 x $(1+ 0.1)^4$ = £14,641 at the end of four years (that is, at Year 4 if it is now Year 0).

The principle of discounting is that if we wish to have £S in n years' time, we need to invest a certain sum now (Year 0) at an interest rate of r% in order to obtain the required sum of money in the future. This is illustrated in the following example.

Example

If we wish to have £14,641 in four years' time, how much money would we need to invest now at 10% interest per annum? (Think of this as being the reverse of the compounding calculations we have already looked at.)

Using our compounding formula, $S = X (1 + r)^n$

Where X	=	the original sum invested
r	=	10%
n	=	4
S	=	the sum we want to achieve = £14,641

£14,641 = $X(1 + 0.1)^4$

£14,641 = X times 1.4641

so X $= \dfrac{£14,641}{1.4641} = £10,000$

So £10,000 now, earning interest at 10% per annum, is the equivalent in value of £14,641 after four years. We can therefore say that £10,000 is the present value of £14,641 at year four, at an interest rate of 10%.

The term 'present value' refers to the amount of money which must be invested now for n years at an interest rate of r%, to earn a given future sum of money at the time it will be required.

1.3 Variations in the Rates of Return from Asset Classes

Learning Objective

6.1.3 Understand how the rates of return from the main asset classes vary

Between 1980 and 2011, investments in different asset classes produced historical returns in the following ranges:

*   S&P equities are estimated to have returned around 7.8% per year.
*   Corporate bonds are estimated to have returned around 6.1% per year.
*   Treasury bills are estimated to have returned around 1.6% per year.

It would be tempting to look at these figures and simply invest in equities. However, the historic volatility of equities is much higher than fixed income, which in turn is higher than cash deposits. Therefore, the time available to invest is a key factor in deciding which asset class or classes to invest in.

The longer the available time, the higher the percentage can be invested in equities. As the 'deadline' approaches (for example, starting to draw a pension income from the portfolio), the assets could be switched into progressively less volatile assets. The returns may not be as high, but nor will they be as low.

2. Identification, Measurement and Management of Investment Risk

2.1 Main Investment Risks

Learning Objective

6.2.1 Understand the main investment risks and their implications for investors and investment selection: currency risk; interest rate risk; issuer risk; equity risk; commodity risk; property risk; liquidity risk

2.1.1 Currency Risk

Currency risk is the risk arising from fluctuations in the value of currencies against one another. A UK resident whose home currency is sterling and who buys stocks or bonds in other currencies, such as the US dollar, faces currency risk.

Suppose that a UK investor buys shares in a US company which does most of its trading in the US:

*   the share price in US dollars fluctuates on the US stock market – this is market risk
*   additionally, the value of sterling fluctuates against the US dollar – this is currency risk.

The sterling value of the investment will fluctuate as a result of two effects:

1. The changing dollar share price.
2. The changing US dollar/sterling exchange rate.

In fact, sterling investors are still exposed to currency risk even when investing in the UK, as many UK companies do much of their business abroad. This means that corporate earnings will be affected by exchange rate fluctuations.

For example, if a UK company makes goods in the UK using domestically sourced raw materials, and then exports its products to the eurozone countries, it is exposed to the risk of a rise in the value of sterling against the euro. If sterling rises in value, the euro-priced receipts from the company's eurozone sales will buy fewer pounds than before. This reduces profitability on exports, which, in turn, may reduce the price of the company's financial instruments in the markets.

2.1.2   Interest Rate Risk

Interest rate risk is the risk that interest rates move against the investor. For example:

- an investor borrows at a fixed rate of interest of 5% over three years to finance an investment. During this period interest rates move down to 2% but the loan is still locked into a rate of 5%
- an investor opens a bank deposit account that pays a variable rate of interest linked to the Bank of England base rate. If the Bank of England reduces interest rates then the income from the deposit account falls.

Interest rate risk can also affect an investor's capital, since the price of fixed income securities (ie, bonds) moves in the opposite direction to interest rates.

2.1.3   Issuer Risk

When companies and governments wish to raise funds, one option is for them to issue bonds. Bonds come in many flavours, but most of them promise that in return for an upfront payment by an investor they will provide a predictable stream of interest payments (coupons), followed by a final repayment of their face value (capital or principal repayment).

Bonds are traded on secondary markets, and the main advantages of holding bonds are:

- for fixed-income bonds, a regular, fixed and predictable flow of income: even if the issuer has poor profits in a given year, it must still pay interest on its bonds – whereas dividends on equities, being paid from profits, are at risk in an unprofitable year
- a range of income yields to suit different investment and tax situations
- for most bonds, a fixed maturity date (although some bonds have no **redemption** date and others may be repaid over a range of dates – some at the investor's option and some at the issuer's option)
- a higher place in the 'pecking order' if the issuer defaults than investors who have equities in the same company.

They therefore have a useful role to play in portfolios for investors who need:

- a secure home for their funds
- a dependable level of income, or
- a source of future funds for an anticipated expense or liability.

Issuer risk is the risk that the bond issuer, whether a government or a corporate, gets into financial difficulties and cannot keep up the interest payments, or defaults on the final repayment.

Government bonds are sometimes thought of as having no default risk. However, although government guarantees do reduce the risk of holding government bonds, it is not eliminated altogether and governments do, from time to time, default. This risk is known as sovereign risk.

Apart from issuer risk, the other main risk associated with holding bonds is unanticipated inflation risk. This is the risk of inflation rising unexpectedly and, therefore, eroding the real value of the bond's coupon payments and redemption payment.

2.1.4 Equity Risk

The returns from investing in equities come from:

- **capital growth** – if the company does well the price of its shares should go up
- **income** – through the distribution by the company of its profits as dividends.

However, investing in equities carries risks that can affect:

- **the income** – if the company is not as profitable as hoped, the dividends it pays may not keep pace with inflation; indeed they may fall or even not be paid at all. Unlike bond coupons, dividend payments are not compulsory
- **the capital** – the share price may fall, or fail to rise in line with inflation or with the performance of other, less risky investments.

Certain specific factors that affect the riskiness of investment in shares are:

- liquidity risk (see chapter 7)
- growth risk
- volatility risk
- strategic risk of the issuing institution.

Growth Risk

Many investors' objective in buying shares is to secure capital growth, through an appreciation in the share price. Others invest for income, but usually also hope for this to grow too – so that their income keeps pace with inflation.

But investing for growth involves risk. Will the investor's shares rise (or fall) in price and will the company make enough profits to pay steady and rising dividends?

If the company does not do well or, indeed, if the stock market as a whole is performing badly, share prices fall. An investor who has to sell his shares at that point may make a loss.

If a company is 'wound-up' – put into liquidation, with all its assets being sold to pay off its liabilities (debts), the ordinary shareholders are the last people in line for any payout. Thus, there is the possibility there might not be enough money left to give them a payout at all; all the money might be spent on paying off the company's creditors (including, of course, its bondholders).

The reward for taking on this level of risk is that if the company does very well, investors may make large capital gains with no 'cap' on how high these could be. If profits remain strong, they should receive stable and rising dividends.

Volatility Risk

Volatility is the term used to describe the degree to which an investment is prone to swings in pricing. Even an investment which appreciates dramatically in price can carry unacceptable levels of volatility if the investor wants to hold something which performs more predictably.

It is possible to measure the (historic) volatility of a given share by looking at its previous price swings. This can then be compared with the returns the share has also historically provided, and these can be looked at against the risk and return of other investments. For example, this comparison can be made against the returns available on investments regarded as virtually risk-free such as government issued Treasury Bonds.

Professional investment managers do this to assess whether the additional returns, which they believe an investment may offer, are worth the additional volatility (ie, risk) to their investors: shares that are volatile are regarded as higher risk because their performance can change, quickly and in either direction, over a short period.

Investors can compare the returns they are receiving against the volatility of the shares they hold. Of two shares with similar returns, the one with the lower standard deviation (volatility of returns) will (to date) have given a better return for the amount of risk incurred.

Strategic Risk of the Issuing Institution

Shares are issued by companies, and their performance is linked to the fortunes of those companies. Different companies are subject to differing strategic risks (discussed in chapter 1), which are determined by factors such as:

- The nature of their industry and its cyclicality. Some companies provide goods and services which people mainly want during an economic upswing; others trade in goods which people want in a downturn; and still others in things that people need regardless of the state of the economy.
- The competence of the management. No matter how impressive a company's business model or products, its prospects cannot be good if it is not being run by effective managers.
- The financial soundness of the company. A company which is, for example, over-geared (ie, over-leveraged) can suffer disproportionately if interest rates rise.

2.1.5 Commodity Risk

A commodity is an asset, all elements of which are identical in the market. So, for example, pure gold is a commodity and when gold is traded people do not pay different amounts for different types of pure gold – there is a worldwide market price for a commodity called gold bullion. Other commodities include oil, sugar and coffee.

Commodities tend to have volatile price movements, often linked to natural events such as harvests. **Commodity price risk** is the risk of an adverse price movement in the value of a commodity.

2.1.6 Property Risk

Property as an asset class is unique in its distinguishing features:

*   Given that each individual property is unique in terms of location, structure and design, the property market can be segmented into a large number of individual markets.
*   Valuation is subjective as property is not traded in a centralised market, so continuous and reliable price data is not available.
*   It requires high up-front costs.
*   It is subject to complex legal considerations and high transaction costs upon transfer.
*   It is highly illiquid as a result of not being instantly tradeable.
*   It is not divisible. As property can only be bought in discrete units, diversification is difficult.
*   The supply of land is finite and its availability can be further restricted by legislation and local planning regulations. Therefore, price is predominantly determined by changes in demand.

The risks associated with property investment include:

Property risk:

*   location of the property
*   the effect of the use of the property on its value
*   the credit quality of the tenants
*   the length of the lease.

Market risk:

*   the effect of changes in interest rates on valuations
*   performance of individual property sectors
*   prospects for rental income growth.

2.1.7 Liquidity Risk

We will discuss liquidity in detail in chapter 7, but in essence, for the purposes of investment selection, liquidity is concerned with the ease with which investment assets can be:

1. **sold for cash** – this is linked to market risk because the investor may need to accept a lower price than anticipated if the need for cash is urgent;
2. **used as collateral against which to secure increased cash inflows** – this is linked to credit risk and market risk as the lower the investor's credit rating, the more collateral will be required to secure a loan.

Investment liquidity risk, therefore, refers to the likelihood of being unable to transform assets into cash within a preferred time, without incurring losses, and is closely linked to both credit and market risk.

2.2 Calculating Asset and Portfolio Investment Risk

Learning Objective

6.2.2 Understand how asset and portfolio investment risk is calculated

There are various ways in which risk, or at least certain aspects of it, can be measured. Usually, risk is measured in terms of the degree of fluctuation, or volatility, that an investment has shown in the past. We can see the volatility of different assets' investment values by looking at graphs of daily share prices or share indices over a period of time.

As described in chapter 5, the volatility in the value of an investment can be quantified mathematically by calculating the standard deviation of the values (as discussed in chapter 5, the standard deviation measures how widely the value of an investment fluctuates around the mean or average). The more volatile the value of an investment is, the greater is the standard deviation:

- An investment with returns that do not vary much from its average return has a low standard deviation. **Low standard deviation implies low risk**.
- An investment with returns that do vary greatly from its average return has a high standard deviation. **High standard deviation implies high risk**.

We can calculate the standard deviation on the basis of past data, on the assumption that there will be a similar level of volatility in the future too, for that investment. Of course, past performance is not a guide to future performance – the investment's track record gives us only an idea of its previous volatility.

Knowing the standard deviation can help us to know the range of different values of return we might expect from an investment. Experience shows that for about **two-thirds** of the time, we can expect the return to be within one standard deviation above or below the average return.

For example, suppose that an investment has an average annual return of 9% and a standard deviation of returns of 4%. Then we can expect that, if we make the investment:

- there is a chance of 2/3 that the annual return will be between 5% and 13%
- there is a chance of 1/3 that the annual return will be below 5% or above 13%.

The volatility, and therefore the risk, of a share, or a fund, can be compared with a benchmark – a standard against which its performance can be compared, either:

- the volatility of the index which relates most closely to that share or fund (for example, a blue chip share's standard deviation might be benchmarked against that of the FTSE 100 Index), or
- for a fund, against other funds in the same sector.

Investments with high volatility involve higher risk; there will be a greater variation in returns than for a lower-volatility investment. Rational investors should be particularly interested to hold investments that produce **higher than average returns** but with **low volatility**.

2.3 Alpha, Beta and Key Investor Ratios

Learning Objective

6.2.3 Understand the significance of alpha, beta and key investor ratios

---

If a fund's performance is reported in isolation, it means relatively little. Is a 10% return over the year a 'good' performance? Yes, if the market only went up by 5% and other funds which invested in similar assets only returned 6%. But it is not so good against the backdrop of a market that rose by 20% and a peer group of similar funds which also rose by that amount.

A benchmark is simply any standard against which it is reasonable to compare the performance of a share or fund. Indeed, the mandates or promotional literature for many funds explicitly set out the benchmark which the fund is intended to be measured against, or which its managers aim to outperform, as discussed below.

Typically, a fund's benchmark will be:

- the performance of the peer group of funds to which it belongs, eg, the performance of the sector of funds as measured by an industry body such as the Investment Association (IA), or
- a relevant market index, eg, a fund investing in blue chip UK equities might be benchmarked against the FTSE 100 index, or
- for certain types of funds, a standard such as the return on a particular government stock or other risk-free asset – so for example certain hedge fund managers state that their aim is to outperform the total return on long gilts by a certain number of percentage points – regardless of the direction of markets.

Benchmarks should be relevant to the market in which the fund itself is invested, and they should be used consistently – the manager should not switch benchmarks simply to show the fund's performance in a better light.

Benchmarks can be used to compare not only the performance of a fund in terms of return, but also in terms of volatility. The beta factor measures the volatility of an investment relative to the market or benchmark. The higher the value of beta for an investment, the greater the movement in its return relative to the market or benchmark.

- A fund with a **beta factor of one** moves in line with the market or benchmark. If the market moves up 5%, the price of this fund is likely to move up 5%. Therefore, index funds should have a beta factor that is equal to or very close to one.
- A fund with a **beta factor greater than one** varies more widely than the market or benchmark. If the market moves up 5%, the price of a fund with a beta of two is likely to move up 10%.

- A fund with a **beta factor of less than one** fluctuates less than the wider market or benchmark. If the market moves up or down 10%, the price of a fund with a beta of 0.5 is likely to move up or down respectively by 5%.

Beta values for funds are generally calculated over a 36-month period, from monthly data. Because beta factors are calculated from historical data, changes in the strategy of a fund, or of its manager, may mean that future performance and volatility differ from the past.

Alpha is another measure used when assessing the performance of a fund or portfolio, and refers to the extent of any outperformance against its benchmark, ie, the difference between a fund's expected returns based on its beta and its actual returns.

A disadvantage of alpha is that it does not distinguish between underperformance caused by incompetence and underperformance caused by fees. For example, managers of index funds do not select stocks, so they do not add or subtract any value. Therefore, in theory, an index fund should have an alpha of zero. Yet many index funds have negative alpha, usually because of the fund's expenses.

In addition to alpha and beta, there are two further key investor ratios:

- the Sharpe ratio
- the information ratio.

The Sharpe ratio makes use of a concept called the 'risk-free return'. The risk-free return rate is the rate that it is assumed can be obtained by investing in financial instruments with no default risk. However, the financial instrument can carry other types of risk, eg, market risk or liquidity risk.

A truly risk-free asset exists only in theory, so, in practice, a short-dated government bond of the relevant currency is used instead.

The Sharpe ratio measures the excess return of a portfolio over the risk-free interest rate, for each unit of risk assumed by the portfolio – risk being measured by the standard deviation of the portfolio's returns. So:

$$\text{Sharpe ratio} = \frac{\text{return on the portfolio} - \text{risk-free return}}{\text{standard deviation of portfolio}}$$

The higher the Sharpe ratio, the better the risk-adjusted performance of the portfolio, and the greater the implied level of active management skill.

The information ratio compares the excess return achieved by a fund over its benchmark, to the fund's tracking error.

Its tracking error is the standard deviation of returns relative to the benchmark. It is a measure of how closely a portfolio follows the index to which it is benchmarked.

The ratio is expressed as follows:

$$\text{Information ratio} = \frac{\text{mean of excess returns}}{\text{standard deviation of excess return from the benchmark}}$$

A fund's performance may deviate from the benchmark due to the investment manager's decisions concerning asset weighting. If it outperforms, the ratio will be positive and if it underperforms it will be negative. A high information ratio is, therefore, a sign of a successful fund manager.

2.4 Key Features and Relevance of Illiquid Assets to Investment Risk

Learning Objective

6.2.4   Understand the key features and relevance of illiquid assets in relation to investment risk: venture capital, private equity and property

2.4.1   Venture Capital

Venture capital is a type of private equity capital (see below), typically provided to early-stage, high-potential, growth companies in the hope of generating a return through an eventual sale of the company once it has become successful. Venture capital investments are generally made as cash in exchange for shares in the invested company.

The entrepreneurial idea that is being funded by the venture capital may require several years to come to fruition. Until that point, there is no market in the firm's shares, so the investment is illiquid.

Venture capital investments offer three main advantages for a portfolio of otherwise 'standard' investments:

1. Tax advantages – In many countries tax relief is given on the investment.
2. The potential for higher returns than can be achieved by mature companies.
3. Lack of correlation with more 'standard' investments – in other words while mainstream bond and equity markets may be declining in value, a start-up company could still be increasing in value.

Clearly, though, there is also a risk that the initial idea being funded is never able to be brought to market, in which case there would be no return on the investment.

2.4.2   Private Equity

Private equity is an illiquid asset class consisting of equity securities in operating companies that are not publicly traded on a **stock exchange**. Investments in private equity involve either an injection of capital into, or the acquisition of, an operating company.

Private equity fund managers often take an active role in the management of the companies they invest in, through having a majority shareholding and/or a seat on the board. They look to add value for their investors by transforming the way the investee company is managed, and may aim to make their money by floating the company on the market after a few years, once its performance has been improved.

Again, the advantages of holding private equity in a portfolio of more 'standard' investments are the potential for higher returns and a lack of correlation with more 'standard' investments – but with the risk of losing the initial investment if the firm fails. In addition, the lack of stock market listing also means a lack of transparency in the firm's operations and finances.

2.4.3 Property

As an asset class, property has consistently provided positive real long-term returns allied to low volatility and a reliable stream of income. An exposure to property can provide diversification benefits to a portfolio, owing to its low correlation with both traditional and alternative asset classes. However, property can be subject to prolonged downturns and, if invested in directly, its lack of liquidity and high transaction costs on transfer really make it suitable only as an investment for the medium to long-term.

2.5 Correlation of Performance between Asset Classes

Learning Objective

6.2.5   Understand the concept of correlation of performance between asset classes

Different asset classes correlate differently with each other. In other words, equity prices could be going up while bond prices are remaining stable and commodity prices are going down.

Asset correlations change over time, and the discipline of '**asset allocation**' is the macro equivalent of diversifying a portfolio to reduce its risk. Before deciding which stocks to pick, a decision must first have been made on which asset-mix to choose.

Asset allocation involves considering the big picture first by assessing the prospects for each of the main asset classes within each of the world's major investment regions against the backdrop of the world economic, political and social environment.

2.6 Tracking Error

Learning Objective

6.2.6   Understand the concept of tracking error

Tracking error is a measure of how closely a portfolio follows the index to which it is benchmarked, and it can be calculated either as a historical or a predictive indicator. Historical tracking error is 'realised' or 'ex post', while predictive tracking error is 'ex ante'.

Historical tracking error is usually calculated as the standard deviation of returns relative to the benchmark and is more useful for reporting performance.

Various types of ex ante tracking error models exist, from simple equity models which use beta as a primary determinant to more complicated multi-factor fixed income models. Ex ante is generally used by portfolio managers to control risk.

As one might expect, index funds should have minimal tracking error.

2.7 Investment Mandate and its Role in Risk Mitigation

Learning Objective

6.2.7   Know the key features of an investment mandate and its role in risk mitigation

A fund's investment mandate is set out by the investment management company, and determines the fund's aims, the limits within which it is supposed to invest, and the investment policy it should follow.

The mandate will typically define:

- the fund's aim, for example 'generation of dividend income' or 'long-term growth'
- any specific strategies it will follow
- the geographic regions it will invest in
- the sectors it will invest in
- the types of securities it will invest in – eg, equities, bonds or commodities
- whether the fund is allowed to short sell and whether it will be hedged
- whether it will be geared and to what extent
- a benchmark index that the fund aims to beat (or match if it is a tracker fund)
- the maximum error in tracking the benchmark
- any investment restrictions placed on the fund.

To ensure that none of the limits in the mandate is breached, the mandate limits will be transformed into more stringent internal limits against which the fund is managed.

The wording of an investment mandate must enable the client to understand what the fund will do. However, investment management firms generally need to prevent the wording from being too specific, or they run the risk of being sued if performance deteriorates and the client can demonstrate that certain details were not adhered to. Fund managers need the combination of the discipline which the mandate enables, and the flexibility to run the fund in the best way over the medium to long term.

2.8 Methods used to Mitigate Investment Portfolio Risk

Learning Objective

6.2.8 Understand the main methods used to mitigate investment portfolio risk: systematic and non-systematic risk; optimisation and diversification; portfolio hedging; short selling and risk transfer

2.8.1 Systematic and Non-Systematic Risk

In the context of a well-run portfolio of stocks which is benchmarked against a peer group or index, there are two reasons that the value of the portfolio changes:

1. It needs to stay close to its benchmark, so as that moves, the portfolio will tend to follow because it keeps its weighting of its constituent stocks broadly in the same ratio as the benchmark.
2. The portfolio manager seeks to gain small advantages over the benchmark by going over- or underweight in certain stocks.

The first scenario – the portfolio moving broadly in line with markets or its benchmark – is referred to as systematic risk and this sort of risk cannot be diversified away.

The second scenario introduces 'non-systematic' or 'specific' risk into the portfolio, but it can be diversified by ensuring that the portfolio has at least 15–20 stocks with low or negative correlations.

As described in chapter 5, the behaviour of a diversified portfolio can be quite different from the behaviour of individual components of the portfolio. The risk of a 'properly' constructed portfolio can display much lower risk characteristics than the average of the risks of its individual assets.

2.8.2 Optimisation and Diversification

Optimisation refers to portfolio construction techniques that obtain the best expected returns from the right mix of correlations and variances. Portfolio optimisation is often called mean-variance (MV) optimisation. The term mean refers to the mean or the expected return of the investment and the variance is the measure of the risk associated with the portfolio. The mathematical problem can be formulated in many ways as permutations of either:

*   minimising the risk for a given return, or
*   maximising the expected return for a given risk.

A diversified portfolio that is invested in multiple instruments whose returns are uncorrelated will have an expected simple return which is the weighted average of the individual instruments' returns. However, its volatility will be less than the weighted average of the individual instruments' volatilities. Diversification means that an investor can reduce market risk simply by investing in many unrelated instruments. The risk reduction is 'free' because expected returns are not affected.

2.8.3 Portfolio Hedging

Hedging is a means of reducing the risk of adverse price movements by taking an offsetting position in a related product. It is a means of insuring against market risk.

Hedging is the taking of offsetting risks. With diversification, risks are uncorrelated. With hedging, they have negative correlations. The main financial instruments used in hedging are derivatives, and in particular, futures and options.

For instance, the portfolio manager may buy a certain equity and realise that they are at risk of losing money if the market declines. This could be hedged by buying a put option. This option gives the buyer the right to sell the stock at a set price (the strike price) within a particular time in the future. The investor is now protected against adverse market movements – if markets go down, the equity price loss will be offset by the profit received in exercising the option.

The decision to hedge is a trade-off between the risk of adverse movement and the cost of the hedge – in this case the purchase price of the option. However, it is difficult to achieve perfect offsetting of the risk because the use of hedging introduces, or exacerbates, other risks such as basis risk (see chapter 5), credit risk and operational risk.

2.8.4 Short Selling

Short selling means selling a security which you do not own, in anticipation of its price reducing so that you can buy it back for less than you sold it for. The stock to be sold needs to be borrowed from someone who does own it.

Shorting is a method of reducing portfolio risk in falling markets – a short position benefits from a decline in the security's price. However, extreme caution should be taken when entering a short trade, since, if the price of the stock starts rising while the position is held, the losses on the position can be unlimited. In fact, some countries' financial regulators have banned short selling in their markets.

2.8.5 Risk Transfer

In chapter 4 on Credit Risk, we discussed ways in which institutions can use credit derivatives to increase or decrease their credit exposure to a particular counterparty for a particular period of time. The same principle also applies to portfolios. A portfolio manager may choose to buy or sell protection (eg, credit default swaps) on fixed income assets whose credit ratings he believes are wrong or about to change in his favour.

2.9 Monitoring, Managing and Reporting of Investments

Learning Objective

6.2.9 Understand how timely and accurate monitoring, management and reporting of investments can enhance the risk management process

Robust risk management processes, including investment management, monitoring and reporting, are key to ensuring an appropriate balance between risk and return.

Many firms run a dedicated investment management committee whose task is to challenge the investment managers and ensure that appropriate monitoring takes place.

There are four main areas where a portfolio will benefit from monitoring, management and reporting:

1. **Peer review with other fund managers in the same firm** – this will help to ensure that, for example, managers are abiding by 'house view' rules and not taking 'unusual' risks.
2. **Risk review with independent risk managers in the firm** – this ensures that the investment process is transparent and duly challenged.
3. **Monitoring for mandate compliance** – systems are commonly used to perform pre- and post-trade compliance checking, for example, ensuring that forbidden stocks are not invested in.
4. **Performance attribution reporting** – this enables the fund manager, and the investors, to better understand which elements within the portfolio are contributing to its returns. Typically, the contribution to overall performance could come from:
   - asset allocation
   - stock selection
   - currency exchange rate impact.

Firm-specific client and internal reporting requirements will determine the extent to which the results of the above monitoring and management processes will be more widely shared.

End of Chapter Questions

Think of an answer for each question and refer to the appropriate section for confirmation.

1. What is the definition of investment risk?
   Answer reference: Chapter Summary

2. In simple terms, what is the relationship between the nominal and real return of an investment?
   Answer reference: Section 1.1

3. What are the two constituent elements of total returns?
   Answer reference: Section 1.1.3

4. What is the formula for calculating compound interest?
   Answer reference: Section 1.2

5. To one decimal place, what are the typical historic returns from equities, bonds and cash investment?
   Answer reference: Section 1.3

6. Commodity risk is one of the seven components of investment risk. Name three others.
   Answer reference: Section 2.1

7. What are the four risk factors for equity investments?
   Answer reference: Section 2.1.4

8. What is asset allocation?
   Answer reference: Section 2.5

9. Give four elements of a typical fund mandate.
   Answer reference: Section 2.7

10. Which portfolio risk can be diversified away, systematic or non-systematic?
    Answer reference: Section 2.8.1

Chapter Seven
Liquidity Risk

This syllabus area will provide approximately 10 of the 100 examination questions

Chapter Summary

A company's survival is dependent upon both its profitability and its ability to generate sufficient cash to support its day-to-day operations. Profitability is clearly important, but even profitable companies will fail if they suffer a liquidity crisis and cannot honour their financial commitments. This is true for all companies, but acutely so for financial services firms whose raison d'être is the collection and redistribution of cash.

The focus of this chapter is on banks' liquidity management because banks directly affect the rest of the financial and economic system. However, it is worth bearing in mind that securities firms also have exposure to funding liquidity risk if, for example, their assets are financed by short-term borrowing from wholesale sources.

On the other hand, investment managers are focused mainly on liquidity within their clients' funds, and individual funds will have different requirements. This even includes, in some cases, the ability to prevent fund cash withdrawals (redemptions) under certain circumstances. In stark contrast, the case of Northern Rock shows just how quickly a bank can fail when it experiences a liquidity crisis.

Northern Rock Case Study – Liquidity Matters

The market turmoil that began in mid-2007 re-emphasised the importance of liquidity to the functioning of financial markets and the banking sector, and the inter-bank wholesale markets finally froze on 9 August.

It became clear that banks would face liquidity problems if the markets were to stay frozen for long. These problems were especially severe for Northern Rock compared to other banks because its business model was based on providing long-term mortgage loans, but funding the loans in significant measure by short-term borrowing in the wholesale inter-bank markets.

The chairman and the chief executive of Northern Rock first discussed these problems with each other on Friday 10 August. On the same day, the regulator contacted the financial businesses that it believed might be at risk from the freezing of financial markets. One of these was Northern Rock.

Northern Rock replied to the regulator on the next working day, Monday 13 August, alerting the regulator to the difficulties that the bank would face if the market freeze continued. Thereafter, the regulator and Northern Rock were in twice-daily telephone contact.

On Tuesday 14 August, the first discussions of Northern Rock took place between the Tripartite Authorities – the Bank of England, the regulator and the Treasury – and the Chancellor of the Exchequer was informed about Northern Rock on that day. The possibility of a support operation was discussed.

The subsequent announcement of government support for the troubled bank increased the public's perception that it was in trouble. Queues started to form at branches of Northern Rock, and ultimately the bank was taken into national ownership.

The term liquidity is used in various ways, all relating to availability of, access to, or convertibility into cash.

- An institution is said to have liquidity if it can easily meet its needs for cash (because it has cash on hand or it can otherwise raise or borrow cash).
- A market is said to be liquid if the instruments it trades can easily be bought or sold in quantity with little impact on market prices.
- An asset is said to be liquid if the market for that asset is liquid.

The common theme in all three contexts is cash. A firm is liquid if it has ready access to cash. A market is liquid if participants can easily convert positions into cash. An asset is liquid if it can easily be converted to cash.

The definition of liquidity risk for our purposes is the risk that a firm has insufficient cash to meet its cash obligations and will either become insolvent, or will suffer losses from borrowing, selling assets at below market price, or paying contractual penalties.

For a bank, virtually every financial transaction or commitment has implications for its liquidity. Effective liquidity risk management helps ensure a bank's ability to meet cash flow obligations, which are uncertain as they are affected by external events and other agents' behaviour.

Liquidity risk management is of paramount importance because a liquidity shortfall at a single bank can have system-wide repercussions, as became apparent during and after the 2008 banking crisis.

In response to that crisis, and to promote better liquidity risk management and to improve resilience to financial market stress, the Basel Committee published a set of *Principles for Sound Liquidity Risk Management and Supervision*. In the run-up to the crisis, many banks had failed to take account of a number of basic liquidity risk management principles when liquidity was plentiful. Many of the most exposed banks did not have an adequate framework that satisfactorily accounted for the liquidity risks posed by individual products and business lines. This meant that incentives at the business level were misaligned with the overall risk tolerance of the bank.

Many banks had not considered the amount of liquidity they might need for contingent obligations, either contractual or non-contractual, as they viewed the funding of these obligations as highly unlikely. Many firms viewed severe and prolonged liquidity disruptions as implausible. They did not conduct stress tests that factored in the possibility of market-wide strain or the severity, or duration, of the disruptions. Contingency funding plans were not always appropriately linked to stress test results and sometimes failed to take account of the potential closure of some funding sources.

1. Identification of Liquidity Risk

1.1 Basic Constituents of Liquidity Risk

Learning Objective

7.1.1 Understand the basic constituents of liquidity risk and how they can arise within the contexts of credit, market, investment and operational risk: maturity ladder; actual and contractual cash receipts; asset liquidity risk; funding liquidity risk

The liquidity of an institution depends on, among other things, its immediate need for cash, how much cash it currently has, its available lines of credit, and how easily it can transform its non-cash assets into cash. Its reputation in the marketplace or credit rating will also have a bearing on its liquidity because counterparties will not lend to firms which appear to be in trouble.

Firms' approaches to credit and market risks have traditionally been somewhat segregated (although this approach is changing as the industry's treatment of securitisation, which combines both risk types, continues to mature). However, a firm's liquidity risk has always been intrinsically linked to its internal and external risk factors and controls. It cannot be treated in isolation from:

- financial controls, such as the cash flow statement
- instruments which generate cash
- instruments which require cash for margin calls
- credit risks which include the risk of default on a loan or bond obligation, as well as the risk of a guarantor or derivative counterparty failing to meet its obligations
- market risks, such as the risk of loss through not being able to trade in a market or obtain a price on a desired product when required. This can occur in a market due either to a lack of supply or demand or to a shortage of market makers
- operational risks, such as the failure of a major outsource supplier whose replacement requires immediate and significant amounts of cash
- business risk, such as a change in the environment which renders a firm's business strategy obsolete, eg, the withdrawal of favourable tax treatment for certain financial products.

In these respects, liquidity risk is like operational risk – difficult to quantify, yet all-pervasive. However, whereas an operational risk issue can continue undetected for some time until it becomes a critical issue, the effects of a liquidity squeeze is measured in days, and even intra-day issues can cause significant disruption to the firm.

Ultimately, impaired liquidity can result in insolvency and can have repercussions for the market as a whole, causing tighter liquidity conditions in the affected markets and resulting in systemic risk.

Tools to help identify liquidity risk include the construction of a maturity ladder, and analysis of actual and contractual cash receipts.

1.1.1   The Maturity Ladder

A maturity ladder is a useful device for comparing cash inflows and outflows, both on a daily basis and over a series of specified time periods. The analysis of net funding requirements involves the construction of a maturity ladder and the calculation of a cumulative net excess, or deficit, of funds at selected maturity dates.

A bank's net funding requirements are determined by analysing its future cash flows based on assumptions about the future behaviour of assets, liabilities and off-balance-sheet items, and then calculating the cumulative net excess or shortfall over the time frame for the liquidity assessment.

In constructing the maturity ladder, a bank has to allocate each cash inflow or outflow to a given calendar date. As a preliminary step to constructing the maturity ladder, cash inflows can be ranked by the date on which assets mature or a conservative estimate of when credit lines can be drawn down.

Similarly, cash outflows can be ranked by the date on which liabilities fall due, the earliest date a liability holder could exercise an early repayment option, or the earliest date contingencies can be called. Readily marketable assets may be 'slotted in' to the earliest point in the maturity ladder at which they could be liquidated. Banks or supervisors should consider what discount should be applied to assets which are 'slotted in' in this way to reflect market risks.

Significant interest and other cash flows should also be included. In addition, certain assumptions can be made based on past experience. The difference between cash inflows and cash outflows in each period (the excess or deficit of funds) becomes a starting point for a measure of a bank's future liquidity excess or shortfall at a series of points in time.

In the following table, a maturity ladder, based on contractual maturities, is represented by placing sources and amounts of cash inflows on one side of the page and sources and amounts of outflows on the other.

Day one: Cash inflows		Cash outflows		Excess/ (shortfall)
Maturing assets	100	Maturing liabilities with contractual maturities	50	
Interest receivable	20			
Asset sales	50			
Drawdowns on committed lines	10	Interest payable	10	
		Other deposit runoffs	30	
		Drawdowns on committed lines	10	
Total	**180**	**Total**	**100**	**80**
Day two: Cash inflows		Cash outflows		Excess/ (shortfall)
Maturing assets	100	Maturing liabilities with contractual maturities	70	
Interest receivable	20			
Asset sales	55			
Drawdowns on committed lines	10	Interest payable	20	
		Other deposit runoffs	40	
		Drawdowns on committed lines	50	
Total	**185**	**Total**	**180**	**5**
Day three to day 15: Cash inflows		Cash outflows		Excess/ (shortfall)
Maturing assets	130	Maturing liabilities with contractual maturities	90	
Interest receivable	50			
Asset sales	60			
Drawdowns on committed lines	20	Interest payable	30	
		Other deposit runoffs	40	
		Drawdowns on committed lines	80	
Total	**260**	**Total**	**240**	**20**
Day 16 to day 30: Cash inflows		Cash outflows		Excess/ (shortfall)
Maturing assets	160	Maturing liabilities with contractual maturities	130	
Interest receivable	80			
Asset sales	90			
Drawdowns on committed lines	40	Interest payable	60	
		Other deposit runoffs	80	
		Drawdowns on committed lines	80	
Total	**370**	**Total**	**350**	**20**

Aside from the liquidity needs arising from business activities, the maturity ladder must also reflect the need for excess funds to support other operations. For example, many large banks provide clearing services to correspondent banks and financial institutions that generate significant and not always easily predictable cash inflows and outflows, the amounts of which depend on the clearing volumes of the correspondent banks. Unforeseen fluctuations in these volumes can deplete a bank of needed funds.

Net overhead expenses, such as rent and salary, are also sources of cash outflows. Future strategic commitments will also require cash at different points in time and these should therefore be included on the ladder.

A maturity ladder will never show the complete picture, because, for example, derivative cash flows are not predictable because they have a very broad range of possible outcomes. However, the probability that the cash flows shown on the ladder will actually appear at the right time can be fine-tuned by considering actual and contractual cash receipts.

1.1.2   Actual and Contractual Cash Receipts

There are three main reasons why actual and contractual cash flows shown in the maturity ladder will differ from the actual cash receipts.

1. It is not possible to estimate with certainty the cash flows from all instruments. Many types of financial instruments do, indeed, have contractually specified cash flows, which can be predictably estimated. However, some types of financial instruments, such as derivatives, have a very broad range of possible contractual outcomes. In these cases, statistical modelling techniques are used to provide ranges of cash flow likelihoods.
2. Even when cash flows can be properly estimated, the existence of credit risk means that the cash may not materialise on the due date – or at all. As discussed in chapter 4, many instruments are exposed to the risk that the counterparty will not honour its contractual obligations. If this credit risk is significant, then the single number to be included in the maturity ladder needs to be risk-weighted, using the techniques discussed in chapter 4.
3. The business may not wish to hold the instrument until maturity. Even without credit issues occurring, the way that the business uses financial instruments will often result in the actual cash flows being significantly different from the contractually stated position.

1.1.3   Asset Liquidity Risk

Liquidity is a broad term referring to all the cash and near-cash resources available to a firm, and it is helpful to draw a distinction between asset liquidity and liability liquidity.

We will consider liability liquidity below, but asset liquidity is cash obtained from mature or divested (sold) assets, or the use of these assets as collateral in secured funding, such as repurchase (**repo**) agreements.

There are two main factors that determine the liquidity risk of the firm's assets:

1. Potential marketability – how easily they can be sold for cash. This is linked to market risk.
2. How easily the assets can be used as collateral against which to secure increased cash inflows. This is linked to credit risk.

So asset liquidity risk refers to the likelihood of being unable to transform assets into cash within a preferred time period without incurring losses; it is closely linked to both credit and market risk.

1.1.4 Funding Liquidity Risk

The term 'funding liquidity' usually refers to the way in which a firm obtains liquidity from the liability side of its balance sheet. Liability liquidity tends to refer to unsecured funding obtained from depositors, third parties and the wholesale markets. So the term 'funding liquidity risk' refers to the likelihood that the bank's funding will not be available when required.

Funding liquidity risk is closely linked to the perceived level of credit risk that a bank poses to third parties to whom it might need to turn for emergency funding.

1.2 Potential Impact of Liquidity Risk

Learning Objective

7.1.2   Understand the potential impact of liquidity risk within an individual firm and across the wider financial system

When liquidity risks materialise within a specific firm, it may not be able to meet its obligations as they fall due. The firm will face a loss in this case due to the cost of borrowing to meet those obligations, or through facing contractual penalties for non-payment. Ultimately, illiquidity will result in insolvency.

As discussed in chapter 2, banks are treated differently by regulators and governments because of their special role in providing liquidity to the economy. They facilitate trade by bridging the gap between short-term cash requirements and longer term cash flows – by borrowing short to lend long.

When a bank such as Northern Rock suffers a liquidity shortage, what it needs to do is attract more funds from depositors, or from the wholesale money markets.

What actually happens is that as soon as depositors hear of problems, they start trying to withdraw their savings, forcing the bank to sell assets, perhaps at a loss, or to try and raise finance in more expensive markets – assuming that these markets have not been affected by the same liquidity shortage.

This can quickly become a negative self-reinforcing process, and without regulatory or government intervention the bank fails. Bank failure has contagion effects because consumers start to lose confidence in the banking system as a whole, rather than simply the failed bank – and queues start forming outside other banks too.

2. Measurement of Liquidity Risk

2.1 Funding Liquidity Risk Analysis

Learning Objective

7.2.1 Understand the importance of funding liquidity risk analysis: liquidity gap analysis, stress testing, expected future funding requirement

2.1.1 Liquidity Gap Analysis

Modern banks rely on a number of sources for their funding. For example, retail depositors, larger wholesale depositors and the money markets. Funding is therefore spilt between different areas of the organisation such as the retail division and capital markets division.

Negative net future cash flows over a given time period represent a major source of liquidity risk. Before a liquidity gap analysis can be performed, a technique called cash matching is used to understand a firm's or portfolio's liquidity risk, by examining all net future cash flows. A firm or portfolio is cash matched if:

- every future cash inflow is balanced with an offsetting cash outflow on the same date, and
- every future cash outflow is balanced with an offsetting cash inflow on the same date.

Gap analysis then aggregates the cash flows into maturity brackets and checks if cash flows in each bracket net to zero. As a simple example, consider a portfolio whose cash flows all mature in less than three years. We can group the maturities into five brackets:

- 0–3 months
- 3–6 months
- 6–12 months
- 12–24 months
- 24–36 months.

The following table illustrates a gap analysis using our brackets and hypothetical cash flows.

Bracket (months)	0–3	3–6	6–12	12–24	24–36
Cash inflows (£m)	130	165	90	60	50
Cash outflows (£m)	130	25	90	70	50
Gap	0	140	0	−10	0

A liquidity gap is any net cash flow for a bracket, so there is a positive gap of £140 million for the three to six month bracket, and a negative gap of £10 million for the 12–24 month bracket. Having derived this information, the bank can then arrange to correct the future liquidity gaps where necessary.

Shortcomings of Liquidity Gap Analysis

One disadvantage of liquidity gap analysis is that it does not consider credit risk, and assumes all cash flows will occur. A further shortcoming is that it cannot handle options in a meaningful way. Options have cash flows whose magnitudes – and sometimes timing – is highly uncertain, and therefore the cash flows cannot be allocated to a certain time bracket.

2.1.2 Stress Testing

Stress testing is a technique for assessing how outcomes differ when individual inputs to a system are changed or stressed. Before any liquidity stress testing can be undertaken, a bank must first collect its contractual liquidity data from across all its businesses – perhaps using the sort of liquidity gap analysis that we looked at above.

Once that has been done, the bank should set out how it expects normal behaviour to impact the resulting liquidity risk. These normal assumptions should be clearly documented and can be based on historical data – since, by definition, they represent what customers have done previously.

Stress testing will then take those normal assumptions and tailor them to the particular area being tested. Some stress information can be readily based on historical observation – eg, volatility of the value of collateral – while others will, of necessity, be based on subjective assumptions. It is important that the normal assumptions are used as a starting point or base case and that any movement away from the norm is recorded, together with the underlying argument for the move.

2.1.3 Expected Future Funding Requirement

In estimating 'normal' future funding needs, banks use a number of approaches:

- analysing historical patterns of roll-overs, draw-downs and new requests for loans
- conducting statistical analysis taking account of seasonal and other effects believed to determine loan demand (eg, for consumer loans)
- making subjective high-level business projections
- undertaking a customer-by-customer assessment for its larger customers and applying historical relationships to the remainder.

2.2 Uses and Limitations of the Key Measures of Asset Liquidity Risk

Learning Objective

7.2.2 Know the uses and limitations of the key measures of asset liquidity risk: bid-offer spread, market depth, immediacy and resilience

The key measures of asset liquidity risk are:

- bid-offer spread
- market depth
- immediacy
- resilience.

2.2.1 Bid-Offer Spread

The bid-offer (sometimes synonymously referred to as bid-ask) spread is the difference between the prices quoted by market makers for an immediate sale to them (the bid) and an immediate purchase from them (the offer). The size of the bid-offer spread is a measure of the liquidity of the market. To compare the liquidity of different assets, the ratio of the spread to the asset's mid-price can be used. The smaller the ratio, the more liquid the asset is. A limitation is that the bid-offer spread reflects the size of the transaction cost, as well as the liquidity of the market.

2.2.2 Market Depth

Market depth is a measure of the volume of transactions necessary to move prices – the deeper the market, the higher the volume needed to move prices. Depth is important because when selling an asset quickly to secure liquidity, a market that is not deep will result in the price of the assets falling and, hence, a need to sell more assets with further resulting prices falls.

Typically, the markets for various assets fall across a spectrum ranging from the very deep market for equities in blue-chip companies, such as the FTSE 100, to markets such as those for very specific types of commercial/industrial property or private equity. One drawback of relying on measures of market depth when anticipating methods of realising 'emergency' liquidity from asset sales is that market depth can change very rapidly.

2.2.3 Immediacy

Immediacy is a measure of the time it takes to achieve a deal in a market. It depends on the existence of market makers to buy from sellers, and sell to buyers. Without market makers, each seller would have to find their own buyer and vice versa.

Immediacy is not simply a feature of the price. For example, during 2008 in the interbank markets, LIBOR rose significantly above the Bank of England base rate and yet banks would still not lend to each other because of fears over credit risk and not being able to 'get their money back'.

2.2.4 Resilience

Resilience is a measure of the speed with which prices return to equilibrium following a large trade. The more liquid the market, the faster the prices return to equilibrium.

3. Management of Liquidity Risk

Banks clearly need liquidity to remain solvent, but if they carry too much liquidity their profits will suffer, which can also lead to future problems. Banks need to perform a balancing act, and that is why liquidity risk needs very careful management.

In summary, the process for managing liquidity risk is fourfold:

- a bank must be able to readily determine its contractual liquidity position
- a bank should then overlay that view with assumptions about normal behaviour
- it should then undertake stress testing by reviewing how the normal assumptions change under the various stress scenarios
- given the results of the stress tests the bank can then assess its current level of liquidity provision, establish the cost of contingency arrangements, and compare the associated liquidity risk levels to its risk appetite and profitability goals.

The bank can then use certain techniques to ensure that it stays within its risk appetite and profitability goals. These include:

- setting and monitoring liquidity limits
- setting and monitoring counterparty credit limits
- performing scenario analyses
- using liquidity at risk techniques
- ensuring diversification
- considering behavioural analysis.

Banks and certain other financial services firms are required by their regulator to submit details of their approach to the management of liquidity risks. In the UK this takes the form of a process called the 'Individual Liquidity Adequacy Assessment' (ILAA). Firms that are subject to the ILAA regime must provide their regulator with:

- a full and complete review of the firm's liquidity position, access to liquidity, composition of its liquid assets, contractual and behavioural wholesale and retail deposit assumptions, and secured and unsecured funding profiles under business-as-usual conditions and under a prescribed set of stress tests
- a review of liquidity risk governance
- a statement of the firm's liquidity risk appetite

- liquidity stress testing policies, processes, and methodologies
- the assumptions used for liquidity stress test scenario development and those defining operational constraints on stress testing and management remedial actions
- contingency funding plans
- management information and reports, along with processes and procedures used for the identification, measurement, monitoring, and management of liquidity risk within the firm, and
- a review and justification of the firm's assessment of its liquidity requirement.

3.1 Managing Liquidity Risk

Learning Objective

7.3.1 Understand the main ways in which liquidity risk can be managed: liquidity limits; counterparty credit limits; scenario analysis; liquidity at risk; diversification; behavioural analysis; funding methods

It is different for investment managers

The cash flow and liquidity requirements for an investment management firm are more predictable than for a bank. In addition, investment funds' liquidity risks are managed differently from banks' liquidity risks – a fund needs to remain as liquid as its prospectus or mandate says it will. The prospectus must make the liquidity risks clear and may, in addition, specify gate provisions that can be applied to limit the level of redemptions under certain circumstances.

3.1.1 Liquidity Limits

A bank should set limits to control its liquidity risk exposure. These limits would impose a ceiling on the projected net funding requirement along the maturity ladder discussed above. There should also be a set of corresponding escalation procedures for each limit breach.

For example, a commonly employed type of limit constrains the size of cumulative contractual cash flow mismatches (eg, the cumulative net funding requirement as a percentage of total liabilities) over various time horizons. This type of limit may also include estimates of outflows resulting from the drawdown of commitments or other obligations of the bank.

Funding concentration limits place upper limits on the use of wholesale funding and retail funding. Simply stated, the objective of such measures is to ensure that, even under stress conditions, available liquidity exceeds liquidity needs.

For a global bank, the limits may vary by time zone, since access to liquidity will depend on the time of day. At the beginning of the global trading day, during Asia-Pacific trading hours, the limits may be less severe because more time is available to mobilise funding sources or, if necessary, initiate asset sales to generate additional liquidity. As the day proceeds and currency zones begin to close, the limits should become tighter, with the strictest limits applied later in the day when only the US markets are available.

3.1.2 Counterparty Credit Limits

Certain liquidity issues arise from a bank's counterparties' inability to fulfil their settlement obligations. This can either be because of financial problems with the counterparty, or because of problems with inter-bank payment failures and data mismanagement.

Failure to process payment transactions in a timely manner may result in payment failures which, in times of extreme market conditions, can disrupt the bank's liquidity management. Therefore, to reduce its liquidity risks, the bank needs to maintain intra-day counterparty credit limits in addition to those discussed in chapter 4.

3.1.3 Scenario Analysis

There are a number of drivers which can increase the likelihood of liquidity risk. These include:

- market concerns over availability of credit
- general market and economic conditions
- global shocks.

Evaluating whether a bank is sufficiently liquid depends on the behaviour of cash flows under these and other different conditions. Three specific scenarios then provide useful benchmarks:

1. A bank's 'going-concern' condition.
2. A bank-specific crisis.
3. A general market crisis.

Under each scenario, a bank should try to account for any significant positive or negative liquidity swings that could occur.

1. The going-concern scenario establishes a benchmark for the 'normal' behaviour of balance sheet-related cash flows in the ordinary course of business at a bank. This scenario is useful in managing a bank's use of deposit and other debt markets. By establishing such a benchmark, a bank can manage its net funding requirements so that it is not faced with very large needs on any given day, thus avoiding the impact of temporary constraints on its ability to roll over liabilities because of market disruptions or concerns about its condition.
2. Assessing liquidity under the second scenario, a liquidity crisis at an individual bank that remains confined to that bank, provides one type of 'worst-case' benchmark. The key underlying assumption in this scenario is that many of the bank's liabilities could not be rolled over or replaced and would have to be repaid at maturity so that the bank would have to wind down its books to some degree. While a severe liquidity crisis at an individual bank usually stems from a fundamental, bank-specific problem, a bank's ability to honour its deposit maturities under such conditions can provide the time that the bank would need to address the underlying problem. If a bank can weather such a 'worst-case' scenario, it can almost certainly survive less drastic firm-specific problems.
3. The last scenario is some form of general market crisis where liquidity is affected at all banks in one or more markets. The key underlying assumption that banks need to make in this scenario is that severe tiering by perceived credit quality would occur, so that differences in funding access among banks or among classes of financial institutions would widen, benefiting some and harming others. Although some banks may believe that central banks would ensure that key markets continued to function in

some form, severe market disruption would not necessarily be prevented. For bank management, this represents a second type of 'worst-case' scenario that a bank would wish to weather.

A supervisor or central bank may find this third scenario to be of particular interest when surveying the liquidity profile of the entire banking sector. The collective results would suggest the size of the total liquidity buffer in the banking system, and the likely distribution of liquidity problems among large institutions, if the banking system as a whole experienced a shortage of liquidity.

A bank will need to assign the timing of cash flows for each type of asset and liability by assessing the probability of the behaviour of those cash flows in the scenario being examined. These decisions about the specific timing and the size of cash flows are an integral part of the maturity ladder's construction under each scenario. For example, for each funding source, a bank would have to decide whether the liability would be:

- repaid in full at maturity
- gradually run off over the next few weeks
- virtually certain to be rolled over or available if tapped.

The bank's decisions will be guided by its experience of historical liquidity flow and a knowledge of market conventions, but management judgment will also need to play a significant part, especially in crisis scenarios. Uncertainty will always be present when choosing between possible behaviour patterns, and so banks need to err on the side of caution by assigning later dates to cash inflows and earlier dates to cash outflows.

Hence, the timings of cash inflows and outflows on the maturity ladder (shown above) will differ between the going-concern approach and the two crisis scenarios. The next table shows the day one positions of the maturity ladder under the alternative scenarios.

Day One of the Maturity Ladder under Alternative Scenarios

Cash inflows	Normal business conditions (1)	Institution-specific crisis (2)	General market crisis (3)
Maturing assets	100	100	90
Interest receivable	20	20	10
Asset sales	50	60	0
Drawdowns	10	0	5
Total	**180**	**180**	**105**
Cash outflows			
Maturing liabilities	50	50	50
Interest payable	10	10	10
Deposit runoffs	30	100	60
Drawdowns on lending commitments	10	60	75
Total	**100**	**220**	**195**
Liquidity excess/ (shortfall)	80	(40)	(90)

In constructing the going-concern maturity ladder, conservative assumptions need to be made about the behaviour of cash flows that can replace the contractual cash flows. For example, many maturing loans would be rolled over in the normal course of business and some proportion of transactions and savings deposits would also be rolled over or could be easily replaced.

In a bank-specific crisis scenario, it is assumed that a bank will be unable to roll over or replace many or most of its liabilities and that it may have to wind down its books to some degree.

The assumptions under the third scenario, a general market crisis, may differ quite sharply from the assumptions made for a bank-specific crisis. For example, a bank may believe, based upon its historical experience, that its ability to control the level and timing of future cash flows from a stock of saleable assets in a bank-specific funding crisis would deteriorate little from normal conditions.

However, in a general market crisis, this capacity may fall off sharply if few institutions are willing or able to make cash purchases of less liquid assets. On the other hand, a bank that has a high reputation in the market may actually benefit from a flight to quality as potential depositors seek out the safest home for their funds. Banks may also anticipate that central banks would ensure that key markets continued to function but not necessarily without significant disruption.

Lessons from the Scenarios

In examining the cash flows arising from a bank's liabilities in the two crisis scenarios, a bank could ask the following basic questions:

1. Which sources of funding are likely to stay under any circumstance, and can these be increased? Some core deposits generally stay with a bank because retail and small business depositors may rely on the public-sector safety net to shield them from loss, or because the cost of switching banks, especially for some business services such as transactions accounts, is prohibitive in the very short run.
2. Which sources of funding can be expected to run off gradually if problems arise, and at what rate? Is deposit pricing a means of controlling the rate of runoff?
3. Which maturing liabilities or liabilities with non-contractual maturities can be expected to run off immediately at the first sign of trouble? Are there liabilities with early withdrawal options that are likely to be exercised?
4. Does the bank have back-up facilities that it can draw down?

Non-banks, such as securities firms, also benefit from constructing liquidity risk scenarios. Firms whose activities may generate contingent commitments should forecast contingent liability requirements by analysing their trading positions under various market scenarios. Scenario analysis enables the firm to evaluate any potential cash requirements arising from early termination, collateral, and other credit provisions normally found in the firm's derivative contracts.

3.1.4   Liquidity at Risk

We have seen in chapters 4 and 5 that Value-at-Risk (VaR) can be used to estimate the likely future value of credit and market instruments. The same approach can also be used to estimate the likelihood of liquidity shortages within a firm.

We showed earlier that a maturity ladder can give a forward-looking picture of a bank's funding requirements. There are certain shortcomings with this approach though, because the cash flows for many financial instruments cannot be predicted with any certainty. An alternative approach is for the bank to use its historic financial data to work out the size and frequency of its past funding requirements.

A series of 'funding amount' brackets can be defined, similar to those used for the liquidity gap analysis described above. The actual net funding amounts over a defined time interval are counted and then put into the corresponding bracket. For example, amounts between £20 million and £16 million might be counted 14 times, whereas those between £16 million and £12 million might be counted 18 times and so on.

Once the historic funding requirements have been assigned to their brackets, the brackets can be arranged as a distribution. Typically, there will be a cluster of commonly required funding amounts in the middle of the distribution, with lower amounts and higher amounts spread out on either side to form the tails.

Exactly as with market VaR and credit VaR, the **Liquidity at Risk (LaR)** distribution gives the bank an idea of its likely funding requirement over a given time period at different confidence levels.

3.1.5   Diversification

A firm with a sufficiently flexible funding strategy should be able to reduce its liquidity risk by diversifying its liquidity resources. Its liquidity resources should be diversified according to:

- the type of liquidity instruments held
- the currency of the funding
- the counterparties used
- the firm's liability term structure, and
- an assessment of the availability of markets for the realisation of the liquid assets and funding.

A firm should also be aware that the degree of diversification in its liquidity resources can be compromised, particularly in periods of stress, by a number of factors, including but not limited to:

- reduced or terminated funding provision from some counterparties as a result of the firm's credit-rating being downgraded or its financial condition deteriorating
- disputes over the terms of legally binding commitments to lend which delay the provision of funding
- the closure or reduced capacity of markets previously used by the firm for raising funding
- reliance on a small number of brokers to access funding sources, and
- positive correlations in the behaviour of different funding sources and liquid assets (see chapter 5).

3.1.6 Behavioural Analysis

To evaluate the cash flows arising from a bank's liabilities – for example, customer deposits – a bank needs to examine the behaviour of its liabilities under normal business conditions. This would include establishing:

- the normal level of rollovers of deposits and other liabilities
- the effective maturity of deposits with non-contractual maturities, such as demand deposits and certain types of savings accounts
- the normal growth in new deposit accounts.

Withdrawals from instant access deposit accounts, whether by individuals or businesses, are particularly difficult to predict. Many banks therefore conduct a statistical analysis that takes account of seasonal factors, interest rate sensitivities, and other macroeconomic factors.

For example, for each funding source a bank would have to decide whether the liability would be:

- repaid in full at maturity
- gradually run off over the next few weeks, or
- virtually certain to be rolled over or available if tapped.

For some large wholesale depositors, a bank may also undertake a customer-by-customer assessment of the probability of rollover.

3.1.7 Funding Methods

As discussed above, liquidity can be obtained from both sides of the balance sheet. On the liability side, firms can obtain funding in many forms, both secured and unsecured, from a variety of lenders and for differing maturities.

It is important to avoid a concentration in any particular type of funding, and common funding sources are:

- wholesale money markets
- securitisation of loan portfolios
- retail deposits
- loan facilities with the central bank.

On the asset side, less liquid assets can be used as collateral to obtain liquidity through the use of repurchase agreements (repos and securities lending) or posted as collateral to support various trading strategies for the creation of liquidity. Loan repayments also provide a source of liquidity.

Each liquidity source, be it on the asset or liability side of the balance sheet, has its own characteristics in terms of cost, availability, maturity and, importantly, liquidity risk. Effective liquidity risk management makes best use of the potential from both sides of the balance sheet, taking into account the risks and costs of each type of liquidity source.

3.2 Calculating a Simple Example of a Cash Netting Agreement

Learning Objective

7.3.2   Be able to calculate a simple example of a cash netting agreement

As discussed in chapter 4, netting agreements reduce the exposure of a bank to outstanding amounts owed to it by its counterparties. The example below illustrates the benefit of netting agreements in the case of counterparty failure.

Example

Delta Bank has an exposure of $40 million to each of two hedge funds, Phoenix Partners and Vapour Capital. In both cases, the bank has assets (profitable positions) of $100 million and liabilities (losing positions) to the counterparty of $60 million. There is a netting agreement in place with Phoenix Partners.

A major market event causes both funds, Phoenix and Vapour, to implode. Unsecured creditors of both funds will receive 40¢ on the dollar.

With netting

*   Owed to Phoenix   <60m>

*   Owed by Phoenix   100m

*   Make claim for net amount   40m

*   Recovery 40%   16m

In this case an asset of $40 million has become a cash inflow of $16 million.

Without netting

*   Owed to Vapour   <60m> PAID

*   Make claim for gross amount   100m

*   Recovery 40%   40m

*   Net payment   <20m>

In this case an asset of $40 million has become a cash outflow of $20 million.

3.3   Market Dislocation

Learning Objective

7.3.3   Understand the concept and implications of market dislocation

---

Markets are generally held to work in a certain way – if everything was completely random then no-one would invest. There are certain key principles that are relied upon when making investment decisions, and also when making everyday purchase decisions. One such principle is that if the price of something is reduced then there will be more people interested in buying it.

However, at certain points in the business cycle, markets occasionally stop clearing at any price. Economic experience has shown that when liquidity disappears, no-one will lend, regardless of price. This is an example of market dislocation.

The behaviour of banks and central banks becomes unpredictable during times of market dislocation. For example, no matter how low the central bank sets interest rates, banks may still not lend to each other.

In fact, often, the interbank rates continue to rise even while interest rates are falling. No matter how much liquidity the central bank provides, banks simply hold on to it and will not pass it on in the form of customer loans. This is because they fear becoming insolvent if they have insufficient liquidity to fund their short-term operations.

The implications of market dislocation are:

- companies find it harder to borrow, which means they are more likely to fail, thus making the economic situation worse and causing bank profits to fall further
- consumers find that they cannot obtain mortgages, thus prolonging any fall in house prices
- central banks lose the use of interest rates as their main economic lever. Interest rates can only go as low as zero and once this point is reached, the economy risks entering into deflation.

End of Chapter Questions

Think of an answer for each question and refer to the appropriate section for confirmation.

1. What is the definition of liquidity risk?
   Answer reference: Chapter summary

2. What sort of cash flows does a maturity ladder compare?
   Answer reference: Section 1.1.1

3. Give one reason why a maturity ladder can never capture all flows.
   Answer reference: Section 1.1.2

4. What are the four key measures of asset liquidity risk?
   Answer reference: Section 2.2

5. What can the ratio of the bid-offer spread to an asset's mid-price be used to indicate?
   Answer reference: Section 2.2.1

6. In the context of liquidity risk, what is resilience the measure of?
   Answer reference: Section 2.2.4

7. Why are Counterparty Credit Limits a useful tool for the management of liquidity risk?
   Answer reference: Section 3.1.2

8. What does LaR stand for?
   Answer reference: Section 3.1.4

9. What are the four common funding sources for a bank?
   Answer reference: Section 3.1.7

10. What term is used to describe a period during which markets will not clear at any price?
    Answer reference: Section 3.3

Chapter Eight
Model Risk

This syllabus area will provide approximately 6 of the 100 examination questions

Chapter Summary

Models play an important role in the analysis, measurement and management of risk. In recent years, firms have applied models to increasingly complex areas of risk and with more ambitious scope, while the markets and products in which they are used have also broadened and changed.

This increasing use of models reflects the extent to which they can improve business decisions – but models also have important limitations which need to be appreciated in order to avoid misusing the output of the model.

These limitations include not only the direct cost of resources necessary to develop and implement models properly. There are also the potential indirect costs of relying on models, grouped under the term model risk, which is defined as the possibility of adverse consequences arising from decisions based on models that are incorrect or misused.

This chapter will consider the use of models, and the management of model risk, with reference to the models commonly used to identify and measure credit, operational, market and liquidity risks.

The word 'model' refers to any method or approach in which statistical, economic, financial or mathematical theories, techniques and assumptions are used to transform input data into quantitative estimates. This definition also covers quantitative approaches whose inputs are partially or wholly qualitative or based on expert judgment, provided that the output is quantitative in nature.

It can be seen from this definition that simply using a spreadsheet for calculations, such as commission payments, does not constitute a model. An element of judgement is required to establish whether an application is a model by the above definition, but even if a business application is not a model, it will still require careful design and maintenance, especially if important decisions are influenced by its output. An area of IT called end-user-computing (EUC) focusses on helping non-IT staff to manage their own-developed applications to achieve scaleability and robustness.

The use of models invariably presents model risk. Model risk can lead to financial loss, poor business and strategic decision-making, or damage to a firm's reputation.

Model risk is an operational risk and occurs primarily for two reasons:

1. The model may have fundamental errors and may produce inaccurate outputs when viewed against the design objective and intended business uses. The mathematical calculation and quantification exercise underlying any model generally involves application of theory, choice of sample design and numerical routines, selection of inputs and estimation, and implementation in information systems. Errors can occur at any point from design through to implementation. In addition, shortcuts, simplifications or approximations used to manage complicated problems could compromise the integrity and reliability of outputs from those calculations. Finally, the quality of model outputs depends on the quality of input data and assumptions, and errors in inputs or incorrect assumptions will lead to inaccurate outputs.
2. The model may be used incorrectly or inappropriately. Even a fundamentally sound model producing accurate outputs consistent with the design objective of the model may exhibit high model risk if it is misapplied or misused.

Model risk should be managed like other types of risk and firms should identify the sources of risk and assess its magnitude. With an understanding of the source and magnitude of model risk in place, the next step is to manage it properly. We will consider the methods used to manage model risk in section 2 on Effective Governance of Risk Modelling below.

The focus of this chapter will be the use of models to identify and measure risk, but it is important to bear in mind that models are used for a wide variety of other business purposes, including:

- informing business decisions, for example, through analysing business strategies or estimating credit exposures for lending decisions
- conducting stress testing, for example, to assess balance sheet capital adequacy
- valuing exposures, instruments or positions
- providing the real-time signal for algorithmic securities trading.

1. Overview of Model Risk

1.1 The Benefits and Limitations of Modelling

Learning Objective

8.1.1 Know the benefits and limitations of modelling

1.1.1 The Benefits of Modelling

The world in which we live is inherently complex. The human mind is unable to deal with concepts and relationships that lie beyond a certain level of complexity, such as the economy or the ecosystem. For that reason, models that represent the important aspects of real-world entities in a simplified form can be enormously helpful.

A good analogy of the way in which models represent reality is the relationship between a map and the terrain which it represents. A relatively small map can portray the important geographical aspects of a large area of land in a way that allows the whole to be viewed and understood in a manageable form. In the same way, models are simplified representations of the real-world relationships that exist between observed characteristics, values and events.

The benefit that a well-constructed risk model brings to a business can be immense. A proprietary risk model that enables an unclear and complicated reality to be represented in a way that enables sound investment decisions to be made can be a source of real competitive advantage.

The successful use of models also speeds up decision-making through the automation of complex methods. Models can also facilitate results that have greater accuracy, and easier repeatability. Repeatability then enables 'what-if' analyses to be performed by varying individual inputs to observe the effect(s) on the outputs.

Case Study: Long Term Capital Management (LTCM)

LTCM provides a real-world example of model-based competitive advantage. LTCM ran an initially very successful model-based hedge fund that generated very high returns in its first few years. The majority of the firm's partners held Ph.Ds, and the board members included Myron Scholes and Robert Merton, who won the Nobel Prize for Economics for their work on valuing derivatives.

LTCM built and used complex mathematical models to take advantage of fixed-income arbitrage deals, called 'convergence trades', usually with government bonds. The firm achieved considerable competitive advantage through its innovative use of models, and major investors in the fund included Barclays, Credit Suisse, Deutsche Bank, Goldman Sachs, Merrill Lynch, Société Générale and UBS.

1.1.2   The Limitations of Modelling

Models, by their very nature, have specific limitations which must be respected when applying the model's outputs. This is because, as discussed above, models are simplifications of specific aspects of reality, so any attempt to 'reuse' their outputs for purposes other than that for which they were designed can have adverse consequences.

Case Study continued: LTCM

The success of LTCM's model-based strategy meant that its capital base grew rapidly. Pressure grew to invest that capital, but there were only limited numbers of convergence trades available for the fund to undertake. This led LTCM to move into more aggressive trading strategies which were different from the convergence trades on which its reputation and success had been built. By late 1997 the firm was taking extremely large positions in areas such as merger arbitrage in which bets are taken on whether or not corporate mergers would be completed.

In 1998 LTCM lost $4.6 billion in less than four months following the Russian financial crisis, and the fund closed in early 2000. In its annual report, one of its corporate investors, Merrill Lynch, observed that mathematical risk models *'may provide a greater sense of security than warranted; therefore, reliance on these models should be limited'*.

LTCM's experience shows how misuse or over-reliance on a model, especially attempts to use its output in ways that are inappropriate, can lead to highly sub-optimal outcomes.

In any firm, the simplifying or limiting assumptions that were made when building its models need to be well understood by those using them.

These limiting assumptions include:

* **The shape of any underlying distribution used by the model** – for example, if market returns are assumed to be normally distributed, then the model will not be suitable for instruments whose returns are not normally distributed.
* **The relationship between the past and the future** – although investors are constantly told that past performance does not provide a guide to future returns, many models do assume that the future will be similar to the past. This assumption is especially important in the context of model risk because it may be hidden from the end users of the outputs.

- **The state of the business environment at the point when the model was designed** – unless models are updated in line with changes to the business environment, their usefulness over time will be limited.
  - For example, a firm might use Value-at-Risk (VaR) to monitor market risk. When the VaR measure was implemented, perhaps the firm's traders took little or no basis risk (see chapter 5 on Market Risk) so it was coded with a fixed spread assumption. If traders have since started taking significant basis risk, they may not realise that the model is failing to capture it.
  - Another example, might be a brokerage firm that is expanding its derivatives operation into emerging markets. If the firm fails to modify its pricing models to reflect the lack of liquidity in these markets, it will underestimate the cost of hedging its positions.

Another limitation when using models is the tendency to focus on the maximum loss at less than the 100% confidence level. For example, knowing that the loss at the 95% confidence level is £5 million tells the model's users nothing about how much could be lost in the five days out of 100 on which that value is exceeded – except that it will be upwards of £5 million. For this reason, stress testing is extremely important as a means of understanding extreme outcomes which the model may fail to capture.

Decision-makers need to understand the limitations of a model to avoid using it in ways that are not consistent with the original intent. Limitations come in part from weaknesses in the model due to its various shortcomings, approximations and uncertainties. Limitations are also a consequence of assumptions underlying a model that may restrict the scope to a limited set of specific circumstances and situations.

The shorter the time lag between (i) implementing the output of a model and (ii) being able to assess the value of that implementation, the easier it is to gauge the model's accuracy. In the case of high-frequency trading (HFT), for example, the models that drive the trading decisions will typically execute those decisions in small fractions of a second. If the profit and loss (P&L) being generated by the trading decisions is calculated in real time, then the models can be automatically shut down if the P&L dips below a certain level.

1.2 Examples of Some Commonly Used Models

Learning Objective

8.1.2   Know the major models utilised in operational, credit, market and liquidity risks

The following common risk models will be described in this section:

- An operational risk scenario model.
- Credit Value-at-Risk.
- Market Value-at-Risk.
- Liquidity-at-Risk.

Examples of the way each model works are given, but it must be borne in mind that different firms implement these models in different ways.

1.2.1 Operational Risk Scenario Modelling

In chapter 2 on International Risk Regulation, we described how firms need to hold sufficient capital to guard against unexpected operational risk losses. One approach to calculating the required level of capital is to use operational risk scenario modelling.

Risk workshops are typically held with senior risk and business personnel to ensure good quality model inputs, and the participants are asked to consider plausible but unlikely scenarios that could have a significant impact were they to occur.

The workshop outputs capture, amongst other things, estimates for each scenario of:

- the frequency with which such a scenario might occur
- the typical loss were it to occur
- the severity of the loss that could occur in an extreme case.

In order to arrive at the level of capital necessary to cover the potential scenarios, the loss impacts and frequencies are subjected to a modelled stress. Key to this stress is the conversion of the impacts for each scenario into a non-normal distribution to reflect the fact that, should it occur, (a) the actual impact could be greater than the extreme impact estimate, and (b) it could occur more than once in a given year.

Operational risk loss events are not 'normally distributed', but instead follow a distribution that exhibits fat tail characteristics. This is intuitively the case in so far as firms have far more low level losses than catastrophic ones. There are various commonly used distributions which exhibit 'fat tail' characteristics, and scenario impact distributions are often simulated with a lognormal distribution.

Having established the estimates from the business areas, it is important to account for the fact that the scenario participants would typically be able to draw on only about 20 years of experience when assessing the impacts. In other words, their extreme impact estimates represent only a one in 20-year view (ie, a 95% confidence level).

Lognormal Impact Distribution for Single Operational Risk Scenario

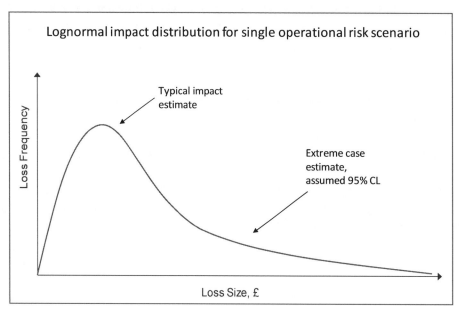

Lognormal impact distribution for single operational risk scenario

Typical impact estimate

Extreme case estimate, assumed 95% CL

Loss Frequency

Loss Size, £

© Andrew Brand

Firms may require their operational risk capital to cover a higher severity than 1 in 20, and common severity levels include one in 200 (ie, a 99.5% confidence level) and one in 1,000 (ie, a 99.9% confidence level). The impacts and likelihoods estimated by the business are therefore 'stretched' in a controlled, repeatable fashion by using a Monte Carlo simulation process (see chapter 5) to take multiple random readings off the plotted lognormal curve, governed by the frequency of each scenario. The results are then sorted by impact. The required confidence level impact is then selected from the sorted results. This stress can be performed per scenario, and also across groups of scenarios to arrive at the capital figures for different parts of the firm.

1.2.2 How the Monte Carlo Simulation Process Works

This description uses 100,000 iterations to keep the maths simple, although, in reality, more iterations would be required as explained below. The simulation considers the impact estimates separately from the frequency estimates.

Deriving the Likelihood of Occurrence

To determine the likelihood of each scenario occurring on any particular iteration (or 'year'), a distribution algorithm called the Poisson distribution is commonly used. Over the 100,000 iterations, the number of times a scenario occurs will equate to its estimated frequency (eg, 10%), but the Poisson distribution allows a more realistic occurrence pattern.

In reality, we would not expect a 10% ('1 year in 10') event to occur exactly once every decade. Such an event may occur twice this decade and then not occur again for 30 years, at which point perhaps it occurs three times over the following five years. Over two centuries (ie, 200 iterations) a long-run average occurrence of once per decade would be expected, but in order to discover the worst year in 200, especially with several scenarios under consideration, the process needs to allow for many scenarios happening in the same year and then not happening again for several iterations.

Deriving the Impacts

Using the typical and extreme impact values estimated during the scenario workshops, a lognormal curve is plotted for the impact distribution of each scenario, with the typical estimate providing the mode, and the extreme estimate providing a point at the 95% confidence level. The curve is then used to select a random impact each time the scenario occurs.

After each iteration, the impacts are summed for all scenarios that occurred on that iteration. After 100,000 iterations the summed impacts for every iteration are sorted, with the worst at the top. The required confidence level is then selected – for 99.5% this would be the 99,500th row from the bottom. This figure gives the one in 200 year loss resulting from all the scenarios over a one-year time horizon.

It is important to note that the impact of any individual scenario that contributed to the 99,500th row of the summed impacts may not be the one in 200 worst impact for that particular scenario. To derive the figure for each scenario separately, the impacts per scenario are also sorted for each iteration (rather than summing all scenarios for each iteration and sorting the summed values). The required confidence level is then selected for each individual scenario: again, for a 99.5% confidence level, this would be the 99,500th row from the bottom.

Unless the model assumes a correlation of one between all scenarios (in other words, that when one scenario happens they all happen), adding up the 99.5% impacts of each of the individual scenarios will produce a total that is greater than the 99.5% impact for all summed scenarios. This so-called portfolio effect or diversification benefit reflects reality in that not all operational risk scenarios will occur in a given year.

Although this example has used 100,000 iterations, a higher number of iterations would actually be necessary in order to ensure that the difference between neighbouring values at the required confidence level is small enough to ensure stability.

The principles involved in this discussion of operational risk scenario modelling also apply to the modelling of credit, market and liquidity risks as described below.

1.2.3   Credit Risk Modelling: Credit Value-at-Risk

An example of credit risk modelling is the attempt to predict the value of a bond in one year's time according to its probability of moving from one credit rating to another.

Ratings agencies publish these 'credit migration' probabilities, so, knowing what the rating in one year might be, we can work out the corresponding value of the bond at that point. Because the credit migration is only a probability, the standard deviation is also published (see chapter 5 on Market Risk). It is this that enables us to plot a distribution and read off the value at the required probability.

For a portfolio of bonds, a similar approach is used, although the correlations between the bonds also need to be taken into account to define any diversification benefit (these concepts are also explained in chapter 5 on Market Risk).

The probabilities (ie, the confidence levels) are expressed as a percentage that a given value will not be exceeded. So the model would enable us to say, *'The credit VaR of our portfolio over a one-year time horizon is £5 million at the 95% confidence level'*.

1.2.4 Market Risk Modelling: Market Value-at-Risk

Market Value-at-Risk is a widely used measure that, in simple terms, expresses the maximum market loss that can occur with a specified confidence over a specified period.

Because there is clearly uncertainty about how much could be lost over the specified time horizon, the VaR measure includes the level of confidence that the specified loss will not be exceeded. For example, if a portfolio has a one-day 5% VaR of £1 million, the probability that the portfolio will fall in value by more than £1 million over a one-day period is 0.05.

There are several ways to perform VaR analysis (see chapter 5), one of which is historical simulation: this involves looking back at what actually happened in the past and basing our view of the future on that analysis. The method uses historic analysis of the portfolio's risk factor values to estimate its risk exposure in the future.

The steps are as follows:

1. Identify the risk factors that affect the returns of the portfolio such as:
    *   individual stock prices
    *   individual stock volatilities
    *   the correlations between the stocks.
2. Select a sample of actual historic risk factor changes over a given period of time – say, the last 500 trading days.
3. Systematically apply each of those daily changes to the current value of each risk factor, revaluing the current portfolio as many times as the number of days in the historical sample.
4. List out all the resulting portfolio values, ordered by value, and, assuming the required VaR is at the 95% confidence level, identify the value that represents the fifth percentile of the distribution in the left-hand tail.

VaR: The Historical Simulation Approach

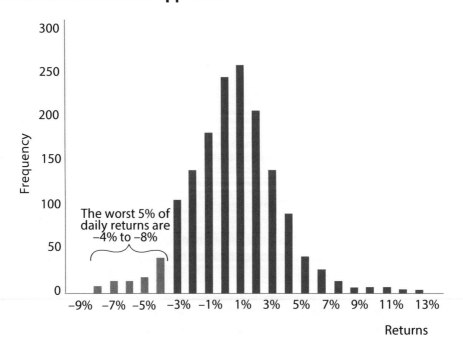

© Andrew Brand

1.2.5 Liquidity Risk Modelling: Liquidity-at-Risk (LaR)

We have seen above that VaR can be used to estimate the likely future value of market and credit instruments. The same approach can also be used to estimate the likelihood of liquidity shortages within a firm.

We showed in chapter 7 on Liquidity Risk that a maturity ladder can give a forward-looking picture of a firm's funding requirements. There are certain shortcomings with this approach though, because the cash flows for many financial instruments cannot be predicted with any certainty. An alternative approach is for the firm to use its historic financial data to work out the size and frequency of its past funding requirements.

A series of 'funding amount' brackets can be defined. The actual net funding amounts over a defined time interval are counted and then put into the corresponding bracket. For example, required amounts between £20 million and £16 million might be counted 14 times, whereas those between £16 million and £12 million might be counted 18 times and so on.

Once the historic funding requirements have been assigned to their funding amount frequency brackets, the brackets can be arranged as a distribution. Typically there will be a cluster of commonly required funding amounts in the middle of the distribution, with lower amounts and higher amounts spread out on either side to form the tails.

Exactly as with market VaR and credit VaR, the LaR distribution gives the firm an idea of its likely funding requirement over a given time period at different confidence levels.

2. Effective Governance of Risk Modelling

Learning Objective

8.1.3   Understand the principles of effective governance of risk modelling

The Federal Reserve document *Supervisory Guidance on Model Risk Management* lays out the elements of a sound model risk governance framework covering:

- the roles and responsibilities of different parts of the organisation including the board, senior management, internal audit and the use of external resources
- the use of policies and procedures and the importance of a model inventory and good documentation.

Developing and maintaining strong governance, policies, and controls over the model risk management framework is fundamentally important to its effectiveness. Even if model development, implementation, use and validation are satisfactory, a weak governance function will reduce the effectiveness of overall model risk management.

2.1 The Roles and Responsibilities of Different Parts of the Organisation

2.1.1 Board of Directors and Senior Management

Model risk governance is provided at the highest level by the board of directors and senior management when they establish a firm-wide framework for model risk management. The framework should include standards for model development, implementation, use and validation.

While the board is ultimately responsible for the framework, it generally delegates to senior management the responsibility for its execution and maintenance.

Duties of senior management include:

- establishing adequate policies and procedures and ensuring adherence to them
- assigning competent staff with clear model ownership established and with potential conflicts of interest identified and addressed
- overseeing model development and implementation
- establishing model risk controls: evaluating model results, ensuring effective challenge, reviewing model validation and internal audit findings, and taking prompt remedial action when necessary
- recognising the potential need for the creation of provisions for trades where the model is known to have limited capability to fully represent reality.

Board members should ensure that the level of model risk is within their risk appetite, and should direct changes where appropriate. These actions will set the tone for the whole organisation in relation to the importance of model risk and the need for active model risk management.

2.1.2 Internal Audit

A firm's internal audit function should assess the overall effectiveness of the model risk management framework, including the framework's ability to address model risk for individual models and in the aggregate. To accomplish this, internal audit staff should possess sufficient expertise in relevant modelling concepts as well as their use in particular business lines. If certain internal audit staff perform day-to-day validation activities, then they should not be involved in the assessment of the overall model risk management framework.

2.1.3 External Resources

Although model risk management is an internal process, a firm may decide to engage external resources to help execute certain activities related to the model risk management framework. Whenever external resources are used, the firm should specify the activities to be conducted in a clearly written and agreed-upon scope of work.

A designated internal party from the firm should be able to understand and evaluate the results of the design, validation and risk-control activities conducted by external resources. The firm should also have a contingency plan in case an external resource is no longer available or is unsatisfactory.

2.2   Policies, Procedures and Documentation

Consistent with good business practice, firms should formalise model risk management activities with board-level policies and the procedures to implement them. All aspects of model risk management should be covered by the policies, for example:

- model risk definition
- assessment of model risk
- acceptable practices for model development, implementation and use
- appropriate model validation activities
- governance and controls over the model risk management process.

Policies should emphasise testing and analysis, and promote the development of targets for model accuracy, standards for acceptable levels of discrepancies, and procedures for review of, and response to, unacceptable discrepancies.

The prioritisation, scope and frequency of validation activities should also be addressed in these policies. They should establish standards for the extent of validation that should be performed before models are put into production, and for the scope of ongoing validation. For models based on historical analysis, back-testing is an important method for benchmarking the outputs of the model against 'reality' once reality has 'caught up'. In other words, a model that gives a figure for VaR in one week's time should be constantly back-tested against the actual market position one week later.

The policies should also detail the requirements for validation of vendor models and third-party products.

Finally, the policies should require maintenance of detailed documentation of all aspects of the model risk management framework, including an inventory of models in use, results of the modelling and validation processes, and model issues and their resolution.

The board or its delegates should periodically review the policies to ensure consistent and rigorous practices across the organisation.

End of Chapter Questions

Think of an answer for each question and refer to the appropriate section for confirmation.

1. What is the definition of model risk?
    Answer reference: Chapter Summary

2. What distribution is commonly used to model operational risk impacts?
    Answer reference: Section 1.2.1

3. In the context of model risk mitigation, what would the duties of senior management include?
    Answer reference: Section 2.1.1

4. A firm's internal audit function should assess the overall effectiveness of the model risk management framework. Which internal audit staff should not be involved in this assessment?
    Answer reference: Section 2.1.2

5. What would typically be covered by a model risk policy?
    Answer reference: Section 2.2

Chapter Nine

Risk Oversight and
Corporate Governance

This syllabus area will provide approximately 5 of the 100 examination questions

Chapter Summary

A company is a distinct legal entity, separate in law from its shareholding owners. The day-to-day running of the company is the responsibility of the board of directors.

Directors are responsible for ensuring the success of the business and its compliance with relevant regulations such as financial reporting, health and safety, employment law, tax and **corporate governance**.

A director is defined in law according to what they do, rather than their actual job title. In other words, even a person not formally appointed to the board might be deemed a director if their role could be considered equivalent to that of a director, or if they have acted as a director. This person is known as a 'shadow' director.

The members of the board of directors are accountable to the company's shareholders for their actions in carrying out their stewardship function. Therefore, a mechanism is needed to ensure that companies are run in the best long-term interests of their shareholders. This mechanism is known as 'corporate governance'. Each jurisdiction has its own rules and standards of business practice, and so the following sections will use the UK as an example.

Depending on the type and size of the firm, corporate governance will typically comprise of the board itself, a risk committee, an audit committee and a remuneration committee. In terms of managing risk throughout the firm, a concept known as the three lines of defence is often referred to. This outlines the way in which:

- the business managers and staff own and manage their risks (first line)
- the risk and compliance functions work independently but with the business to advise and challenge the management of risk (second line), and
- the audit function independently assesses both risk and the business (third line).

Honesty and integrity are key to good corporate behaviour, and the ethics of a firm will be strongly influenced by the culture set by the board and reinforced by the other committees and management structures.

1. Risk Governance within Financial Services Organisations

1.1 Principal Oversight Functions

Learning Objective

9.1.1 Understand the general roles, responsibilities and relationships between the principal oversight functions and the role of senior management: board of directors, risk committee, risk management, compliance, internal and external auditors, internal and external legal support, regulatory oversight

Principal Oversight Functions showing Typical Organisational Relationships

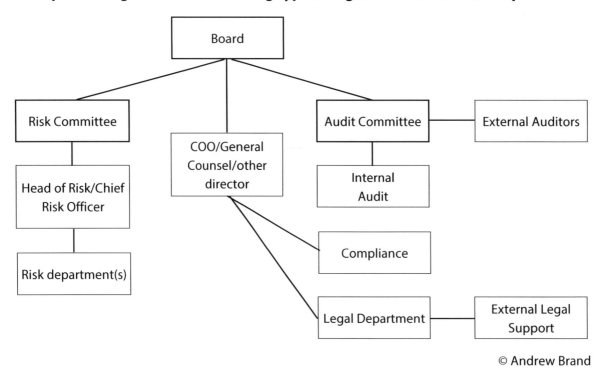

© Andrew Brand

1.1.1 Board of Directors

The board's risk responsibilities typically cover the following areas:

- determining the company's approach to risk, including setting or approving its risk appetite
- setting and instilling the right culture throughout the organisation
- monitoring the company's exposure to risk and the key risks that could undermine its strategy, reputation or long-term viability
- identifying the risks inherent in the company's business model and strategy, including risks from external factors
- overseeing the effectiveness of management's mitigation processes and controls, and
- ensuring the company has effective crisis management processes.

1.1.2 The Risk Committee

At most banks and other financial services firms, the board delegates the management of risk to a risk committee. This is obligatory for larger firms but smaller firms have also chosen to set up board risk committees in the pursuit of good practice. The risk committee will typically:

- ratify the key policies and associated procedures of the firm's risk management activities
- monitor the effectiveness of these key policies
- translate the overall risk appetite of the firm, approved by the board, into a set of limits that flow down through the firm's executive officers, business divisions and sub-committees.

The exact names for each of these sub-committees tend to vary across the industry, as do their specific duties. A typical firm has a senior (or group) risk committee to oversee risk management practices and detailed reporting. Junior (or divisional) risk committees that look at specific types of risk, such as credit risk (see chapter 4) or market risk (see chapter 5), often report to the senior/group risk committee. Investment management firms may also have risk committees specific to fund risks, while their main risk committee will tend to focus on firm risks.

The risk management committee of the board is responsible for independently reviewing the identification, measurement, monitoring and controlling of all risk types. This includes the adequacy of policy guidelines and systems.

1.1.3 Risk Management

The resources to coordinate and monitor risks of all types are generally provided by a centralised risk management function which is independent from the business areas it serves. For firms with a board risk committee, the risk management function is often accountable to this committee and is typically tasked with:

- ensuring that the firm has a robust and consistent risk management and control framework
- providing support, oversight and challenge on the firm's risk appetite statements
- owning the top-level strategic risk assessment process
- monitoring the firm's risk profile against its risk appetites
- playing a leading role in defining and embedding the firm's risk culture
- providing risk training across the firm
- working with other oversight functions such as compliance and audit to provide a comprehensive, robust and efficient assurance framework.

In addition, for all risk types, the risk management function would typically:

- oversee and challenge the risk and control self-assessment programme to capture expected risks
- oversee and challenge the firm's scenario analysis to capture unexpected extreme risks
- help to define, and subsequently challenge, the key risk indicators (KRIs) used for risk monitoring
- ensure issues are properly escalated, assisting with root-cause analysis for incidents and losses, and tracking any associated actions
- test risk models and key controls within the business, and recommend improvements
- advise on risk-based process mapping
- support the firm's risk IT system(s)
- benchmark the firm's risk control framework against industry good practice.

1.1.4   Compliance

Compliance and risk management are not the same, although some of their duties overlap and certainly the compliance function is an important component of a firm's overall risk management.

It is crucial that laws and regulations are followed, and that exceptions are noted and corrected in a timely manner – to do otherwise would represent a significant risk to the firm. So, while there is clearly some overlap between compliance and risk management, each function nevertheless has a different agenda.

Compliance focuses primarily on ensuring that all laws, regulations and internal rules are followed. Risk management focuses on ensuring that risks are understood, and that proactive decisions are made about which risks to take and which to manage or avoid.

Compliance risk is a significant factor in the overall risk framework of financial services firms. It is not limited to simple compliance with laws and regulations; it also encompasses sound fiduciary principles, prudent ethical standards, client documents, internal policies and procedures, and other contractual obligations.

Some examples of issues that could raise an institution's level of compliance risk are:

*   substandard client account acceptance and review processes
*   shortcomings in the ethical culture and expertise of management and staff
*   weak internal compliance systems and training programmes.

The compliance function has the same dilemma as the risk function – the need to be an adviser of the business on the one hand and the need to monitor relevant activities on the other. Compliance teams need to find a careful balance between the fundamentally different mindsets and approaches required by the proactive 'trusted adviser' versus the more reactive 'independent watchdog'. The 'independent watchdog' will report deviations to an appropriate level of management or, if appropriate, to the board of directors.

Effective compliance and risk management is a collaborative process that makes use of all the various control functions within the organisation, such as risk management, internal control, fraud detection, legal and human resources.

For example, the risk management function could help to detect potential compliance risks by identifying visible lapses that might indicate a more pervasive pattern of non-compliant behaviour 'below the water-line'. The human resources function would be involved in its role as the expert in managing people, communicating expected behaviours, designing appropriate appraisal and reward structures and determining disciplinary measures.

1.1.5   Chief Risk Officer/Director/Head of Risk

To assure a strategic focus on risk management at a high level, firms should assign specific senior responsibility for all risk management across the entire organisation. In most cases this would be to a head of risk or chief risk officer (CRO). The CRO/head of risk should be independent of line management and have sufficient influence to have a meaningful impact on decisions.

The CRO/head of risk management may oversee a single group called the risk management department. Professionals working within that department, called risk managers, are responsible for facilitating the taking of applicable financial risks by the other departments within the firm.

In larger firms, there may be more specialisation and the CRO/head of risk management might oversee staff with specific responsibility, for example:

- market risk management
- credit risk management
- operational risk management.

Each of these people, in turn, might oversee a respective department or team. Alternatively, the CRO may simply manage market and credit risk teams, and the operational risk team might report to another senior manager.

Each firm must determine how best to achieve a strong corporate 'risk voice', and often this has been successfully done by having the CRO report directly to the CEO. Alternatively, the CRO is given a seat on the board. In many cases, the CRO will report directly to the risk committee of the board.

Some firms make it a practice for the CRO to report regularly to the full board to review risk issues and exposures, as well to the risk committee. A strong, independent voice will mean that the CRO has a mandate to bring to the attention of both line and senior management, or to the board, any situation that could materially violate risk appetite guidelines.

1.1.6   Internal and External Audit

Internal audit plays an important role in the risk control framework as part of the 'third line of defence'. It provides an independent, internal assessment of the effectiveness of the firm's processes, controls and procedures. It also independently assesses the effectiveness of the risk management process.

By performing regular business reviews, internal audit assesses whether the firm's processes and procedures are adequately controlled, up-to-date and performed in accordance with manuals and documentation.

It also acts as a 'dry run' for external audits and regulatory examiners. Internal audit must have an unrestricted mandate to review all aspects of the transaction life cycle and be totally independent of senior managers and their departments who are subject to the review. It is considered sound practice for internal audit to report to the board of directors through the audit committee.

Identification of Errors and Breaches

There is a crossover with the operational risk management process in that internal audit also involves the identification of risk issues and potential or actual control failures and breaches. However, auditing is aimed more at checking the control environment on a 'snapshot' basis (eg, once every six months), highlighting issues (audit points) but leaving 'cause-effect' analysis and solution implementation to the business.

Operational risk management, on the other hand, monitors risk on a continuous, day-to-day basis, allowing more dynamic and strategic management. Audit information should, therefore, be used as an input to operational risk management.

Departmental operational risk assessments (see chapter 3) can, in turn, be used to create a risk-based audit plan.

External auditors are required to audit the annual accounts and to report to the members of the company whether, in their opinion, the annual accounts:

1. Have been prepared in accordance with the Companies Act.
2. Give a 'true and fair view'.

Additionally, and of great assistance to the risk oversight function, a firm's external auditors produce specialised reports for the board and external clients; these give assurance that the firm's control environment works as designed.

1.1.7   Internal and External Legal Support

Legal risk arises from:

1. Uncertainty due to legal actions.
2. Uncertainty in the applicability or interpretation of contracts, laws or regulations.

Depending on an institution's circumstances, legal risk may entail such issues as the following:

- **Contract formation** – what constitutes a legitimate contract? Is an oral agreement sufficient or must there be a legal document? What sort of documentation is required?
- **Legality of derivatives transactions** – in some jurisdictions there are issues relating to whether certain derivatives could be deemed gambling contracts and thus made unenforceable.
- **Netting agreements** – under what circumstances will a close-out netting agreement be enforceable?
- **Contract frustration** – might unforeseen circumstances invalidate a contract? For example, if a contract is linked to an index or currency which ceases to exist, will the contract become invalid?

Legal risk can be a particular problem for institutions which transact business across borders. Not only are they exposed to uncertainty relating to the laws of multiple jurisdictions, but they also face uncertainty as to which jurisdiction will have authority over any particular legal issue.

Larger firms tend to have in-house legal departments which are bolstered by contract staff from external law firms during busy periods or when specialist advice is required. Smaller firms tend to rely on external advice, perhaps maintaining just one or two in-house lawyers.

In either case, financial services firms typically require good quality legal advice on matters such as:

- institutional client mandates
- regulatory compliance issues
- underwriting Initial Public Offerings (IPOs)

- international markets and cross-border activities
- enforcement, disciplinary matters and dispute resolution
- compliance procedures
- internet/e-commerce contract law
- money laundering
- employment contracts and third party vendor agreements.

1.1.8 Regulatory Oversight

The regulator itself also carries out a key oversight role. For larger firms, this involves lengthy and in-depth on-site visits looking at all the important aspects of the way in which the firm is run. Even for smaller firms, processes such as the Internal Capital Adequacy Assessment (ICAAP) (see chapter 2) mean that the regulator receives detailed reports on the way in which the firm is managing its risks and capital.

1.2 Structural Framework

Learning Objective

9.1.2 Understand the structural framework and high level processes of key business functions in relation to risk identification and management

Having described the framework for risk governance at the board level, we need to consider the mechanism(s) that enable the board's intentions to be propagated down throughout the firm. In other words, the part played by key business functions in relation to risk identification, management, and conformity to the board-agreed risk appetite.

The firm's risk committee recommends to the board an amount at risk (ie, risk appetite or tolerance) that it is prudent for the board to approve. In particular, the risk committee determines:

- the amount of financial risk (ie, market risk, credit risk, liquidity and investment risk), and
- the amount of non-financial risk (ie, operational risk and strategic risk)

to be assumed by the firm as a whole, in line with the firm's business strategies.

The board approves the firm's risk appetite each year, based on a broad set of risk measures (see chapter 1). The board delegates the authority to oversee risk to the risk committee, whose membership, depending on the type of firm, typically includes:

- a non-executive director (NED) as chair
- the chief risk officer (CRO)
- the chief financial officer (CFO)
- the chief investment officer (CIO) for investment management firms
- potentially a risk representative from any parent firm
- other non-executive directors.

The risk committee might hold a strategic risk scenario identification workshop each year in order to ensure that the overall risk focus of the firm remains on track.

The risk committee then delegates to the CRO the authority to:

- make decisions on its behalf
- set business-level risk limits
- approve risks in excess of these limits, within the overall risk limits approved by the board.

Consequently, the CRO is responsible for:

- the firm's risk management strategy
- the firm's risk policies and risk methodologies
- ensuring that the firm's infrastructure can support its risk management objectives.

The risk committee provides a detailed review and approval (say, annually) of each business unit's risk limits, and delegates the monitoring of these limits to the CRO. The CRO may order business units, or advise fund managers, to reduce or close out their positions because of concerns about market, liquidity, credit, operational or other risks.

Risk monitoring responsibilities are also delegated to department heads of the various business units. For example, at an investment bank, the head of global trading is likely to be responsible for the risk management and performance of all trading activities and in turn, then delegates the management of limits to the business managers. The business managers are responsible for the risk management and performance of the business and they, in turn, delegate limits to the bank's traders.

Within an investment management firm there may be risk sub-committees which exist to enable the fund managers to explain their strategies, and to present their risk profile for challenge and debate. These committees may be organised by asset type (eg, bonds, equities and property) or by risk type (eg, credit, liquidity, market).

Within many firms there is also an operational risk committee – sometimes referred to as a controls committee. The operational risk/controls committee is typically made up of both business and risk staff. The role of the committee is to make sure that business decisions are in line with the firm's desired risk/reward trade-offs, and that financial and operational risks are managed appropriately at the department or business line level.

It is important to bear in mind that governance arrangements vary considerably across different firms. The key to a successful structure is to ensure that committees (with clear terms of reference) exist to cover the risks for each 'common area' of the firm's business, however those areas are defined.

At the department level, operational risks and controls would be assessed, perhaps annually, through risk workshops, desk-based reviews or some other mechanism. The business risk/controls committee provides a forum where department heads can be required to bring the results of these assessments for challenge and debate. Any departmental losses or KRIs that have exceeded their predefined escalation threshold would also be examined for trend analysis and the setting of preventative actions.

1.3   Three Lines of Defence

Learning Objective

9.1.3   Understand the principles of the three lines of defence

To ensure that risks are understood and managed, many firms have adopted the so-called three lines of defence model.

1. The first line of defence is the **business management** which has day-to-day ownership, responsibility and accountability for assessing, controlling and managing risk.
2. The second line of defence is performed by the **independent risk functions** (including compliance), working with the business to provide support and challenge on risk management, and helping to set risk appetite and strategy, define risk reporting and ensure the adequacy of risk mitigation.
3. The third line of defence is provided by **internal audit** who provide independent assurance on the first and second lines, and the appropriateness and effectiveness of policy implementation and internal controls.

1.4   Key Challenges

Learning Objective

9.1.4   Understand the key challenges of implementing risk governance structure, policies and procedures: appropriate authority and autonomy, segregation of duties, relationship of risk managers to the business

In chapter 1 we discussed the role of strategic risk takers (the CEO and board), and the delegation to front-office staff of the tactical risks necessary to implement the strategy.

For this process to work, a strong risk governance structure is required, and within that structure the appropriate role of risk managers needs clear definition. The role of risk managers is to facilitate effective communication between the two risk-taking groups.

Risk managers enable strategic risk-takers to communicate 'downwards' through appropriate policies, procedures and risk limits. Risk managers also enable tactical risk-takers to communicate 'upwards' by preparing risk reports that describe the risks they are taking.

A risk manager needs to measure and report risk within a robust risk governance structure. It is the job of the traders, fund managers and other front-office staff to decide what sort of risks to take. However, there are various organisational challenges to implementing a risk governance structure with the 'right' policies and procedures:

*   establishing and maintaining the appropriate authority and autonomy of risk managers
*   keeping a clear segregation of duties between risk-taking staff and risk managers
*   relationship of risk managers to the business.

In the earlier discussion on the influence of risk management within the firm, it was suggested that the CRO/head of risk should be independent of the line management. However, unless the reporting lines for all staff working in the risk function are independent of the staff taking the risks, risk managers will not be truly autonomous. Without autonomy, the authority of risk managers is diminished.

Ideally, to achieve risk management autonomy, staff that take risks should have no input to the performance appraisals, compensation or promotion of risk managers. The alternative is that risk managers become fearful of giving 'bad' news in case their appraisal ratings are affected.

Risk managers do not take risks on the firm's behalf but may have been provided with personal lending authority to approve risks that will be underwritten by the business. Furthermore, they do not advise on which risks to take but can and should suggest suitable mitigants to ensure risks taken are adequately addressed ie, in line with the firm's risk appetite. Risk managers and their teams must not take risks, they must analyse the risks that the revenue-generating staff are taking and provide independent reports on these risks to senior management.

Once risk staff start taking risks, or even advising on which ones to take, the segregation of duties between those who take risks, and those who monitor and report on them starts to blur.

There is a view that staff should not be able to switch from one role to the other. Those hired into risk management should stay in risk management; those hired as risk takers stay as such. Otherwise risk staff may start worrying more about their move into a front-office role than about objectively monitoring and reporting on the risks of front-office staff.

1.4.1   Relationship of Risk Managers to the Business

Although segregation of duties is of key importance when implementing the risk structure's policies and procedures, it also introduces a further challenge. The senior managers who formulate the firm's risk framework are necessarily one step removed from the actual business areas whose risks the framework is designed to help manage.

The same lack of proximity to the business can also become a challenge for heads of large departments and other senior staff.

It is therefore important that risk managers, and other senior managers, find ways of keeping close to the business areas within their oversight or charge. They need to combine good management information with walking the floor and talking to staff at the coalface.

1.5 Risk Governance Implementation

Learning Objective

9.1.5 Understand the main challenges to risk governance implementation that can arise in planned or unplanned change-related scenarios

Setting up the risk governance structure is not a one-off exercise. Corporate changes, whether planned or unplanned, must take the current governance structure into account, and also (in the case of planned changes) any upgrading that might be required as a result of the change.

Such planned changes could include acquiring a firm and merging it with the existing business. Careful thought needs to be given to how its existing governance structure will be merged with the acquiring firm's governance structure – and how any gaps or overlaps will be managed.

To be prepared for unplanned changes, such as senior managers leaving the firm, succession plans must exist for each member of the firm's key committees. A succession plan might reveal that in fact certain roles have no obvious successor. This will give the firm an opportunity to nominate and prepare a member of staff to be the successor or, in the case of NEDs, to develop relationships with future potential candidates.

2. Culture and Leadership

Learning Objective

9.2.1 Know the main factors determining a firm's risk and control culture: governance and policies; risk appetite/risk tolerance; transparency; integrity, ethics and social responsibility; education and development

Excellent risk management begins with the culture of the firm. This section describes the main factors that determine a firm's risk and control culture.

2.1 Governance and Policies

A risk-focused governance structure enables risk to be taken seriously at the top of the firm and, importantly, to be seen as being taken seriously. However, for a firm to embed a risk culture, its written policies must also emphasise, and enable, a focus on risk management.

Key policies and approaches that will tend to enable a risk culture include the following:

- **Staff remuneration policy** – is remuneration linked to risk management?
- **Staff appraisal process** – is risk management a key objective, with accountability for risk management being a priority for the whole institution?

- **Risk policy** – is it comprehensive enough to cover the firm at all levels, yet succinct enough to be read and understood? Is it easily available within the firm? Is it required reading?
- **Risk function(s) independence** – how independent is the head of risk/chief risk officer? How much authority does the role carry?
- **Calibre of risk personnel** – how much is the firm willing to pay for high-quality risk personnel with the people skills necessary to convey to staff the importance of good risk management? A basic essential need is for risk management to have a sufficient amount and quality of resources to fulfil its roles, and it is the responsibility of senior management and, ultimately, the board to ensure that it does.
- **Escalation and whistle-blowing processes** – are these clearly defined and made as easy as possible for staff wishing to report bad news?
- **Code of conduct** – what responsibilities, behaviours, and standards of ethics are expected to be followed by all?

2.2   Risk Appetite/Risk Tolerance

A particularly important governance technique is for senior management to adopt, and periodically to affirm, the firm's risk appetite (see chapter 1 – risk appetite is the type and amount of risk that a firm is willing to accept in the pursuit of its business objectives).

This involves understanding the firm's current risk profile and trends (which is the current implicit risk appetite) and monitoring the firm's ongoing performance against its desired risk appetite. The board should understand the general outlines of the risk appetite as established and assure itself that management has properly considered the firm's risks and has applied appropriate processes and resources to manage those risks.

The firm's risk appetite should be clearly connected to its overall business strategy and capital plan. Business planning, which tends to be driven by earnings goals in a competitive environment, needs to involve the risk management function from the beginning of the planning process. This means that targets can be tested to see how they fit with the firm's risk appetite, and any potential **downsides** can be assessed. Equally important is clear communication to the appropriate staff about the firm's risk appetite and risk position.

2.3   Transparency

In 2015, the Bank for International Settlements (BIS, see chapter 2) updated its *Corporate governance principles for banks*. Principle 12 (Disclosure and transparency) states that the governance of the bank should be adequately transparent to its shareholders, depositors, other relevant stakeholders and market participants.

In support of this principle, it recommends public disclosure of the following topics, on the bank's website or in its annual reports:

- board structure (eg, membership, selection process, qualifications, other directorships, criteria for independence, material interests in transactions or matters affecting the bank) and senior management structure (eg, responsibilities, reporting lines, qualifications and experience)

- basic ownership structure (where a bank is state-owned, an ownership policy that defines the overall objectives of state ownership, the state's role in the corporate governance of the bank, and how it will implement its ownership policy)
- organisational structure (eg, general organisational chart, business lines, subsidiaries and affiliates, management committees)
- information about the incentive structure of the bank (eg, remuneration policies, director and executive compensation, bonuses, stock options)
- the bank's code or policy of business conduct and/or ethics, any applicable governance structures and policies, the content of any corporate governance code and the process by which it is implemented, as well as a self-assessment by the board of its performance relative to this code or policy
- the bank's policy on conflicts of interest, including any bank matters for which members of the board or senior management have material interests either directly, indirectly, or on behalf of third parties.

Internal transparency is also important because it ensures that risks can be uncovered and dealt with quickly. The key to internal transparency is good and open communication, and a lack of public blame for specific incidents.

Mistakes create opportunities to learn, and determining the actual cause of mistakes is key to avoiding them in the future. The firm should maintain a robust, comprehensive database of losses and near misses, which includes cause and cost – and action(s) to prevent recurrence.

Senior managers should prevent the emergence of a 'blame culture'. To sack or reprimand staff during the incident's management and resolution will cause people to cover up problems in future. Therefore, the performance appraisal process must pick up poor general performance at an early stage and staff must feel that the right thing to do is admit their mistakes when specific issues arise.

2.4 Integrity, Ethics and Social Responsibility

The preservation of a financial firm's brand and franchise value is based on its reputation. This, in turn, is based on its core ethical values, such as integrity, trust, confidentiality, fairness and professionalism. Firms thrive when they account for the needs and interests of all stakeholders. These include clients, employees, shareholders, any parent company, service providers, government authorities, financial regulators and other users of the environment in which they operate.

2.5 Education and Development

An important element of a firm's risk and control culture is the way it educates its people. This extends the necessary board-level education on risk management down to process and control education for staff on the 'front-line'. So, for example, boards need to be given the means to understand risk appetite and the firm's performance against it, whereas staff need to understand where in the overall process their role fits.

2.6   Reducing Risk

Learning Objective

9.2.2   Understand how appropriate management of these factors can add value and reduce risk

---

The set of techniques and processes described earlier, which enable an appropriate risk culture, are not cheap to implement. However, without them, the firm risks becoming ever more compartmentalised, with each member of staff being concerned only with their own area because of a lack of shared vision, resources, communication and knowledge flowing through the organisation. This is known as the 'silo effect'.

Organisations need to understand that risk management is more than a methodology and a set of tools to be imposed on the operations of a business. It is a way of doing business that enables firms to derive the greatest value from every opportunity without jeopardising the existing value of the organisation.

When staff throughout the firm appreciate why what they do is important, and how it fits with what other staff are doing, then a feeling of ownership and professional care is better able to flourish. Staff begin to anticipate problems, both internal and external, before they arise – and, when issues occur, staff take personal responsibility to ensure speedy resolution.

2.7   Moral Hazard

Learning Objective

9.2.3   Understand the principle of moral hazard as it relates to appropriate and ethical behaviour in a business environment

---

Moral hazard describes the possibility that people will behave differently when protected from the effects of the risks that they take. For example, a person with car insurance may be less cautious about the way they drive, because the negative consequences (damage to the car) would be the responsibility of the insurance company.

In a corporate setting, moral hazard exists whenever staff stand to gain by behaving in ways that may not benefit the company or may not be in line with company policy or the company's risk management strategy and/or guidelines. This can range from careless behaviour when inputting data on computer systems, through to taking excessively high risks in the knowledge that bonuses will have been paid before the risk crystallises.

Organisations can significantly moderate self-interested behaviour by encouraging a climate of honesty and care. This means emphasising the importance of ethical decisions and rewarding staff for acting ethically. Many firms define a formal 'Code of Conduct', which describes the company's values and the corresponding expectations of staff behaviour.

End of Chapter Questions

Think of an answer for each question and refer to the appropriate section for confirmation.

1. What is corporate governance?
    Answer reference: Chapter Summary

2. Give two typical duties of the board of directors.
    Answer reference: Section 1.1.1

3. Give three examples of tasks for which the risk committee would be responsible.
    Answer reference: Section 1.1.2

4. Give three examples of areas of business in which financial services firms need legal advice.
    Answer reference: Section 1.1.7

5. Which corporate role would chair a public firm's main risk committee?
    Answer reference: Section 1.2

6. Which line of defence would compliance fit into?
    Answer reference: Section 1.3

7. What is meant by the three lines of defence?
    Answer reference: Section 1.3

8. Name three key policies that would tend to enable a risk culture.
    Answer reference: Section 2.1

9. Give four of the six items that BIS recommend should be publicly disclosed by a bank to achieve governance transparency.
    Answer reference: Section 2.3

Chapter Ten
Enterprise Risk Management (ERM)

This syllabus area will provide approximately 5 of the 100 examination questions

Chapter Summary

The diagram below is a sub-set of the one presented at the start of this workbook, but adapted just to show the key areas of an enterprise risk management framework.

Enterprise Risk Management (ERM)

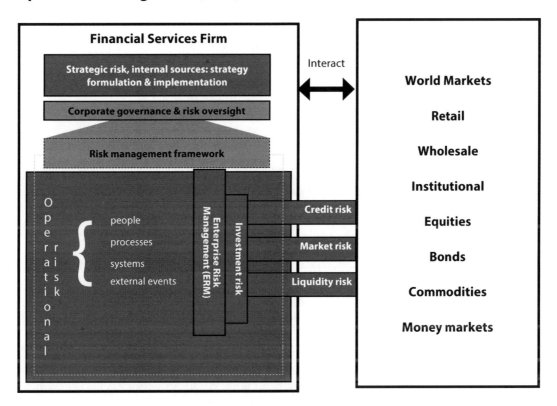

© Andrew Brand

The Basel Committee's enhanced Pillar 2 guidance sets clear expectations for boards of directors and senior management to:

- understand the firm-wide risk profile
- aggregate firm-wide exposure information in a timely manner using easy to understand and multiple metrics
- define the risk appetite in a way that considers long-term performance
- set clear incentives across the firm to control risk exposures and concentrations in accordance with the stated risk appetite.

Enterprise risk management (ERM) will enable firms to meet this challenge.

Understanding the different risks to which a financial services firm is subject is key to a firm's success, and for this reason risk information is regularly reported up the chain of command. Separate reporting mechanisms have traditionally been used for separate risk types, but, increasingly, firms are recognising the need to group the risk types together and report on them collectively in order to see the 'big picture'.

10

ERM is a method of providing the firm with a succinct view of all its key risk information, thus enabling the senior team to make balanced, firm-wide risk decisions. ERM enables firms to:

- Define a common understanding of risk and a common risk language.
- Aggregate risk information from the whole firm across all risk types, asset types and business lines:
  - risk types include: business/strategic, operational, credit, market, liquidity
  - asset types include: bonds, equities, cash, commodities
  - business lines include: corporate finance; trading and sales; retail banking; commercial banking payment and settlement; agency services; asset management; retail brokerage.
- Present the summarised risk information quickly and succinctly enough to enable better management decision-making.
- Compare the firm's risk profile to the available risk capital.
- Use the firm-wide risk view to define and fine-tune the firm's risk appetite.
- Assign the firm's limited resources to the areas of most relative risk.

1. Overview of Enterprise Risk Management (ERM)

1.1 Definitions of Enterprise Risk and ERM

Learning Objectives

10.1.1   Know the definitions of enterprise risk and ERM

Risk management is the practice of using processes, methods and tools for managing risks and uncertainties. Risk management focuses on identifying what could go wrong, evaluating which risks should be dealt with and implementing strategies to deal with them.

A common definition of ERM is the process of applying the discipline of risk management to all the risks a firm faces to understand and manage them, not only individually, but also in the way that they relate to each other.

ERM is also known as integrated risk management or firm-wide risk management.

1.2　How Enterprise Risk Relates to Corporate Governance

Learning Objectives

10.1.2　Understand how enterprise risk relates to the process of corporate governance and board responsibilities

In chapter 9 we discussed the fact that governance and risk management is, in the first instance, the responsibility of the board and senior management of a firm, undertaken as part of their duties to shareholders and the regulators. In many firms this responsibility is formally delegated to a risk committee which provides oversight of senior management activities in managing credit, market, liquidity, operational and other risks.

This senior oversight responsibility is common to any well-designed risk management process. The difference with an ERM approach is that because it integrates the management of all risks, those with corporate governance responsibilities are able to see a single view of the firm's risk profile.

1.3　Industry Regulation and Sound Practice

Learning Objectives

10.1.3　Understand how industry regulation and sound practice have combined to influence the development and implementation of ERM programmes

Industry regulation, such as Basel Pillar 2 (ICAAP), is currently driving firms towards an enterprise risk management approach without necessarily referring to it as ERM.

In chapter 2 we saw that to produce an ICAAP, firms have to:

1. Define and quantify their overall risk exposure across all risk types.
2. Stress and scenario test this exposure.
3. Compare the results to the available capital.

Of these three steps, the first is the most challenging. Once a firm can define and quantify its overall risk exposure across all risk types then the next two steps are more straightforward.

However, the act of 'defining and quantifying its overall risk exposure across all risk types' is what ERM also seeks to do. Therefore, firms who take ICAAP seriously have a good chance of being able to implement an enterprise risk management framework as part of the ICAAP programme.

1.3.1　Sound Practice

Sound practice approaches to risk management already recognise that operational, credit and market risks are often linked, and so should not be considered in isolation. The following example, using an investment management firm as an illustration, shows how market, operational and credit risks may move together in response to external events.

If an economic shock causes market volatility to increase, then the investment manager's risk indicators will register an increase in market risk because volatility is one of the input factors for its Value-at-Risk (VaR) models. An increase in market volatility will often be accompanied by an increase in 'buy and sell' decisions as the investment management firm and its clients seek to rebalance their asset allocations. This, in turn, will mean an increase in back-office activity to support these reactive asset reallocation decisions. Increasing back-office volumes will mean an increased chance of errors in the process chain, so operational risk is also increasing.

If the economic shock reduces market levels sufficiently, then some organisations will start to struggle, and may default on their debt payments. This then leads to an increase in credit risk for any of the investment management firm's funds which are holding defaulting bonds.

It can be seen, then, that market, operational and credit risks can move together in response to various events. An ERM approach will show the indicators across all the firm's risk types, and when one risk indicator starts to increase, the links through to the other risks can be clearly seen.

1.4   Goals and Challenges of Establishing an ERM Programme

Learning Objectives

10.1.4   Understand the main goals and challenges of establishing and implementing an ERM programme in relation to: exception-based escalation, aggregation, accountability

The goals of an ERM programme will include:

- designing and implementing the methods for collating firm-wide information on all risk types, asset types and business lines
- enabling decision-making through aggregated risk reporting
- allowing comparison of the firm's risk profile to the available risk capital
- setting clear accountability and incentives across the firm to control risk exposures and concentrations in accordance with the stated risk appetite.

There are many challenges to implementing an ERM programme, both technical and cultural, and these will be discussed under the headings below.

1.4.1   Cultural Aspects of Implementing and Establishing an ERM Programme

An effective ERM programme requires the active involvement of several different areas of the firm including credit risk, market risk, operational risk, compliance, finance and others. This means that identifying the right executive sponsor for the programme is extremely important. The sponsor will need to be senior enough to ensure that the right resources are available – while still being able to grasp the detail of what the programme is attempting to achieve. The sponsor will also play a vital part in ensuring acceptance throughout the firm for this new way of reporting all risk types.

Because the different risk departments use similar, but not identical, vocabulary, there is often scope for misunderstanding when these departments are required to work together. Establishing a common risk language or glossary across the firm is important to enable this collaborative work – and will also help to embed the approach within the firm.

Firms have experienced challenges in combining their 'financial' (credit and market) risk teams, with their operational risk teams to form a single unit. The main challenge has been the different cultures and skill-types required to perform these very different roles. The leadership of these combined teams requires more than simply an understanding of multiple risk types; high-quality people management skills are also required.

1.4.2 Exception-Based Escalation Challenges

Managing the different risks to which a financial services firm is subject is key to the firm's success, and for this reason the following types of risk information are reported up the chain of command:

- periodic reporting of risk and control information
- immediate escalation of risks as they materialise, and controls as they fail.

An ERM framework encompasses so much information which could potentially be escalated and actioned, that, without an exception-based approach, it may not be clear to the senior teams which actions should be prioritised. Thresholds and limits should be established across the firm for individual risk types, and these should then be used to build an ERM 'escalation matrix'. An escalation matrix is a table showing potential incident types and who should be alerted at different points of severity.

Interconnectedness within the firm also means that major incidents often require input from several departments for their resolution. Even with an ERM framework in place, it remains a challenge to ensure that incidents are not escalated in a piecemeal fashion by the different departments that are involved. A piecemeal approach makes it more difficult for senior managers to properly prioritise and coordinate their actions when the information they receive is coming from several disparate sources.

1.4.3 Data Aggregation Challenges

Grouping risk data into comprehensive yet manageable reports is clearly a key goal of any ERM programme, but this also presents challenges. These fall into three inter-related categories:

- **measurement** – the need to ensure that comparisons can be made between the various measurement techniques used across different risk types
- **timescales** – linked to the measurement challenge, different risk types are normally considered over very different timescales
- **combining the data** – having established a common approach to measurement and timescales, the data then needs to be combined and summarised to enable succinct reports that can be readily understood and acted upon.

Measurement Aspects

Confidence levels and time-frames both need to be consistent across all measured risks to aggregate risk meaningfully. Without these conditions, it will not be possible to compare risks on a like-for-like basis.

The chosen measurement approach(es) also need to enable direct comparisons between asset classes. In other words, it will not be sufficient to use, for example, tracking errors to measure equity risk, and **duration** to measure bond risk because these have different units of measurement. This consideration was one of the drivers behind the growing popularity of VaR – a measure that, if used carefully, can yield useful and comparable results across disparate risk types.

Timescale Aspects

As discussed in previous chapters, a set of integrated VaR models will enable risks to be compared across different asset and risk classes. The models would include market VaR, credit VaR and liquidity VaR, and a modified VaR approach can also be used to estimate future operational risk, based on key scenarios.

However, the challenge lies in amalgamating the necessarily short-term market risk VaR (days) with the medium-term credit and liquidity risk VaR models (weeks and months), and the longer term operational risk VaR model (months and years).

There are further timescale challenges in the actual production of the ERM reports. They can be slow to produce because of:

- the complexity involved in collecting and transforming the inputs from disparate sources
- the need to add narrative to the data in order that the senior team can quickly understand and act on the key points.

Combining the Data

As well as the challenges involved in combining data across different asset and risk classes, it is also important to distinguish between the (i) the firm's risks and (ii) its clients' risks to avoid inflating the risk profile through double-counting:

- **Firm risks** – the firm's risks are those which either impact (a) just the firm itself, or (b) its clients in such a way that they need to be compensated:
  - (a) the firm is impacted when its own resources are reduced in value through credit, market, investment, liquidity or operational risks
  - (b) the firm is also impacted when it needs to compensate clients for errors. In some cases this compensation is a regulatory requirement; in other cases the firm will choose to pay compensation in order to protect its reputation.
- **Client risks** – a client's risks are those which impact the client, but do not require the firm to pay compensation when they occur.
  For example, when managing funds on behalf of clients, there is an understanding that markets fall as well as rise. Therefore, if a client fund decreases in value because of systematic market risk, clients would not normally expect compensation.

However, there would be an indirect consequence for the firm which needs to be captured as part of the management of enterprise risk. This indirect consequence is the reduction in fees earned by the firm when the value of client holdings falls. In other words, the VaR on client funds can be translated into an earnings at risk figure for the firm.

1.4.4 Accountability

A visible ERM programme should increase accountability in three main ways:

1. Where departments or named individuals are included as risk or control owners in the ERM reports seen by senior managers, those departments and individuals often become very keen to ensure that they carry out their role effectively.
2. If a risk materialises, senior executives know which specific department or individual has responsibility for ensuring its resolution.
3. As specific accountability becomes more visible, other members of staff know they do not need to try to resolve certain issues 'just in case' and, hence, can become more productive in the areas for which they are accountable.

1.5 Business Functions that Participate in an ERM Programme

Learning Objectives

10.1.5   Know the most relevant business functions that participate in an ERM programme

The following business functions would typically participate in an ERM programme:

*   Strategic planning. In chapter 1 we discussed business risk in two sections: internal and external. For an ERM programme, the external threats and opportunities would be distilled by the strategy team into the currently relevant drivers, with any strategic initiatives to address them.
*   The finance department would provide information on available capital and future earnings. Liquidity risks could also be provided by finance, or, for certain firms, by the treasury desk.
*   The appropriate risk departments would provide the information for ERM reporting – typically the liquidity, credit, market and operational risk teams.

The operational risk team(s) would potentially also provide information on:

*   losses over a certain threshold
*   the controls environment
*   business continuity planning
*   insurance arrangements.

The internal audit department plays a key role, but independently of the provision of risk information. Its role is to audit the ERM framework to ensure it is accurate and robust, and to evaluate its effectiveness and recommend improvements.

End of Chapter Questions

Think of an answer for each question and refer to the appropriate section for confirmation.

1. What is the definition of enterprise risk management (ERM)?
    Answer reference: Section 1.1

2. Which area of industry regulation is driving firms towards ERM?
    Answer reference: Section 1.3

3. Describe three goals of an ERM programme.
    Answer reference: Section 1.4

4. What are three data-related challenges to implementing an ERM programme?
    Answer reference: Section 1.4.3

5. In addition to the appropriate risk departments, name one other business function that would need to be involved in an effective ERM programme.
    Answer reference: Section 1.5

Glossary

Alpha

Alpha is a measure of the performance of a fund or portfolio, and refers to the extent of any outperformance against its benchmark. In other words, it is the difference between a fund's expected returns, based on its beta, and its actual returns. Alpha gives an indication of the value added by the fund manager to the fund's performance.

Asset Allocation

The process of deciding a portfolio's asset classes before deciding upon sector and stock selection.

Back Testing

The practice of comparing actual data with predicted data in order to ensure the veracity of a predictive model.

Balance Sheet

A financial statement that summarises a company's assets, liabilities and shareholders' equity at a specific point in time.

Basis Risk

The risk of a difference in the impact of market factors on the price of two similar instruments.

Beta

The covariance between the returns from a security and those of the market relative to the variance of returns from the market.

Bilateral Arrangement (of Collateral)

Both parties post collateral for the value of their total obligation to the other.

Bottom-Up Measurement

A method of measuring operational risk that builds up a detailed profile of risks occurring in each process, aggregating these risks to provide overall measures of exposure for the department or the firm as a whole.

Business Risk

The risk of loss due to an adverse external environment, such as high inflation affecting labour costs; an over-competitive market reducing margins or legal, tax or regulatory changes in the markets.

Central Counterparty (CCP)

The guarantor of contracts normally, but not necessarily, for exchange-traded products, usually the clearing house of an exchange.

Collateral (Margin)

An asset held by a lender on behalf of an obligor, under certain agreed conditions, as security for a loan or borrowed assets. An acceptable asset used to cover a margin requirement.

Corporate Governance

The mechanism that seeks to ensure that companies are run in the best long-term interests of their shareholders.

Commodity Price Risk

This is the risk of an adverse movement in the price of a commodity.

Compliance Risk

The risk to earnings or capital arising from violations, or non-conformance with laws, rules, regulations, prescribed practices or ethical standards.

Confidence Level

An assessment of the probability that an event will occur, usually expressed as a percentage.

Confirmation Process

The process of agreeing the details of a transaction with a counterparty.

Correlation

The degree of co-movement between two variables determined through regression analysis and quantified by the correlation coefficient. Correlation does not prove that a cause-and-effect or, indeed, a steady relationship exists between two variables as correlations can arise from pure chance.

Coupon

The predetermined rate of interest applying to a bond over its term expressed as a percentage of the bond's nominal, or par, value. The coupon is usually a fixed rate of interest.

Credit Default Swap

A bilateral financial contract in which one counterparty (the protection buyer) pays a periodic, or one-off, fee (typically expressed in basis points on the notional amount), in return for a contingent payment by the other counterparty (the protection seller) following a credit event of a reference entity.

Credit Derivatives

Specialised products that allow the transfer of credit exposure between parties.

Credit Event

An adverse change such as bankruptcy, insolvency, receivership, material adverse restructuring of debt, or failure to meet payment obligations when due.

Credit Exposure

The amount that can potentially be lost if a debtor defaults on their obligations.

Credit Limits

The maximum limits for lending set by financial institutions to prevent too much exposure to a particular firm or counterparty.

Credit Rating

An assessment of the credit worthiness of a firm that is used by lenders to manage their credit exposure.

Credit Risk

The potential loss of earnings or capital due to an obligor's failure to meet the terms of a contract or otherwise failing to perform as agreed.

Credit Risk Premium

The difference between the interest rate a firm pays when it borrows and the interest rate on a default-free security, such as a government bond.

Current Exposure

The current obligation outstanding.

Deposit insurance

The provision of insurance against bank failure. Depending on the scheme type, depositors with the failed bank will be compensated for some or all of their unrecovered capital.

Derivative

An instrument whose value is based on the price of an underlying asset. Derivatives can be based on both financial and commodity assets.

Detective Controls

Operational controls that detect errors once they have occurred in order to prevent further losses.

Direct Market Risk Factors

The factors that have a direct bearing on an instrument's price, such as the financial performance of a company and the health of its balance sheet.

Distribution Analysis

A statistical means of using historical data to predict future events.

Diversification

A means of reducing overall risk by choosing to take risks that are weakly correlated.

Downside

The negative aspect of incurring risk.

Duration

A first order measure of the exposure of fixed income products to changes in the risk factor of interest rates.

Equity

That which confers a direct stake in a company's fortunes. Also known as a company's ordinary share capital. In terms of financial instruments, the words 'stocks', 'shares' and 'equities' are used interchangeably.

Financial Conduct Authority (FCA)

The body responsible for regulating conduct in retail and wholesale markets, for supervising the trading infrastructure that supports those markets and for the prudential regulation of firms not prudentially regulated by the Prudential Regulation Authority (PRA).

Financial Risk

The quantifiable likelihood of loss or less-than-expected returns.

Financial Services Act 2012

The Act of Parliament that altered the regulatory framework in the UK by abolishing the Financial Services Authority (FSA) and introducing the Prudential Regulation Authority (PRA) and the Financial Conduct Authority (FCA).

Forward

A derivatives contract that creates a legally binding obligation between two parties for one to buy and the other to sell a prespecified amount of an asset at a prespecified price on a prespecified future date. As individually negotiated contracts, forwards are not traded on a derivatives exchange.

Frequency Distribution

Data either presented in tabulated form or diagrammatically, whether in ascending or descending order, where the observed frequency of occurrence is assigned to either individual values or groups of values within the distribution.

Future

A derivatives contract that creates a legally binding obligation between two parties for one to buy and the other to sell a prespecified amount of an asset at a prespecified price on a prespecified future date. Futures contracts differ from forward contracts in that their contract specification is standardised so that they may be traded on a derivatives exchange.

Hedging

A means of reducing the risk of adverse price movements by taking an offsetting position in a related product.

Inflation

The rate of change in the general price level or the erosion in the purchasing power of money.

Historical Simulation

The simplest method of VaR calculation that uses actual historic data to estimate risk exposure in the future.

Indirect Market Risk Factors

The factors that have an indirect bearing on an instrument's price, such as interest rate levels, economic events, political and environmental effects.

Inside Information

Information relating to a security, or an issuer, which is not publicly known and which would affect the price of the security if it was made public.

Integration

The third stage of money laundering; integration is the stage at which the laundered funds appear to be of legitimate provenance.

Interest Rate Risk

The risk of adverse movements in interest rates.

Issuer Risk

The risk of default, with respect to redemption or interest servicing, when one institution holds debt securities issued by another institution.

Key Performance Indicators (KPIs)

Quantifiable measures to gauge performance in terms of meeting strategic and operational goals.

Key Risk Indicators (KRIs)

Objective measurement criteria that measure a firm's ongoing risk status.

Layering

The second stage of money laundering in which money or assets are typically passed through a series of transactions to obscure their origin.

Legal Risk

The risk of loss due to the unenforceability of contracts or documents.

Lender of Last Resort

The provision of 'last resort' credit to banks – a function usually performed by the Central Bank.

Liquidity at Risk

The use of historic financial data to work out the size and frequency of a firm's past funding requirements and hence determine the likely future funding requirements.

Loan Loss Reserves

Reserves held by a bank against the possibility of loans not being repaid – and hence the income stream from the loans not being realised.

Loan Sales

The practice of a firm making a loan to a company and then selling the loan to other institutions or investors.

Loss Given Default (LGD)

The estimated loss that a firm would incur at a specific time if a counterparty defaulted.

Market Liquidity Risk

The risk of loss through not being able to trade in a market or obtain a price on a desired product when required.

Market Risk

The potential loss of earnings or capital arising from changes in the value of financial instruments.

Mean

A measure of central tendency established by summing the observed values in a data distribution and dividing this sum by the number of observations. Also known as the arithmetic mean, it takes account of every value in the distribution.

Median

A measure of central tendency established by the middle value within an ordered distribution containing an odd number of observed values or the arithmetic mean of the middle two values in an ordered distribution containing an even number of values.

Mode

A measure of central tendency established by the value or values that occur most frequently within a data distribution.

Money Laundering

The process whereby criminals attempt to conceal the true origins of the proceeds of their criminal activities, and to give them the appearance of legitimacy by introducing them into the mainstream financial system.

Negative Correlation

An inverse, or opposite relationship between two factors.

Netting

The practice whereby two parties who exchange multiple cash flows during a given day agree bilaterally to net those cash flows to one payment per currency, thereby reducing settlement risk. Multi-lateral netting between a group of counterparties is performed by a clearing house.

Normal Distribution

A distribution whose values are evenly, or symmetrically, distributed about the mean. Depicted graphically, a normal distribution is plotted as a symmetrical, continuous, bell-shaped curve.

Normal Distribution Curve

A common form of probability distribution which is continuous, symmetrical about its mean and is defined by its mean and standard deviation.

Notional Amount

The amount (in an interest rate swap, forward rate agreement, or other derivative instrument) or each of the amounts (in a currency swap) to which interest rates are applied (whether or not expressed as a rate or stated on a coupon basis) in order to calculate periodic payment obligations.

Obligor

A party that has a financial obligation to another party.

Outsourcing

The transfer of an aspect of a firm's business to a third party who will carry the risk exposure for a fee.

Pillar 1

The rules in the Basel Capital Accord that define the minimum levels of regulatory capital to risk weighted assets.

Pillar 2

The supervisory review pillar of the Basel Capital Accord, which requires supervisors to undertake a qualitative review of a bank's capital allocation techniques and compliance with relevant standards.

Pillar 3

The disclosure requirements of the Basel Capital Accord, which facilitate market discipline.

Placement

The first stage of money laundering in which money is introduced into the financial system.

Portfolio

A collection of investments with one or more common features which makes their collective management possible or desirable.

Potential Exposure

The likely maximum loss (for a specified confidence level) in the event of default at a particular point in time.

Pre-Settlement Risk

The risk that an institution defaults prior to settlement when the instrument has a positive economic value to the other party.

Preventative Controls

Operational controls that prevent errors occurring.

Price Level Risk

The risk of potential adverse changes in the price of a financial instrument.

Price Uncertainty

The uncertainty of knowing whether market prices will move in a favourable or adverse direction.

Probability Distributions

Mathematical functions that describe the probabilities of possible outcomes occurring. They are depicted as graphs with the 'probability of occurrence' on the vertical axis and the 'possible outcome' on the horizontal axis.

Probability of Default (PD)

The estimated likelihood that a counterparty will default on an obligation.

Process

A set of activities that allows the firm to deliver its product. A process takes a collection of inputs and turns them into desired outputs by adding value to them.

Prudential Regulation

The aspect of financial services regulation which deals with firms' financial resources.

Redemption

The repayment of principal to the holder of a redeemable security.

Regression Analysis

A statistical technique used to establish the degree of correlation that exists between two variables.

Repo

Short for 'repurchase', this is the sale and repurchase of bonds between two parties: the repurchase being made at a price and date fixed in advance. Repos are categorised into general repos and specific repos.

Risk

The hazard or chance of bad consequences or loss occurring.

Risk Factor

An environmental effect that influences the price of a financial instrument or value of a portfolio.

Risk Profile

The types of risks that are faced by a firm and its exposure to those risks.

Sample

A statistical term applied to a representative subset of a particular population. Samples enable inferences to be made about the population.

Scenario Analysis

A subjective method of highlighting potential risk issues in order to allow preventative action to be taken.

Securitisation

The packaging of rights to the future revenue stream from a collection of assets into a bond issue.

Settlement

The fulfilment of contractual commitments such as payment of cash for securities. The conclusion of a securities transaction by delivery against payment.

Settlement Risk

The risk that an expected payment of an asset/ security or cash will not be made on time or at all.

Short Position

The position following the sale of a security not owned or selling a derivative.

Spread

The difference between similar financial measures, for example the difference between the bid and offer prices of an instrument, or between market interest rates and a central bank base rate.

Standard Deviation

A measure of dispersion. In relation to the values within a distribution, the standard deviation is the square root of the distribution's variance.

Stock Exchange

An organised marketplace for issuing and trading securities by members of that exchange.

Stop-Loss Limit

The specified maximum loss that a firm is prepared to make.

Strategic Risk

The risk of loss due to a sub-optimal strategy being employed and associated with the way the institution is managed. For instance, a competitor or product strategy may be employed that fails to maximise the return on the investment made.

Stress Testing

A means of testing the accuracy of VaR models against 'extreme' market event scenarios.

Underwriting Standards

The standards that financial institutions apply to borrowers in order to evaluate their creditworthiness and therefore limit the risk of default.

Unilateral Arrangement (of Collateral)

One party gives collateral to the other.

Value-at-Risk (VaR)

The maximum loss that can occur with a specified confidence over a specified period of days.

Variance

A measure of dispersion. In relation to the values within a distribution, the variance is the mean of the sum of the squared deviations from the distribution's arithmetic mean.

Volatility

A measure of the extent to which investment returns, asset prices and economic variables fluctuate. Volatility is measured by the standard deviation of these returns, prices and values.

Volatility Risk

The risk of price movements that are more uncertain than usual affecting the pricing of products.

Multiple Choice
Questions

The following additional questions have been compiled to reflect as closely as possible the examination standard that you will experience in your examination. Please note, however, they are not the CISI examination questions themselves.

1. Which of the following is the BEST reason for using detective controls?

    A. To reduce the likelihood of risk occurring

    B. To prevent a risk occurring

    C. To reduce the impact if a risk occurs

    D. To provide feedback in the risk reporting process

2. Which of the following distributions is commonly used for modelling operational risk?

    A. Lognormal

    B. Abnormal

    C. Normal

    D. Exponential abnormal

3. Which of the following items forms part of the expected loss calculation?

    A. Probability of Default

    B. Expected Default

    C. Initial Default

    D. Unexpected Default

4. Which of the following is a means of reducing credit risk within a portfolio?

    A. Outsourcing

    B. Top-slicing

    C. Diversification

    D. Equalisation

5. The Basel Committee's mandate is to:

    A. Enhance understanding of supervisory issues and improve the quality of banking supervision worldwide

    B. Publish best practice standards on risk and banking

    C. Serve as a bank for central banks, and foster international monetary and financial cooperation

    D. Establish a worldwide legal framework to force countries to regulate their banks

6. What is the minimum level of capital required to be held by banks as protection against the realisation of financial risk?

    A. 6%

    B. 8%

    C. 10%

    D. 12%

7. Which of the following items could appear under either the inflow or the outflow columns of a maturity ladder?

    A. Maturing assets

    B. Interest receivable

    C. Asset sales

    D. Drawdowns on committed lines

8. Which of the following would most contribute to model risk?

    A. Difficulty in hiring risk staff who can obtain regulatory approval for the model

    B. Lack of netting agreements between counterparties

    C. Data errors in the model's inputs

    D. The programming language used to construct the model

9. Operational risk is defined as the loss arising from four distinct causes. Which of the following is one of these causes?

    A. Systems issues

    B. Market issues

    C. Credit issues

    D. Governance issues

10. A maturity ladder is a device for:

    A. Comparing currency pairs across the intra-day trading period

    B. Comparing cash inflows and outflows, over a specified time period

    C. Assessing the liquidity of financial controls, such as the cash flow statement

    D. Analysing which instruments require cash for margin calls

11. Where Value-at-Risk back testing shows unsatisfactory differences between the estimates and reality, what action is normally taken?

    A. Additional capital is sought

    B. The model methodology is revised

    C. A report is immediately issued to the regulator

    D. Extra hedging is arranged

12. An assessment of a risk that excludes the beneficial effects of mitigating controls is called:

    A. Gross risk

    B. Net risk

    C. Target risk

    D. Residual risk

13. Risk is not synonymous with uncertainty; variability that can be quantified in terms of probabilities is best thought of as 'risk', whereas 'uncertainty' describes:

    A. Variability that can only be quantified with advanced statistics

    B. Variability that cannot be quantified at all

    C. A more subjective view of risk quantification

    D. A less subjective view of risk quantification

14. Which of the following models is used in financial services?

    A. Regulatory dynamics

    B. Heidelberg's uncertainty principle

    C. Market Value-at-Risk

    D. Relativity theory

15. The key role of the compliance function is to ensure that the firm:

    A. Follows all applicable laws and regulations

    B. Issues guidelines on collateral and margin usage

    C. Has an independent risk department

    D. Accurately compiles reports of its assets and liabilities

16. Which of the following statements BEST describes settlement risk?

    A. The risk of losses caused by the failure of a firm to pay its creditors

    B. The risk of loan default where money is lent to a customer

    C. The risk that occurs when there is a non-simultaneous exchange of value and one party defaults

    D. The risk that an institution defaults before settlement when the instrument has a positive economic value to the other party

17. The report of the external auditors forms an important part of the firm's publicly available financial statements, it must:

    A. Be filed by the internal audit department with the regulator

    B. Give a true and fair view.

    C. Replace the firm's risk profile to be used by the operational risk department

    D. Be carefully disposed of with the firm's other confidential material

18. Which of the following items would be most likely to appear on a retail credit scoring questionnaire?

    A. Gross risk

    B. Number of children

    C. Years in current job

    D. Probability of default

19. The volatility of an investment's value can be quantified mathematically by calculating the investment's:

    A. Alpha

    B. Inter-quartile range

    C. Beta

    D. Standard deviation

20. Which of the following statements BEST describes hedging?

    A. It is a means of reducing market risk

    B. It is a means of reducing credit risk

    C. It limits operational risks

    D. It is a cost-free method of insurance

21. Operational controls are commonly utilised in which of the following risk mitigation strategies?

    A. Avoid the risk

    B. Retain the risk

    C. Accept the risk

    D. Transfer the risk

22. Which of the following would be considered as a defence against cyber theft?

    A. Software prevention

    B. Enabling media controls

    C. Managing IT user privileges

    D. Locking away important papers each night

23. Which of the following factors could affect the riskiness of investment in shares?

    A. The investor's credit rating

    B. Quantification of the investor's operational risk scenarios

    C. Platform stability

    D. Strategic risk of the issuing institution

24. The risk of a difference in the impact of market factors on the price of two similar investments is known as:

    A. Volatility risk

    B. Basis risk

    C. Settlement risk

    D. Liquidity risk

25. A portfolio's tracking error is a measure of:

    A. Its volatility relative to the volatility of the FTSE 100

    B. Its Sharpe ratio

    C. How closely it follows the index to which it is benchmarked

    D. Its underperformance resulting from systematic risk

26. Which of the following is not a duty of the operational risk department?

    A. Benchmark best industry practice

    B. Provide risk oversight and monitoring

    C. Ensure issues are properly escalated and track the actions arising from operational risk incidents

    D. Own the firm's operational risks

27. Which of the following is a measure of asset liquidity risk?

    A. Bid-offer spread

    B. Flow turbulence

    C. Liquid pool urgency

    D. Dynamic granularity

28. Which of the following regulatory influences has most contributed to the development of ERM programmes?

    A. ICAAP

    B. Pillar 1

    C. Pillar 3

    D. The Sarbanes-Oxley Act

29. Which of the following statements regarding the credit risk management function of a bank is TRUE?

    A. It owns the majority of the bank's credit risks

    B. It transfers responsibility for credit risk exposure to the board

    C. It monitors compliance with the bank's credit policy

    D. It ensures credit limit compliance through credit risk insurance

30. Consistent confidence levels are fundamental to which of the following challenges to establishing an enterprise risk management programme?

    A. Aggregation

    B. Cultural

    C. Firm risks vs client risks

    D. Choice of timescale

31. Which of the following areas forms a Pillar of the Basel Accord?

    A. Minimum capital requirements

    B. Reinsurance needs

    C. Conflicts of interest

    D. Credit risk quantification

32. Within a simple risk framework, which of the following key activities would normally be carried out at board level?

    A. Assessing the risks

    B. Managing risk on a day-to-day basis

    C. Monitoring risk and associated controls

    D. Setting risk policies

33. Where an investor deals on the basis of information which is not known to the market, this is BEST described as:

    A. Moral hazard

    B. Money laundering

    C. Market abuse

    D. Operational risk

34. Which of the following types of risk is excluded from the Basel Committee's definition of operational risk?

    A. Legal risk

    B. Process risk

    C. Reputation risk

    D. Systems risk

35. Which of the following is an attribute of a normal distribution curve?

    A. It is symmetrical about its standard deviation

    B. It is plotted about its median

    C. Its average value is always greater than its standard deviation

    D. It is defined by its standard deviation and its mean

36. Bond one has a rating of AAA and Bond two has a rating of BBB. This means that Bond one:

    A. Has a better credit risk rating

    B. Has a worse credit risk rating

    C. Has a better business risk rating

    D. Has a worse business risk rating

37. The risk of loss through being unable to obtain a price on a product when required is which ONE of the following types of market risk?

    A. Commodity risk

    B. Basis risk

    C. Liquidity risk

    D. Volatility risk

38. If a fund's beta value increased from 0.55 to 0.85, what does this indicate?

    A. Competitiveness has improved

    B. Volatility has increased

    C. Charges have been increased

    D. Performance has moved more in line with the market

39. What term is normally used to describe the possibility that people behave differently when protected from the effects of the risks they take?

   A. Ethical culture

   B. Integrity

   C. Moral hazard

   D. Governance

40. Which management approach addresses the premises and people aspects of a serious outage?

   A. A business continuity plan

   B. Disaster recovery

   C. Working from home

   D. Working from a back-up location

41. Which of the following types of risk is least likely to be mitigated through the use of diversification?

   A. Capital risk

   B. Issuer risk

   C. Management risk

   D. Systematic risk

42. Why might internal and external drivers of a company`s business risks be best addressed together?

   A. To benefit from economies of scale

   B. Because they may overlap

   C. To avoid compliance breaches

   D. To minimise the scope for error

43. If someone deposits criminally obtained banknotes in a bank account, what stage of the money laundering process does this represent?

   A. Integration

   B. Layering

   C. Phasing

   D. Placement

44. What is the risk exposure for Firm C under a netting agreement for the following transactions if Firms A and B default?

    Firm A owes Firm C £40 million

    Firm B owes Firm C £20 million

    Firm C owes Firm A £50 million

    Firm C owes Firm B £40 million

    A. £20 million
    B. £30 million
    C. £40 million
    D. £50 million

45. A general move in the regulatory style from a statutory-based approach to a principles-based approach usually results in:

    A. An increase in enforcement penalties
    B. An increase in regulatory staff
    C. A reduction in the number of specific rules
    D. A reduction in the level of investor protection

46. Which of the following processes would be considered to provide a firm-wide risk management approach?

    A. Operational risk policy
    B. Enterprise risk management
    C. Value-at-Risk models
    D. Cost-based provisioning

47. An effective market risk management function will ensure that the VaR measurement process is:

    A. Monitored by the company secretary
    B. Monitored externally rather than internally
    C. Carried out by the compliance department
    D. Carried out in conjunction with other methods

48. Which of the following is an input to loss causal analysis?

    A. Value-at-Risk calculations
    B. Actual and contractual cash receipts
    C. Historical loss data
    D. Correlation coefficients alpha and beta

49. Which of the following statements is an advantage of credit derivatives?

    A. They help to reduce concentrations of credit risk

    B. They reduce market volatility

    C. They replace the need for diversification

    D. They allow credit risk to be monitored

50. Deposit insurance schemes are designed to:

    A. Enable depositors to offset their cash balances against life insurance premiums

    B. Prevent bank runs by reassuring depositors that their funds are safe

    C. Prevent bank runs by enabling banks to deposit collateral with the central bank

    D. Enable regulators to assess the creditworthiness of a lending institution

51. As a result of a risk assessment visit to a firm by the regulator, shortcomings were identified. In order to address this problem, the regulator will typically require:

    A. An increase in the firm`s regulatory fees

    B. Implementation of a mitigation programme

    C. The removal of a firm's licence to operate

    D. The engagement of an external consultancy firm to analyse the situation

52. Which two occurrences could be counted as credit events.

    A. Bankruptcy or failure to publish corporate accounts

    B. Bankruptcy or insolvency

    C. Failure to maintain regulatory reporting deadlines or publish corporate accounts

    D. Failure to maintain regulatory reporting deadlines or insolvency

53. Volatility risk is one type of market risk; name three more.

    A. Settlement, currency, basis

    B. Liquidity, issuer, basis

    C. Settlement, issuer, counterparty

    D. Liquidity, currency, basis

54. Which of the following risks are listed in the seven Basel operational risk event types?

    A. Internal fraud, moral hazard and money laundering

    B. Internal fraud, external fraud and damage to physical assets

    C. Internal fraud, market abuse and money laundering

    D. Internal fraud, damage to physical assets and moral hazard

55. Which of the following is an external stakeholder that could present a source of risk for a business?

    A. The board of directors

    B. A major institutional investor

    C. The firm's staff

    D. The Chief Risk Officer

56. A limitation of using credit ratings for bonds is that they:

    A. Ignore historical data

    B. Are primarily opinion based

    C. Only measure liquidity risk

    D. Cannot be downgraded once allocated

57. In the context of liquidity risk at a specific firm, the fact that some of its financial instruments have a very broad range of possible outcomes means that:

    A. The firm should avoid using them

    B. Such instruments can form useful hedges against liquidity risk

    C. The firm's maturity ladder can never completely capture all future cash flows

    D. All the firm's future cash flows can be perfectly predicted

58. What are two main ways in which operational loss data is used to manage operational risk?

    A. To set escalation thresholds and perform loss causal analysis

    B. To monitor the probability of default (PD) and perform loss causal analysis

    C. To set escalation thresholds and monitor the probability of default (PD)

    D. To monitor the probability of default (PD) and estimate the exposure at default (EAD)

59. With an inflation rate of 2% and a real return on an investment of 5%, 7% is normally described as the investment's:

    A. Nominal return

    B. Final coupon

    C. Internal rate of return

    D. APR

60. Gross (ie, inherent) risk is:

    A. A measure of the risk without taking controls into account

    B. A measure of the risk after taking controls into account

    C. A measure of the risk that affects the firm's pre-tax position

    D. A measure of the risk that affects the firm's post-tax position

61. Credit risk is defined as the risk of loss caused by:

    A. The failure of a counterparty to meet its obligations

    B. The failure of a counterparty or issuer to meet its obligations

    C. The failure of an issuer to meet its obligations

    D. The failure of a third party to honour its supply contract

62. Net (ie, residual) risk is:

    A. A measure of the risk that affects the firm's post-tax position

    B. A measure of the risk without taking controls into account

    C. A measure of the risk after taking controls into account

    D. A measure of the risk that affects the firm's pre-tax position

63. What are the three stages of a successful money laundering operation?

    A. Placement, layering and dissemination

    B. Placement, layering and integration

    C. Insider dealing, placement, and integration

    D. Placement, integration and dissemination

64. For large public firms, which corporate role should chair the risk committee?

    A. A non-executive director

    B. The CRO

    C. The CEO

    D. An executive director

65. Which of these events was most associated with systemic risk?

    A. The failure of Barings Bank in 1995

    B. The bursting of the dot com bubble in 2000

    C. The attacks of 9/11 in 2001

    D. The failure of Northern Rock in 2008

66. The key step required to perform a historical simulation Market risk VaR calculation is:

    A. Identify the risk factors that affect the returns of the portfolio

    B. Use a monte carlo simulation to obtain a set of likely future risk factor daily changes

    C. Use a monte carlo simulation to apply each daily change to the current value of each risk factor

    D. Apply a monte carlo simulation to the results to obtain the desired confidence level

67. The organisation that fosters international cooperation on banking regulations is the:

    A. G20

    B. World Bank

    C. International Monetary Fund

    D. Bank for International Settlements

68. If a liquidity gap analysis shows a net positive figure for a given time period, this shows that for that period:

    A. Outflows of cash are greater than inflows of cash

    B. Asset sales exceed drawdowns

    C. Inflows of cash are greater than outflows of cash

    D. All the firm's future cash flows can be perfectly predicted

69. A firm's risk appetite is:

    A. The amount of risk that a firm is willing to accept in the pursuit of its business objectives

    B. A measure of how much risk a firm has experienced over the previous 12 months at a 99.5% confidence level

    C. The type of risk that a firm is willing to accept in the pursuit of its business objectives

    D. The type and amount of risk that a firm is willing to accept in the pursuit of its business objectives

70. The risk committee will typically:

    A. Ratify the key policies and associated procedures of the firm's risk management activities

    B. Own the firm's key risks

    C. Work outside the overall risk appetite of the firm to demonstrate its independence

    D. Design and sign off the annual audit plan before the audit committee receive it

71. What are the two main components of market abuse?

    A. Insider information and market manipulation

    B. Insider information and money laundering

    C. External fraud and market manipulation

    D. External fraud and money laundering

72. The risk of contagion describes:

    A. A situation where the failure of one firm has a knock-on effect on the confidence placed in other firms in the industry

    B. A situation where poor business practices result in risk being inadequately managed throughout the industry

    C. A situation in which a flu (or other) pandemic causes staff shortages throughout the financial service industry

    D. A situation where cyber defences break down and allow a virus or other malware to penetrate the firm's IT systems

73. If interest rates rise by 2%, the market value of a specific bond is likely to:

    A. Rise

    B. Fall

    C. Become more stable

    D. Become more volatile

74. Which statistical measure is also commonly known as the 'average'?

    A. The variance

    B. The median

    C. The mean

    D. The mode

75. In the context of credit risk, an example of concentration risk would be:

    A. An uneven distribution of exposures to individual borrowers

    B. Caused by a boundary operational risk event

    C. The risk that remains after all other credit mitigations are in place

    D. Caused by a boundary market risk event

76. Which of the following methods is used by the Basel Committee on Banking Supervision to change the way that banking supervision is implemented at national level?

    A. Setting minimum standards for the regulation and supervision of banks

    B. Encouraging secrecy in supervisory approaches and techniques

    C. Forcing local legislators to follow the international regulatory laws laid down by the BIS

    D. Exchanging information on the history of the banking sector and financial markets

77. What is the main reason for a bank's risk management staff to be involved in product development projects from a very early stage?

A. To keep the terms as competitive as possible

B. To enable them to advise on the likelihood and impact of any delays

C. To maximise the projected revenue of the product

D. To help coordinate the interests of all relevant stakeholders

78. As the volatility of returns increases, what happens to the standard deviation?

A. It gets higher

B. It gets lower

C. It stays the same

D. It depends on the distribution

79. The ratio of the bid/offer spread to an asset's mid price can be used to compare the characteristics of different assets. What does it mean if a bond has a higher ratio than an equity?

A. The bond is more liquid than the equity

B. The bond is more volatile than the equity

C. The equity is more liquid than the bond

D. The equity is more volatile than the bond

80. For any given investment, what are the two constituent elements of its total returns?

A. Its income production, and any capital gains (or losses) it generates

B. Its nominal return and its real return

C. Its pre-tax and its post-tax returns

D. Its initial value and its outperformance relative to its benchmark

81. Name three credit rating agencies.

A. Fitch, Smith and Lehman

B. Lehman, Smith and S&P

C. Lehman, Moody's and S&P

D. Fitch, Moody's and S&P

82. Which type of risk does resilience measure?

A. Market risk

B. Liquidity risk

C. Credit risk

D. Investment risk

83. Models are MOST useful to firms because:

    A. They prevent unknown losses

    B. They facilitate close interaction between Risk and Compliance staff

    C. They reassure the regulator that the firm understands the quantification of its risks

    D. They enable a complex reality to be more easily understood

84. What are the three different approaches to calculating VaR?

    A. Historical simulation, Quadratic, Monte Carlo simulation

    B. Market-based, value-based, risk-based

    C. Historical simulation, Parametric, Monte Carlo simulation

    D. Volatility, Price, Correlation

85. A fund manager is able to outperform the market and so has a positive:

    A. Beta

    B. Delta

    C. Alpha

    D. Benchmark

86. Which of the following is an example of systemic financial risk materialising and damaging to the economy?

    A. The credit crisis that started in 2007

    B. The attack on the World Trade Centre in 2001

    C. The bursting of the dot com bubble in 2000

    D. The rapid reduction in oil prices in 2015

87. What characterises the approach to regulatory capital taken by Pillar 1 of the Basel Accord?

    A. It uses formula(s) to calculate regulatory capital

    B. It allows firms to design their own approach to quantifying their risks

    C. It is based on consultants' best practice

    D. It is a formality and the regulators do not take it into account

88. In the context of credit risk, collateral is:

    A. A set of credit scoring cards used to rate retail customers

    B. The risk that remains after all other credit mitigations are in place

    C. An asset held by a lender on behalf of an obligor, under certain agreed conditions, as security for a loan

    D. The damage caused by the failure of a counterparty or issuer

89. The market risk appetite within an investment management firm is more likely to be defined:

    A. Across the board
    B. Per fund
    C. Per fund manager
    D. Per territory

90. One disadvantage of liquidity gap analysis is that:

    A. It only considers cash inflows
    B. It can only be conducted for a firm's base currency
    C. It cannot be automated
    D. It does not consider the impact of credit risk on future cash flows

91. Political change is unlikely to cause:

    A. A rise or fall in the markets in which firms invest
    B. An increase or decrease in demand for the products which the industry sells
    C. Changes to the legislative and regulatory environment in which financial services firms operate
    D. A failure of the firm's IT systems

92. What is the relationship between the variance and the standard deviation?

    A. The variance is the square root of the standard deviation
    B. The standard deviation is the square root of the variance
    C. The standard deviation is the square of the variance
    D. The variance is the same as the standard deviation

93. A credit default swap (CDS) can BEST be thought of as:

    A. A way to avoid margin calls
    B. A currency hedge
    C. An insurance contract
    D. A financial reserve

94. Which of the following is an attribute of a normal distribution curve?

    A. It is positively skewed
    B. 68.3% of the data will be within one standard deviation either side of the mean
    C. 95.5% of the data will be within one standard deviation either side of the mean
    D. Its median is greater than its mean

95. If a bank in the UK faces liquidity issues in a 'normal' market situation, one way it could mitigate the impact is to:

   A. Report the matter to the regulator immediately

   B. Draw down its loan facilities at the Bank of England

   C. Recalibrate its maturity ladder

   D. increase the size of its loan book

96. A firm's network defences can BEST be strengthened against cyber threats via:

   A. Removable media controls

   B. User education and awareness

   C. Penetration testing

   D. User privilege testing

97. Which of the following tests could be described as a stress test?

   A. Using the credit crisis years to assess the position of the firm's balance sheet were it to recur

   B. Altering the interest rate to assess the impact on the firm's earnings and capital position

   C. Assembling the senior executives to walk through a market crash exercise

   D. Altering the interest rate and the inflation rate to assess the impact on the firm's loan book

98. What are the typical historic return rankings from equities, bonds and cash investment?

   A. Cash outperformed bonds which outperformed equities

   B. Bonds outperformed cash which outperformed equities

   C. Equities outperformed bonds which outperformed cash

   D. Bonds outperformed equities which outperformed cash

99. Which line of defence would Compliance fit into?

   A. First line

   B. Second line

   C. Third line

   D. All three lines

100. What is the fundamental principle behind hedging?

   A. An investor can offset the risks of a falling market by purchasing assets at a reduced price

   B. An investor can buy products in one market at a better rate than the domestic market

   C. The risk exposure of one instrument offsets the risk exposure of another instrument

   D. The risk exposure of two instruments moves with the market

Answers to Multiple Choice Questions

1.   **Answer: C**   **Chapter 3**   **Section 6.3.1**   **LO: 3.6.3**

No matter how good a firm's preventative controls are, risks may still materialise. For that reason the firm also needs detective controls which can pick up errors before they spiral out of control. A detective control will not prevent a risk occurring or reduce its likelihood, but it may reduce the impact if the risk occurs. The answer is therefore C.

2.   **Answer: A**   **Chapter 8**   **Section 1.2.1**   **LO: 8.1.2**

Operational risk loss events are not 'normally distributed', but instead follow a distribution that exhibits fat tail characteristics. This is intuitively the case, in so far, as firms have far more low level losses than catastrophic ones. There are various commonly used distributions which exhibit 'fat tail' characteristics, and scenario impact distributions are often simulated with a lognormal distribution. The answer is therefore A.

3.   **Answer: A**   **Chapter 4**   **Section 2.4**   **LO: 4.2.4**

Expected loss is the product of (i) probability of default, (ii) exposure at default and (iii) loss given default. The answer is therefore A.

4.   **Answer: C**   **Chapter 4**   **Section 3.1.6**   **LO: 4.3.1**

Diversification can be used as a means of reducing portfolio credit risk by ensuring that the portfolio is spread across borrowers in different, negatively correlating industry sectors that have an inverse economic relationship to each other. When one industry sector enters a downturn and its borrowers start to default, another sector might be booming. The earnings of some of the loans in the portfolio will therefore offset the losses of others, making it less likely that the portfolio will lose money overall. Therefore diversification is a means of reducing credit risk within a portfolio and the answer is C.

5.   **Answer: A**   **Chapter 2**   **Section 1.2.1**   **LO: 2.1.4**

The Basel Committee is a committee of the Bank for International Settlements (BIS), and the committee's objective is to enhance understanding of supervisory issues and improve the quality of banking supervision worldwide. It does this in many ways, including, but not limited to, publishing best practice standards on risk and banking. BIS itself (but not the Basel Committee) serves as a bank for central banks, and also fosters international monetary and financial cooperation – but these are not objectives of the Committee. Neither BIS nor the Basel Committee have any force in law and so answer D is incorrect. The correct answer is therefore A.

6.   **Answer: B**   **Chapter 2**   **Section 2.1.1**   **LO: 2.2.1**

According to the Basel Accord, the ratio of a firm's capital compared to the sum of its credit, market and operational risks must be greater or equal to 8%. The answer is therefore B.

7.   **Answer: D**   **Chapter 7**   **Section 1.1.1   LO: 7.1.1**

Maturing assets, interest receivable and asset sales all generate cash and would therefore appear under the cash inflows column. Drawdowns on committed lines could refer either to lines extended to a bank's customers, or lines available to the bank from an external source. Therefore the answer is D.

8.   **Answer: C**   **Chapter 8**   **Chapter Summary**

The quality of model outputs depends on the quality of the input data, and so errors in the model's inputs will lead to inaccurate outputs and hence increase the associated model risk. The answer is therefore C.

9.   **Answer: A**   **Chapter 3**   **Section 1.1   LO: 3.1.1**

The BIS definition of operational risk is the risk of loss resulting from inadequate of failed internal processes, people and systems or from external events. Therefore the answer is A.

10.   **Answer: B**   **Chapter 7**   **Section 1.1.1   LO: 7.1.2**

A bank's net funding requirements are determined by analysing its future cash flows over a specified time frame (based on assumptions about the future behaviour of assets, liabilities and off-balance sheet items) and then calculating the cumulative net excess or shortfall over that time frame. A maturity ladder is a device for comparing cash inflows and outflows over a series of specified time periods, and the answer is therefore B.

11.   **Answer: B**   **Chapter 5**   **Section 2.7.2   LO: 5.2.7**

Back testing is the practice of comparing the actual daily trading exposure to the previously predicted VaR figure. It is a test of reliability of the VaR methodology and ensures that the approach is of sufficient quality. If unsatisfactory differences between reality and estimation are found, the VaR model must be revised, and so the answer is B.

12.   **Answer: A**   **Chapter 3**   **Section 5.3.1   LO: 3.5.3**

The net risk score is a view of the risk profile once controls have been taken into account. This is also known as the residual risk score. The target risk score is where management would like the risk score to be, and is used to determine which actions should be taken to move the net score to the target score. The gross risk score is an assessment of the risk profile as if there were no controls in place, in other words the risk exposure if the controls were to fail. The answer is therefore A.

13.   **Answer: B**   **Chapter 1**   **Section 1.1   LO: 1.1.2**

It is useful to distinguish between risk and uncertainty. Some future events lend themselves to analysis based on the probability of other similar events that have already occurred. We can therefore talk about the risk of these events occurring again. Other future events either have no precedent or are the combination of so many interrelating factors. The likelihood of occurrence for these events is therefore uncertain. The answer is B because uncertainty cannot be quantified.

14.   **Answer: C**   **Chapter 8**   **Section 1.2.4**   **LO: 8.1.2**

Market Value-at-Risk measures the market risk at a given confidence level over a given time horizon and the answer is therefore C.

15.   **Answer: A**   **Chapter 9**   **Section 1.1.4**   **LO: 9.1.1**

Firms in heavily regulated industries are required to adhere to the rules that make up the regulatory framework. The remit of the compliance department is to enable that adherence, and so the answer is A.

16.   **Answer: C**   **Chapter 4**   **Section 1.2**   **LO: 4.1.2**

When assets are bought and sold, there has to be a point at which money (or its equivalent) 'changes hands' and this activity is known as settlement. Settlement risk is the risk that one party hands over their asset but the other party is unable or unwilling to reciprocate. As settlement approaches simultaneity, this risk approaches zero. Conversably, the greater the time difference between the two halves of the settlement, the greater the risk that one party will default after the other party has completed. The answer is therefore C.

Answer D refers to pre-settlement risk which is when one party fails before the point of settlement. Money has not 'changed hands' and so it represents the loss of economic value which the non-defaulting party had anticipated.

17.   **Answer: B**   **Chapter 9**   **Section 1.1.6**   **LO: 9.1.1**

The purpose of an external audit is to provide key information to investors and other external stakeholders. It must give a 'true and fair view', so therefore the answer is B.

18.   **Answer: C**   **Chapter 4**   **Section 3.6.1**   **LO: 4.3.6**

The questions on a retail credit scoring questionnaire are designed to assess the likelihood of repayment, and so they include factors that historically have made a difference to whether a customer repays. Typical questions include age, credit history, whether the person's home is owned or rented, and how many years they have been in their job. The answer is therefore C.

19.   **Answer: D**   **Chapter 6**   **Section 2.2**   **LO: 6.2.1**

The volatility in the value of an investment can be quantified mathematically by calculating the standard deviation of the values. This is because the standard deviation measures how widely the value of an investment fluctuates around the mean or average. The more volatile the value of an investment is, the greater is the standard deviation. Therefore the answer is D.

20.   **Answer: A**   **Chapter 5**   **Section 2.1.1**   **LO: 5.2.1**

Hedging is a means of reducing the risk of adverse price movements by taking an offsetting position in a related product. It is a means of reducing market risk and so the answer is A.

21.   **Answer: C**   **Chapter 3**   **Section 6.2**   **LO: 3.6.2**

Neither avoiding the risk nor transferring it to a third party would require the utilisation of controls. Accepting the risk refers to accepting it and not expending resources to mitigate it – which implies that controls are not required. Reducing the likelihood of the risk occurring implies the use of controls and so the answer is C.

22.   **Answer: C**   **Chapter 3**   **Section 6.3.5**   **LO: 3.6.3**

Software prevention is not a viable defence to cyber theft – software needs to be allowed on a firm's network. Enabling media controls would be more likely to allow cyber theft through the use of rogue USB keys and CDs/DVDs. Cyber theft targets information on IT systems so although information can be held on paper, and important papers should be locked away, that is not a defence against cyber theft. Managing IT user privileges ensures that only authorised personnel can access each IT system and therefore the answer is C.

23.   **Answer: D**   **Chapter 6**   **Section 2.1.4**   **LO: 6.2.1**

The strategic risk of the issuing institution will all affect the price of shares in a company, for example through analyst's reports issued to the market. The answer is therefore D.

24.   **Answer: B**   **Chapter 5**   **Section 1.1.4**   **LO: 5.1.1**

Volatility risk is the risk of price movements that are more uncertain than usual affecting the pricing of products. All priced instruments suffer from this form of volatility.

Basis risk occurs when one risk exposure is hedged with an offsetting exposure in another instrument that behaves in a similar, but not identical, manner. If the two positions were truly 'equal and opposite' then there would be no risk in the combined position. Basis risk exists to the extent that the two positions do not exactly mirror each other. The answer is therefore B.

Settlement risk occurs when there is a non-simultaneous exchange of value and one party defaults.

Liquidity risk is the risk of loss through not being able to trade in a market or obtain a price on a desired product when required.

25.   **Answer: C**   **Chapter 6**   **Section 2.6**   **LO: 6.2.6**

Tracking errors measure how closely a portfolio follows (or 'tracks') the index to which it is benchmarked, and can be calculated as the standard deviation of returns relative to the benchmark. Therefore the answer is C.

26.   **Answer: D**   **Chapter 3**   **Section 3.1**   **LO: 3.3.1**

The operational risk department performs many duties, amongst which are benchmarking industry best practice, providing risk oversight and monitoring and ensuring that issues are properly escalated and tracking the actions arising from operational risk incidents. However, the risks themselves are owned by the business not the operational risk department. The answer is therefore D.

27.   **Answer: A**   **Chapter 7**   **Section 2.2.1**   **LO: 7.2.2**

The key measures of asset liquidity risk include bid-offer spread which is the difference between the prices quoted by market makers for an immediate sale (bid) and an immediate purchase (offer). The answer is therefore A.

28.   **Answer: A**   **Chapter 10**   **Section 1.3**   **LO: 10.1.3**

Answers B, C and D are not connected to enterprise risk management (ERM). For most firms Basel Pillar 1 is a formulaic approach to the calculation of capital. Basel Pillar 3 is the public disclosure of a firm's approach to risk. The Sarbanes-Oxley Act is concerned with the signing off of key controls by senior management. However, the Pillar 2 Internal Capital Adequacy Assessment Process (ICAAP) requires a firm (amongst other things) to (i) define and quantify its overall risk exposure across all risk types and (ii) stress and scenario test this exposure. This is similar to the aims of an ERM programme and so the answer is A.

29.   **Answer: C**   **Chapter 4**   **Section 3.3**   **LO: 4.3.3**

The credit risk management function, as part of the second line of defence, does not own any risk itself nor does it transfer responsibility for credit risks between different levels of the firm. Neither does it use credit risk insurance to ensure that credit limits are adhered to. Its main tool is ownership of a strong credit policy and ensuring that it is adhered to. The answer is therefore C.

30.   **Answer: A**   **Chapter 10**   **Section 1.4.3**   **LO: 10.1.4**

Different confidence levels make it impossible to aggregate risk data meaningfully. The answer is therefore A.

31.   **Answer: A**   **Chapter 2**   **Section 2.1**   **LO: 2.2.1**

Pillar 1 is a semi-formulaic approach to the calculation of a firm's minimum capital requirements. Therefore the answer is A. Pillar 2 enables the firm itself to offer its own view of the level of capital it should hold, and enables regulators to compare this to the Pillar 1 minimum, and set the level which they think is most appropriate. In Europe and certain other countries, Pillar 2 is known as ICAAP (Internal Capital Adequacy Assessment Process). Pillar 3 is simply the public disclosure of certain prescribed aspects of the firm's capital and approach to risk management.

32.   **Answer: D**   **Chapter 1**   **Section 1.1**   **LO: 1.1.2**

Assessing, managing and monitoring risks is the responsibility of managers. The board is responsible for setting risk policies and so the answer is D.

33.   **Answer: C**   **Chapter 3**   **Section 1.3**   **LO: 3.1.4**

Market abuse takes two main forms: insider information and market manipulation. An investor dealing on the basis of confidential information is using non-public or 'inside' information and so the answer is C.

34.   **Answer: C**   **Chapter 3**   **Section 1.1**   **LO:3.1.1**

The BIS defines operational risk as *'the risk of loss resulting from inadequate or failed internal processes, people and systems or from external events'*. This definition covers legal risk (including fines, penalties and punitive damage resulting from regulatory actions, as well as private settlements), but excludes reputation risk. The answer is therefore C.

35.   **Answer: D**   **Chapter 5**   **Section 2.5.1**   **LO: 5.2.5**

A normal distribution curve is defined by its standard deviation and its mean and so the answer is D.

36.   **Answer: A**   **Chapter 4**   **Section 2.2**   **LO: 4.2.2**

Both the Standard & Poor's and Fitch ratings use combinations of letters to denote the creditworthiness of an investment. AAA is a higher rating than BBB and so Bond one has a better credit risk rating than Bond two. Therefore the answer is A.

37.   **Answer: C**   **Chapter 5**   **Section 1.1.2**   **LO: 5.1.1**

Commodity risk is the risk of an adverse price movement in the value of a commodity. The price risk of commodities differs considerably from other market risk drivers because most commodities are traded in markets where the concentration of supply in the hands of a few suppliers can magnify price volatility.

Basis risk occurs when one risk exposure is hedged with an offsetting exposure in another instrument that behaves in a similar, but not identical, manner. If the two positions were truly 'equal and opposite' then there would be no risk in the combined position. Basis risk exists to the extent that the two positions do not exactly mirror each other.

Liquidity risk is the risk of loss through not being able to trade in a market or obtain a price on a desired product when required. Therefore the answer is C.

Volatility risk the risk of price movements that are more uncertain than usual affecting the pricing of products. All priced instruments suffer from this form of volatility.

38.   **Answer: D**   **Chapter 6**   **Section 2.3**   **LO: 6.2.2**

An asset with a beta of 0 means that its price is not at all correlated with the market. A positive beta means that the asset generally follows the market. A fund with a beta factor of one moves in line with the market or benchmark. Therefore if a fund's beta value increased from 0.55 to 0.85 it is getting close to one and so its performance has moved more in line with the market. Therefore the answer is D.

39.   **Answer: C**   **Chapter 9**   **Section 2.7**   **LO: 9.2.3**

Moral hazard describes the possibility that people or companies will behave differently when protected from the effects of the risks that they take. For example, mortgage firms may be less scrupulous about lending to high-risk customers when they know that there is a ready market for repackaged sub-prime mortgages. Therefore the answer is C.

40. **Answer: A** **Chapter 3** **Section 6.3.2** **LO: 3.6.3**

The business continuity plan (BCP) addresses the people and premises aspects of a serious outage. Disaster recovery is the process that the IT department own in order to keep the systems running. Working from home and working from a back-up location may be useful activities in the event of a disaster, but the BCP is the management tool that addresses all aspects including staff communication and work-reprioritisation. The answer is therefore A.

41. **Answer: D** **Chapter 6** **Section 2.8.1** **LO: 6.2.7**

In the context of a portfolio of stocks which is benchmarked against a peer group or index, the value of the portfolio changes in line with its benchmark. As the benchmark moves, the portfolio will tend to follow because it keeps its weighting of its constituent stocks broadly in the same ratio as the benchmark. This is referred to as systematic risk and it cannot be diversified away – it is the result of attempting to keep the portfolio moving in line with an index or peer group. The answer is therefore D.

42. **Answer: B** **Chapter 1** **Section 1.6** **LO: 1.1.7**

Risks can arise from inside and outside the firm. Although it can be helpful to categorise internal and external risks separately, their inter-relationship means that it makes sense to consider them together because they may overlap. The correct answer is therefore B.

43. **Answer: D** **Chapter 3** **Section 1.3** **LO: 3.1.4**

The first stage of laundering dirty money is to get it into the financial system. This is known as placement and so the correct answer is D. Subsequent stages involve moving the money around the system to mix it with other funds (known as layering) and finally being able to access the now disguised dirty money as though it had been obtained legitimately (known as integration). There is not a stage known as phasing.

44. **Answer: B** **Chapter 7** **Section 3.2** **LO: 7.3.2**

If there is no netting agreement between two firms then if the first firm defaults while still owing money to the second firm, not only will the second firm not get the money but the second firm will still need to pay out any money it owes to the first firm. However, a netting agreement allows individual sums owed between firms to be 'netted off' before the final amount owed is calculated. Therefore because Firm A owes Firm C £40 million but Firm C owes Firm A £50 million, the net exposure from these transactions is £10 million owed by Firm C to Firm A. Also, because Firm B owes Firm C £20 million but Firm C owes Firm B £40 million, the net exposure from these transactions is £20 million owed by Firm C to Firm B. Therefore the total exposure for Firm C under a netting agreement if Firms A and B default is £10m + £20m = £30m which is answer B.

45. **Answer: C** **Chapter 2** **Section 3.1** **LO: 3.3.1**

There are two broad approaches to financial regulation. One approach is based on specific legal rules which must be obeyed. This is known as the 'statutory approach' and is practised, for example, in the US by the Securities and Exchange Commission (SEC) which regulates non-banking financial activity. The other approach is to set out in more general terms the types of behaviour that are expected of firms and individuals. This is known as the 'principles-based approach' and is practised by, for example, the UK regulatory authorities. Therefore a move in regulatory style from a statutory to a principles-based approach would tend to result in a reduction in the number of specific rules, which is answer C.

46.   **Answer: B**   **Chapter 10**   **Section 1**   **LO: 10.1.1**

A common definition of enterprise risk management (ERM), is the process of applying the discipline of risk management to all the risks a firm faces to understand and manage them, not only individually, but also in the way that they relate to each other. ERM is also known as integrated risk management or firm-wide risk management and hence the answer is B.

47.   **Answer: D**   **Chapter 5**   **Section 2.2**   **LO: 5.2.2**

It is important when using VaR to ensure that it is not used alone, but is combined with stress testing and scenario analysis in order to capture the outliers not caught in the (eg) 99% confidence level. Therefore an effective market risk management function will ensure that the VaR measurement process is carried out in conjunction with other methods, which is answer D.

48.   **Answer: C**   **Chapter 3**   **Section 6.4**   **LO: 3.6.4**

Loss causal analysis uses trends from historical loss data to try and understand the underlying causes of the losses. Fixing the underlying causes rather than the surface symptoms gives the firm a better chance of preventing a recurrence of the loss. The answer is therefore C.

49.   **Answer: A**   **Chapter 4**   **Section 3.1.7**   **LO: 4.3.1**

A credit derivative is a financial instrument that derives its value from an underlying loan or series of loans. Credit derivatives allow a view to be held on the quality of a loan without actually holding the loan itself and so they can be used to improve credit portfolio diversification and hence reduce credit concentrations. The answer is therefore A.

50.   **Answer: B**   **Chapter 1**   **Section 2.2**   **LO: 1.2.2**

A deposit insurance scheme pays depositors who lose money when their bank fails. Banks are more likely to fail when depositors start withdrawing their funds en masse in anticipation of losing them. Widespread withdrawals are less likely when deposit insurance schemes are in place. Therefore deposit insurance schemes help to prevent bank runs and so the answer is B.

51.   **Answer: B**   **Chapter 2**   **Section 3.4**   **LO: 2.3.4**

Regulators have an array of powers that can be applied to firms where shortcomings are identified. These powers can extend (in extremis) to the removal of a firm's licence to operate but typically the initial response would be the imposition of a risk mitigation programme. The answer is therefore B.

52.   **Answer: B**   **Chapter 4**   **Section 2.4.2**   **LO: 4.2.4**

It is important for firms to know when a credit risk has materialised because that will trigger certain actions on the part of the bank and other creditors of the bankrupt firm. Although the term 'credit event' is a recognised industry trigger point, it does not have a precise definition. It is commonly understood to include bankruptcy, insolvency, receivership, or simply a failure to meet payment obligations when due. A credit event can also be simply a credit-rating downgrade.

53.   **Answer: D**   **Chapter 5**   **Section 1.1**   **LO: 5.1.1**

The different types of market risk include: volatility risk, liquidity risk, currency risk, basis risk, interest rate risk, commodity risk, equity risk

54.   **Answer: B**   **Chapter 3**   **Section 1.2**   **LO: 3.1.2**

The Basel operational risk event types are: (1) Internal fraud, (2) External fraud, (3) Employment practices and workplace safety, (4) Clients, products & business practices, (5) Damage to physical assets, (6) Business disruption and systems failures and (7) Execution, delivery, and process management. The answer is therefore B.

55.   **Answer: B**   **Chapter 1**   **Section 1.2.6**   **LO: 1.1.3**

Major institutional investors own large shareholdings in the firm, and this gives them external influence through voting rights. The answer is therefore B.

56.   **Answer: B**   **Chapter 4**   **Section 2.3**   **LO: 4.2.3**

Credit ratings agencies use historical credit data to rate bonds, but the rating itself is simply their opinion of the bond's credit-worthiness. Therefore the answer is B.

57.   **Answer: C**   **Chapter 7**   **Section 1.1.2**   **LO: 7.1.1**

A maturity ladder seeks to capture all cash inflows and outflows. It is not possible to estimate with certainty the cash flows from some types of financial instruments, such as derivatives because they have a very broad range of possible outcomes. Therefore a maturity ladder can never completely capture all future cash flows, so the answer is C.

58.   **Answer: A**   **Chapter 3**   **Section 6.4**   **LO: 3.6.4**

Probability of default (PD) and exposure at default (EAD) are credit risk concepts which cannot be analysed using operational loss data. Operational loss data is used to set escalation thresholds and perform loss causal analysis. The answer is therefore A.

59.   **Answer: A**   **Chapter 6**   **Section 1.1**   **LO: 6.1.1**

The real return is the return the investment provides an investor after stripping out the effects of inflation. The nominal return on an investment is simply the return it gives, unadjusted for inflation. Therefore to get back to the nominal return (of 7%), you add the rate of inflation to the real rate. Therefore the answer is A.

60.   **Answer: A**   **Chapter 1**   **Section 1.7.3**   **LO: 1.1.8**

Gross (ie, inherent) risk is a measure of the full exposure which the firm could face if all controls failed. The risk is assessed without taking controls into account and so the answer is A.

61.   **Answer: B**   **Chapter 4**   **Section 1.1**   **LO: 4.1.1**

The definition of credit risk is the risk of loss caused by the failure of a counterparty or issuer to meet its obligations. The answer is therefore B.

62.   **Answer: C**   **Chapter 1**   **Section 1.7.4**   **LO: 1.2.2**

Net (ie, residual) risk is a measure of the expected exposure the firm faces given the controls it has in place. The risk is assessed in light of the controls and so the answer is C.

63.   **Answer: B**   **Chapter 3**   **Section 1.3**   **LO: 3.1.4**

The three stages to a successful money laundering operation are:

1. Placement – the introduction of dirty money into the financial system.
2. Layering – moving the placed money around the system in order to make it difficult for the authorities to track it.
3. Integration – Once layering has successfully completed, the money is regarded as 'integrated' into the legitimate financial system.

Therefore the answer is B.

64.   **Answer: A**   **Chapter 9**   **Section 1.2**   **LO: 9.1.2**

A non-executive director should chair the risk committee to provide independence from the executive management. The answer is therefore A.

65.   **Answer: D**   **Chapter 4**   **Section 1.2**   **LO: 4.1.2**

Systemic risk exists because the fate of any one part of the financial sector is intimately linked to the fate of the other parts. The failure of Barings Bank did not cause a failure of other banks, nor did the bursting of the dot com bubble or the attacks of 9/11. However, the credit crisis that started in the US housing market caused banks around the world to withdraw from the interbank lending markets as trust in the resilience of other banks evaporated. Northern Rock, a UK bank, had built its business model on borrowing cheaply on the short-term interbank markets, and when these markets seized up, Northern Rock failed. This is an example of systemic risk and so the answer is D.

66.   **Answer: A**   **Chapter 8**   **Section 1.2.4**   **LO: 8.1.2**

Monte carlo simulation is an alternative to a historical simulation, therefore the answer is A.

67.   **Answer: D**   **Chapter 2**   **Section 1.1**   **LO: 2.1.1**

The Bank for International Settlements (BIS) is an organisation which serves as a bank for central banks, and fosters international monetary and financial cooperation. The answer is therefore D.

68.   **Answer: C**   **Chapter 7**   **Section 2.1.1**   **LO: 7.2.1**

Before a liquidity gap analysis can be performed, a technique called cash matching is used to understand a firm's or portfolio's liquidity risk, by examining all net future cash flows. A firm or portfolio is cash matched if:

*   every future cash inflow is balanced with an offsetting cash outflow on the same date, and
*   every future cash outflow is balanced with an offsetting cash inflow on the same date.

Gap analysis then aggregates the cash flows into maturity brackets and checks if cash flows in each bracket net to zero or positive. If the aggregate is positive, it means that for that maturity date, inflows of cash are greater than outflows of cash and so the answer is C.

69.   **Answer: D**   **Chapter 1**   **Section 1.7.2**   **LO: 1.1.8**

Risk appetite describes the measured amounts of the different types of risk (eg Operational, Credit, Market) that the firm is willing to accept in order to implement its business strategy. The answer is therefore D.

70.   **Answer: A**   **Chapter 9**   **Section 1.1.2**   **LO: 9.1.1**

The firm's risks are owned by the business. The risk committee assess risk within the risk appetite of the firm. The Audit Committee receives and signs off the annual audit plan. If the risk committee did this it would compromise the independence of the third line of defence (Audit). Therefore the answer is A.

71.   **Answer: A**   **Chapter 3**   **Section 1.3**   **LO: 3.1.4**

In most jurisdictions there are strict rules in place, enforceable through national and international legal systems, to prohibit certain undesirable practitioner behaviours, collectively known as market abuse; these fall into two overlapping categories – insider information and market manipulation. Money laundering and external fraud are not aspects of market abuse and so the answer is A.

72.   **Answer: A**   **Chapter 1**   **Section 2.2**   **LO: 1.2.2**

The failure of a bank causes customers of other banks to lose trust and withdraw their deposits. Because banks transform deposits into loans, they are unable to return all funds to depositors on demand. This then leads to the failure of subsequent banks and so on. This is known as contagion and so the answer is A.

73.   **Answer: B**   **Chapter 6**   **Section 2.1.2**   **LO: 6.2.1**

Interest rate risk can affect an investor's capital, since the price of bonds moves in the opposite direction to interest rates. In other words, when interest rates rise by 2%, the value of the bond will fall and so the answer is B.

74.   **Answer: C**   **Chapter 5**   **Section 2.3.6**   **LO: 5.2.3**

The mean is the central tendency measure that is most commonly referred to as the 'average'. It is calculated by adding together all of the values in a data set and then dividing that sum by the number of observations in that set to provide the average value of all the data. The answer is therefore C.

75.   **Answer: A**   **Chapter 4**   **Section 3.7**   **LO: 4.3.7**

Concentration risk in credit portfolios arises through an uneven distribution of exposures to individual borrowers (single-name concentration) or within industry sectors and geographical regions (sectoral concentration). The answer is therefore A.

76.   **Answer: A**   **Chapter 2**   **Section 1.1**   **LO: 2.1.1**

The BIS encourages openness, not secrecy. The regulatory guidelines produced by the BIS do not have any force in national or international law, and countries around the world that choose to implement them do so by making changes to their own legal and regulatory processes. The BIS do not specifically exchange information on the history of the banking sector and financial markets, but they do set minimum standards. The answer is therefore A.

77.   **Answer: B**   **Chapter 1**   **Section 1.8**   **LO: 1.1.9**

New products need to be risk managed. If Risk are not involved early on in the process, their involvement may delay the product launch timetable because mitigating the risks of the product is not an 'optional extra'. The answer is therefore B.

78.   **Answer: A**   **Chapter 5**   **Section 2.4**   **LO: 5.2.4**

The more volatile an investment's return is, the greater is the standard deviation. Therefore the answer is A.

79.   **Answer: C**   **Chapter 7**   **Section 2.2.1**   **LO: 7.2.2**

The bid-offer spread is the difference between the prices quoted by market makers for an immediate sale (bid) and an immediate purchase (offer). The size of the bid-offer spread is a measure of the liquidity of the market. To compare the liquidity of different assets, the ratio of the spread to the asset's mid-price can be used. The higher the ratio, the less liquid the asset is and therefore the answer is C.

80.   **Answer: A**   **Chapter 6**   **Section 1.1.3**   **LO: 6.1.1**

Total returns are the returns on an investment both from (1) its income production, and (2) any capital gains (or losses) it generates. Therefore the answer is A.

81.   **Answer: D**   **Chapter 4**   **Section 2.2**   **LO: 4.2.2**

Moody's, S&P and Fitch are credit rating agencies and so the answer is D.

82.   **Answer: B**   **Chapter 7**   **Section 2.2.4**   **LO: 7.2.2**

Resilience is a measure of the speed with which prices return to equilibrium following a large trade. The more liquid the market, the faster the prices return to equilibrium, and therefore the answer is B.

83.   **Answer: D**   **Chapter 8**   **Section 1.1.1**   **LO: 8.1.1**

Models are useful because they allow complex realities to be simplified and better understood. The answer is therefore D.

84.   **Answer: C**   **Chapter 5**   **Section 2.7.3**   **LO: 5.2.8**

VaR can be calculated in three main ways:

1. Historical simulation – this involves looking back at what actually happened in the past and basing our view of the future on that analysis.
2. The parametric (or analytical) approach – this assumes that the distribution of possible returns can be plotted, based on a small number of factors, so that the required confidence level can be 'read off' the graph.
3. Monte Carlo simulation – this involves generating a random set of results based on the actual underlying risk factors and again 'reading off' the graph.

85.   **Answer: C**   **Chapter 6**   **Section 2.3**   **LO: 6.2.3**

Alpha is another measure used when assessing the performance of a fund or portfolio, and refers to the extent of any outperformance against its benchmark, ie, the difference between a fund's expected returns based on its beta and its actual returns. The answer is therefore C.

86.   **Answer: A**   **Chapter 1**   **Section 2.2**   **LO: 1.2.2**

The credit crisis refers to a period where banks were unable to extend credit to borrowers because they had bought and sold assets (often to each other) whose value could no longer be accurately obtained. Banks were unable to trust other banks and so the interbank lending market almost disappeared. Many banks relied on the interbank market to fund daily operations, and so risks that affected one bank spread via the interbank market to other banks. This sort of risk is known as contagion and so the answer is A.

87.   **Answer: A**   **Chapter 2**   **Section 2.1.1**   **LO: 2.2.1**

Pillar 1 sets the minimum regulatory capital requirements and involves applying 'formulaic' methods for calculating the regulatory capital. The answer is therefore A.

88.   **Answer: C**   **Chapter 4**   **Section 3.1.5**   **LO: 4.3.1**

Collateral is an asset held by a lender on behalf of an obligor, under certain agreed conditions, as security for a loan. It can be a physical asset (such as a house that secures a mortgage loan), or can be in the form of cash or securities, and is used by the lender as a form of insurance to reduce credit exposure to a counterparty. The answer is therefore C.

89.   **Answer: B**   **Chapter 5**   **Section 2.2**   **LO: 5.2.2**

A bank trading on its own account has limits applied 'across the board', whereas each fund in an investment management firm could have a different risk appetite for market, credit and other risk types. Therefore the answer is B.

90.   **Answer: D**   **Chapter 7**   **Section 2.1.1**   **LO: 7.2.1**

A disadvantage of liquidity gap analysis is that it does not consider credit risk, and assumes all cash flows will occur. The answer is therefore D.

91.   **Answer: D**   **Chapter 1**   **Section 1.2**   **LO: 1.1.3**

Political changes may well affect the external environment, and through regulation may also impact a firm's internal environment. But they are unlikely to cause a failure of the firm's IT systems and so the answer is D.

92.   **Answer: B**   **Chapter 5**   **Section 2.3.9**   **LO: 5.2.3**

The standard deviation is the square root of the variance and represents the average amount by which the values in the distribution deviate from the mean. The answer is therefore B.

93.   **Answer: C**   **Chapter 4**   **Section 3.1.7**   **LO: 4.3.1**

In the simplest form of CDS, the bank making a loan pays a premium to a third party that, in turn, agrees to make the bank whole in the event of a default on the underlying loan. This transaction resembles an insurance contract, where the insured (the bank that made the loan) pays a premium to a third party (an insurance company) in return for a promise to make the insured whole in the event of a loss. The answer is therefore C.

94.   **Answer: B**   **Chapter 5**   **Section 2.5**   **LO: 5.2.5**

For a normal distribution curve, 68.3% of the data will be within one standard deviation either side of the mean. Therefore the answer is B.

95.   **Answer: B**   **Chapter 7**   **Section 3.1.7**   **LO: 7.3.1**

At times of liquidity stress, there are a number of common funding sources available to a bank such as the wholesale money markets and its loan facilities with the Bank of England. The answer is therefore B.

96.   **Answer: C**   **Chapter 3**   **Section 6.3.5**   **LO: 3.6.3**

Penetration testing attempts to discover weaknesses in the firm's network defences in order to fix them before a cyber attack takes advantage of the vulnerability. The answer is therefore C.

97.   **Answer: B**   **Chapter 5**   **Section 2.8**   **LO: 5.2.9**

The difference between a stress test and a scenario test is the number of variables that are altered. A stress test alters one variable at a time to analyse its effect on the rest of the portfolio. Scenario analysis looks at how the portfolio behaves under conditions of multiple changes. Therefore the answer is B.

98.   **Answer: C**   **Chapter 6**   **Section 1.3**   **LO: 6.1.3**

Investments in different asset classes have typically produced long-term historical returns in the following ranges: Equities are estimated to return about 7.4% per year; Bonds are estimated to return about 3.6% per year; Cash investments are estimated to return around 2.4% per year. The answer is therefore C.

99.   **Answer: B**   **Chapter 9**   **Section 1.3**   **LO: 9.1.3**

Compliance, like Risk, works with but independently of the business. Therefore the answer is B.

100.   **Answer: C**   **Chapter 5**   **Section 2.1.1**   **LO: 5.2.1**

Hedging is a means of reducing the risk of adverse price movements by taking an offsetting position in a related product. It is a means of insuring against market risk. Therefore the answer is C.

Syllabus Learning Map

Syllabus Unit/ Element		Chapter/ Section
Element 1	**Principles of Risk Management**	**Chapter 1**
1.1	**Introduction to Risk in Business** On completion, the candidate should:	
1.1.1	Understand the processes typically used to identify, reduce and manage specific aspects of risk	Chap Summ
1.1.2	Understand the key elements of risk management and the differences between risk and uncertainty	1.1
1.1.3	Know the key external sources of risk and their potential impact on a business: • economic • political • competitive environment, social and market forces • technological including cyber security • shocks and natural events • external stakeholders and third parties	1.2
1.1.4	Understand how the key external sources of risk are typically assessed	1.3
1.1.5	Know the key internal drivers of risk: • strategic • operational • financial	1.4
1.1.6	Understand how the key internal drivers of risk are typically assessed	1.5
1.1.7	Understand the overlapping and interactive nature of external and internal risk drivers	1.6
1.1.8	Understand the following risk concepts: • risk culture and conduct risk • risk appetite • inherent (gross) risk • residual (net) risk • risk profile • risk mitigation	1.7
1.1.9	Understand how risk management protects and adds value to an organisation and its stakeholders	1.8
1.2	**Specific Risks in Financial Services** On completion, the candidate should:	
1.2.1	Know the specific key risks in financial services as defined by the Bank for International Settlements	2.1
1.2.2	Understand the nature of systemic risk and recovery and resolution planning within financial services	2.2

Syllabus Unit/ Element		Chapter/ Section
Element 2	**International Risk Regulation**	**Chapter 2**
2.1	**The Bank for International Settlements** On completion, the candidate should:	
2.1.1	Understand the role of the Bank for International Settlements within the financial services industry	1.1
2.1.2	Know the purposes for which the Basel Committee on Banking Supervision was established, and the drivers it introduced to calculate the capital adequacy of banks	1.2
2.1.3	Understand the high level international guidelines and supervisory standards established by the Basel Committee	1.3
2.2	**Basel Regulatory Capital** On completion, the candidate should:	
2.2.1	Know the purpose, key features and implementation implications of Basel: • Pillars 1, 2 and 3 • Sound Practice Principles • Capital Adequacy Assessment Process (ICAAP)	2.1
2.2.2	Understand the key principles of home-host state regulation	2.2
2.3	**Regulatory Risk** On completion, the candidate should:	
2.3.1	Understand the main differences between statutory and principles-based approaches to financial regulation	3.1
2.3.2	Understand the responsibility of the national regulator to implement supervision measures to address country-specific risks	3.2
2.3.3	Understand the main features of the regulatory framework from the perspective of regulatory risk and implementation: • consumer protection • business standards • regulatory standards	3.3
2.3.4	Understand the purpose and process of risk based regulatory reviews and risk assessment visits	3.4
2.4	**Other Relevant Regulations** On completion, the candidate should:	
2.4.1	Understand the importance of considering other legislation within the processes of risk identification and management	4.1

Element 3	**Operational Risk**	**Chapter 3**
3.1	**Definitions of Operational Risk** On completion, the candidate should:	
3.1.1	Know the definition of operational risk according to the Basel Committee on Banking Supervision	1.1

Syllabus Unit/ Element		Chapter/ Section
3.1.2	Know the Basel operational risk event types and what forms they take: • Internal Fraud • External Fraud • Employment Practices and Workplace Safety • Clients, Products, & Business Practice • Damage to Physical Assets • Business Disruption & Systems Failures • Execution, Delivery & Process Management	1.2
3.1.3	Know where and how the Basel operational risk event types typically arise	1.2
3.1.4	Understand the implications of financial crime in terms of appropriate risk management, both internally and externally	1.3
3.1.5	Be able to distinguish operational risk from: • other forms of risk • further risks that arise as a consequence of operational risk	1.4
3.2	**Operational Risk Policy** On completion, the candidate should:	
3.2.1	Understand the following areas that are addressed by an operational risk policy and what they are designed to achieve: • identification of key officers • define clear roles and responsibilities • segregation of duties • cross functional involvement and agreement	2.1
3.3	**Operational Risk Framework** On completion, the candidate should:	
3.3.1	Understand the key aims of the operational risk management function: • identification and assessment of risks • management of risks • reduction of potential impact and likelihood of occurrence	3.1
3.3.2	Know the stages of an operational risk management framework: • identification • measurement • management and control • management information • monitoring • escalation • remediation	3.2
3.4	**Operational Risk Identification** On completion, the candidate should:	
3.4.1	Understand the purpose of identifying and categorising risks	4.1
3.4.2	Understand the self-assessment (self-certification) method of identifying operational risks	4.2

Syllabus Unit/ Element		Chapter/ Section
3.4.3	Be able to apply risk categorisation to simple, practical examples of normal activity and change-related projects: • people • processes • systems • external events	4.3
3.5	**Operational Risk Assessment and Measurement** On completion, the candidate should:	
3.5.1	Understand the main reasons for assessing and measuring operational risk, and the difficulties involved	5.1
3.5.2	Know the basic terms used in the assessment and measurement of operational risk	5.2
3.5.3	Understand the following methods of assessing operational risk: • impact and likelihood assessment • scenario analysis • bottom-up analysis	5.3
3.5.4	Understand the Key Risk Indicators (KRI) method of measuring operational risk	5.4
3.5.5	Understand how historical loss data can be used in measuring operational risk	5.5
3.5.6	Understand the practical constraints of implementing an operational risk management framework	5.6
3.6	**Managing Operational Risk** On completion, the candidate should:	
3.6.1	Know the purpose of a risk register (risk log) and its core features: • objectives • description of risk • risk ranking • lead person or department • action plan • target and completion dates • sources of assurance and oversight • mitigating controls	6.1
3.6.2	Understand and be able to distinguish between the following methods for reducing operational risk exposure: • risk transfer • risk avoidance • risk mitigation • risk acceptance	6.2

Syllabus Unit/ Element		Chapter/ Section
3.6.3	Know the common methods for operational risk mitigation: • controls • business continuity and contingency planning • outsourcing • insurance • information and cyber security • physical security • financial reserves • risk awareness training • data protection	6.3
3.6.4	Understand how historical loss data can be used in managing operational risk	6.4

Element 4	Credit Risk	Chapter 4
4.1	**Identification of Credit Risk** On completion, the candidate should:	
4.1.1	Understand the key components of credit risk and how they arise: • counterparty risk • issuer risk • concentration risk	1.1
4.1.2	Know the main areas of exposure of counterparty, systematic and issuer risk within banking, securities and investment functions	1.2
4.1.3	Understand credit risk boundary issues as identified within Basel	1.3
4.2	**Credit Risk Measurement** On completion, the candidate should:	
4.2.1	Understand the following techniques for measuring credit risk and what they are designed to achieve: • credit exposure • credit risk premium • credit ratings	2.1
4.2.2	Understand the role and influence of credit rating agencies	2.2
4.2.3	Understand the merits and limitations of using credit ratings to assess credit-worthiness of companies and financial instruments	2.3
4.2.4	Understand the key issues relating to counterparty credit risk and applications in practice: • probability of default (PD) • loss given default (LGD) • exposure at default (EAD) • recovery rates (RR) • credit events • maturity • wrong way risk • non-performing assets	2.4

Syllabus Unit/ Element		Chapter/ Section
4.2.5	Know the basic principles of setting credit limits for trade book and loan product risk management	2.5
4.2.6	Understand the main limitations of credit risk measurement	2.6
4.3	**Credit Risk Management** On completion, the candidate should:	
4.3.1	Understand the following examples of credit risk mitigation, and how they may be typically applied: • underwriting standards • guarantees • credit limits • netting • collateral • diversification • insurance/credit derivatives • credit default swaps • collateralised debt obligations • loan sales and securitisation • central counterparties	3.1
4.3.2	Be able to calculate a simple margin or collateral adequacy calculation	3.2
4.3.3	Understand the role and sound practice features of an effective credit risk management function	3.3
4.3.4	Understand the role of reporting and escalation tools of credit risk management	3.4
4.3.5	Know the Basel key stages of credit risk policy development, modelling and control: • development • validation • approval • implementation • review • post-implementation monitoring	3.5
4.3.6	Understand the methods used to manage credit risk: • credit scoring systems • factor inputs: financial, non-financial and extraordinary • stress testing • segmentation • external ratings • setting limits or caps • internal credit rating • provisioning and impairment • key statistics and key performance indicators	3.6

Syllabus Unit/ Element		Chapter/ Section
4.3.7	Understand the purpose and methods of controlling concentration risk: • single name entity • country, sector and industry risk	3.7
4.3.8	Understand the purpose and principles of controlling trading book risk: • Value-at-Risk (VaR) • confidence levels	3.8

Element 5	Market Risk	Chapter 5
5.1	**Identification of Market Risk** On completion, the candidate should:	
5.1.1	Know and be able to identify the different types of market risk: • volatility risk • market liquidity risk • currency risk • basis risk • interest rate risk • commodity risk • equity risk	1.1
5.1.2	Understand the boundary issues that can arise between different types of market risk	1.2
5.1.3	Be able to apply an understanding of market risk to simple, practical situations	1.3
5.2	**Market Risk Management** On completion, the candidate should:	
5.2.1	Understand the following techniques and their application in managing market risk: • hedging • market risk limits • diversification • high-frequency trading (HFT)	2.1
5.2.2	Understand the role and sound practice features of an effective market risk management function	2.2
5.2.3	Be able to calculate the key measures of dispersion and variance: • mean • median • mode • range • inter-quartile range and quartile deviation • variance • standard deviation	2.3
5.2.4	Understand the relevance and application of measures of dispersion and variance within risk analysis	2.4

Syllabus Unit/ Element		Chapter/ Section
5.2.5	Understand the terms distribution analysis, confidence intervals, normal distribution and fat-tailed distribution, and how they are used within risk analysis	2.5
5.2.6	Understand the following concepts used in risk measurement and control: • probability • volatility • regression • correlation coefficients alpha and beta • optimisation	2.6
5.2.7	Understand the Value-at-Risk (VaR) approach to managing market risk: • VaR limit setting and monitoring for bank trading positions • VaR as a portfolio measure of risk • validation and back testing	2.7
5.2.8	Know the three different approaches to VaR: • historical simulation • parametric • Monte Carlo	2.7.3
5.2.9	Understand the underlying purposes, principles and application of the main types of scenario and stress testing: • extreme event • risk factor • external factor	2.8

Element 6	Investment Risk	Chapter 6
6.1	**The Measurement of Investment Returns** On completion, the candidate should:	
6.1.1	Understand the basic concepts and measurement of investment related returns: • nominal returns • real returns • total returns • holding period return	1.2

Syllabus Unit/ Element		Chapter/ Section
6.1.2	Understand the effects of compound interest and the time value of money	1.3
6.1.3	Understand how the rates of return from the main asset classes vary	1.4
6.2	**Identification, Measurement and Management of Investment Risk** On completion, the candidate should:	
6.2.1	Understand the main investment risks and their implications for investors and investment selection: • currency risk • interest rate risk • issuer risk • equity risk • commodity risk • property risk • liquidity risk	2.1
6.2.2	Understand how asset and portfolio investment risk is calculated	2.2
6.2.3	Understand the significance of alpha, beta and key investor ratios	2.3
6.2.4	Understand the key features and relevance of illiquid assets in relation to investment risk: • venture capital • private equity • property	2.4
6.2.5	Understand the concept of correlation of performance between asset classes	2.5
6.2.6	Understand the concept of tracking error	2.6
6.2.7	Know the key features of an investment mandate and its role in risk mitigation	2.7
6.2.8	Understand the main methods used to mitigate investment portfolio risk: • systematic and non-systematic risk • optimisation and diversification • portfolio hedging • short selling • risk transfer	2.8
6.2.9	Understand how timely and accurate monitoring, management and reporting of investments can enhance the risk management process	2.9

Syllabus Unit/ Element		Chapter/ Section
Element 7	**Liquidity Risk**	**Chapter 7**
7.1	**Identification of Liquidity Risk** On completion, the candidate should:	
7.1.1	Understand the basic constituents of liquidity risk and how they can arise within the contexts of credit, market, investment and operational risk: • maturity ladder • actual and contractual cash receipts • asset liquidity risk • funding liquidity risk	1.1
7.1.2	Understand the potential impact of liquidity risk within an individual firm and across the wider financial system	?
7.2	**Measurement of Liquidity Risk** On completion, the candidate should:	
7.2.1	Understand the importance of funding liquidity risk analysis: • liquidity gap analysis • stress testing • expected future funding requirement	2.1
7.2.2	Know the uses and limitations of the key measures of asset liquidity risk: • bid-offer spread • market depth • immediacy • resilience	2.2
7.3	**Management of Liquidity Risk** On completion, the candidate should:	
7.3.1	Understand the main ways in which liquidity risk can be managed: • liquidity limits • counterparty credit limits • scenario analysis • liquidity at risk • diversification • behavioural analysis • funding methods	3.1
7.3.2	Be able to calculate a simple example of a cash netting agreement	3.2
7.3.3	Understand the concept and implications of market dislocation	3.3

Syllabus Unit/ Element		Chapter/ Section
Element 8	**Model Risk**	**Chapter 8**
8.1	**Overview of Model Risk** On completion, the candidate should:	
8.1.1	• know the benefits and limitations of modelling	1.1
8.1.2	• know the major models utilised in operational, credit, market and liquidity risks	1.2
8.1.3	• understand the principles of effective governance of risk modelling	**2**

Syllabus Unit/ Element		Chapter/ Section
Element 9	**Risk Oversight and Corporate Governance**	**Chapter 9**
9.1	**Risk Governance within Financial Services Organisations** On completion, the candidate should:	
9.1.1	Understand the general roles, responsibilities and relationships between the principal oversight functions and the role of senior management: • board of directors • risk committee • risk management • compliance • internal and external auditors • internal and external legal support • regulatory oversight	1.1
9.1.2	Understand the structural framework and high level processes of key business functions in relation to risk identification and management	1.2
9.1.3	Understand the principles of the three lines of defence	1.3
9.1.4	Understand the key challenges of implementing risk governance structure, policies and procedures: • appropriate authority and autonomy • segregation of duties • relationship of risk managers to the business	1.4
9.1.5	Understand the main challenges to risk governance implementation that can arise in planned or unplanned change-related scenarios	1.5
9.2	**Risk Culture and Leadership** On completion, the candidate should:	
9.2.1	Know the main factors determining a firm's risk and control culture: • governance and policies • risk appetite / risk tolerance • transparency • integrity, ethics and social responsibility • education and development	**2**
9.2.2	Understand how appropriate management of these factors can add value and reduce risk	2.6
9.2.3	Understand the principle of Moral Hazard as it relates to appropriate and ethical behaviour in a business environment	2.7

Syllabus Unit/ Element		Chapter/ Section
Element 10	**Enterprise Risk Management (ERM)**	**Chapter 10**
10.1	**Overview of Model Risk** On completion, the candidate should:	
10.1.1	Know the definitions of enterprise risk and ERM	1.1
10.1.2	Understand how enterprise risk relates to the process of corporate governance and board responsibilities	1.2
10.1.3	Understand how industry regulation and sound practice have combined to influence the development and implementation of ERM programmes	1.3
10.1.4	Understand the main goals and challenges of establishing and implementing an ERM programme in relation to: • exception-based escalation • aggregation • accountability	1.4
10.1.5	Know the most relevant business functions that participate in an ERM programme	1.5

Examination Specification

Each examination paper is constructed from a specification that determines the weightings that will be given to each element. The specification is given below.

It is important to note that the numbers quoted may vary slightly from examination to examination as there is some flexibility to ensure that each examination has a consistent level of difficulty. However, the number of questions tested in each element should not change by more than plus or minus 2.

Element Number	Element	Questions
1	Principles of Risk Management	12
2	International Risk Regulation	7
3	Operational Risk	15
4	Credit Risk	15
5	Market Risk	15
6	Investment Risk	10
7	Liquidity Risk	10
8	Model Risk	6
9	Risk Oversight and Corporate Governance	5
10	Enterprise Risk Management (ERM)	5
Total		**100**

CISI Associate (ACSI) Membership can work for you...

Studying for a CISI qualification is hard work and we're sure you're putting in plenty of hours, but don't lose sight of your goal!

This is just the first step in your career; there is much more to achieve!

The securities and investments sector attracts ambitious and driven individuals. You're probably one yourself and that's great, but on the other hand you're almost certainly surrounded by lots of other people with similar ambitions.

So how can you stay one step ahead during these uncertain times?

Entry Criteria:

Pass in either:

- Investment Operations Certificate (IOC), IFQ, ICWIM, Capital Markets in, eg, Securities, Derivatives, Advanced Certificates; or
- one CISI Diploma/Masters in Wealth Management paper

Joining Fee: £25 or free if applying via prefilled application form **Annual Subscription (pro rata):** £125

Using your new CISI qualification* to become an Associate (ACSI) member of the Chartered Institute for Securities & Investment could well be the next important career move you make this year, and help you maintain your competence.

Join our global network of over 40,000 financial services professionals and start enjoying both the professional and personal benefits that CISI membership offers. Once you become a member you can use the prestigious ACSI designation after your name and even work towards becoming personally chartered.

* ie, Investment Operations Certificate (IOC), IFQ, ICWIM, Capital Markets

Benefits in Summary...

- Use of the CISI CPD Scheme
- Unlimited free CPD seminars, webcasts, podcasts and online training tools
- Highly recognised designatory letters
- Unlimited free attendance at CISI Professional Forums
- CISI publications including *The Review* and *Change – The Regulatory Update*
- 20% discount on all CISI conferences and training courses
- Invitation to the CISI Annual Lecture
- Select benefits – our exclusive personal benefits portfolio

The ACSI designation will provide you with access to a range of member benefits, including Professional Refresher where there are currently over 100 modules available on subjects including Anti-Money Laundering, Information Security & Data Protection, Integrity & Ethics, and the UK Bribery Act. CISI TV is also available to members, allowing you to catch up on the latest CISI events, whilst earning valuable CPD.

Plus many other networking opportunities which could be invaluable for your career.

Revision Express

You've bought the workbook... now test your knowledge before your exam.

Revision Express is an engaging online study tool to be used in conjunction with most CISI workbooks.

Key Features of Revision Express:

- Examination-focused – the content of Revision Express covers the key points of the syllabus
- Questions throughout to reaffirm understanding of the subject
- Special end-of-module practice exam to reflect as closely as possible the standard you will experience in your exam (please note, however, they are not the CISI exam questions themselves)
- Extensive glossary of terms
- Useful associated website links
- Allows you to study whenever you like, and on any device

IMPORTANT: The questions contained in Revision Express products are designed as aids to revision, and should not be seen in any way as mock exams.

Price per Revision Express module: £35
Price when purchased with the corresponding CISI workbook: £105 (normal price: £116)

To purchase Revision Express:

call our Customer Support Centre on:
+44 20 7645 0777

or visit the CISI's online bookshop at:
cisi.org/bookshop

For more information on our elearning products, contact our Customer Support Centre on +44 20 7645 0777, or visit our website at cisi.org/elearning

Professional Refresher

Self-testing elearning modules to refresh your knowledge, meet regulatory and firm requirements, and earn CPD.

Professional Refresher is a training solution to help you remain up-to-date with industry developments, maintain regulatory compliance and demonstrate continuing learning.

This popular online learning tool allows self-administered refresher testing on a variety of topics, including the latest regulatory changes.

There are currently over 100 modules available which address UK and international issues. Modules are reviewed by practitioners frequently and new topics are added to the suite on a regular basis.

Benefits to firms:
* Learning and testing can form part of business T&C programme
* Learning and testing kept up-to-date and accurate by the CISI
* Relevant and useful – devised by industry practitioners
* Access to individual results available as part of management overview facility, 'Super User'
* Records of staff training can be produced for internal use and external audits
* Cost-effective – no additional charge for CISI members
* Available to non-members

Benefits to individuals:
* Comprehensive selection of topics across sectors
* Modules are regularly reviewed and updated by industry experts
* New topics added regularly
* Free for members
* Successfully passed modules are recorded in your CPD log as active learning
* Counts as structured learning for RDR purposes
* On completion of a module, a certificate can be printed out for your own records

The full suite of Professional Refresher modules is free to CISI members, or £250 for non-members. Modules are also available individually. To view a full list of Professional Refresher modules visit:

cisi.org/refresher

If you or your firm would like to find out more, contact our Client Relationship Management team:

+ 44 20 7645 0670
crm@cisi.org

For more information on our elearning products, contact our Customer Support Centre on +44 20 7645 0777, or visit our website at cisi.org/refresher

er

Professional Refresher

Top 5

SCORM COMPLIANT

Integrity & Ethics
- High-Level View
- Ethical Behaviour
- An Ethical Approach
- Compliance vs Ethics

Anti-Money Laundering
- Introduction to Money Laundering
- UK Legislation and Regulation
- Money Laundering Regulations 2017
- Proceeds of Crime Act 2002
- Terrorist Financing
- Suspicious Activity Reporting
- Money Laundering Reporting Officer
- Sanctions

General Data Protection Regulation (GDPR)
- Understanding the Terminology
- The Six Data Protection Principles
- Data Subject Rights
- Technical and Organisational Measures

Information Security and Data Protection
- Cyber-Security
- The Regulators

UK Bribery Act
- Background to the Act
- The Offences
- What the Offences Cover
- When Has an Offence Been Committed?
- The Defences Against Charges of Bribery
- The Penalties

Latest

Cryptocurrencies
- Bitcoin
- Altcoins
- Central Bank Digital Currency and Cryptofiat
- Trading Cryptocurrencies
- The Impact of Cryptocurrencies

Change Management
- Types of Change
- Change Theories
- The Complexities of Change
- Leading Change
- Key Skills and Competencies

Regulatory Update
- General Regulatory Changes
- Sector Changes

Common Reporting Standard (CRS)
- What is the CRS?
- Implementation and Compliance
- Practical Issues
- The Global Perspective

Cross-Border Investment Services
- The UK System
- Overseas Regulation
- Applicability
- Face-to-Face Meetings
- Distance Communications
- Brexit Implications
- Gifts and Entertainment
- Tax Evasion, Money Laundering, and Terrorist Financing

Operations

Best Execution
- What Is Best Execution?
- Achieving Best Execution
- Order Execution Policies
- Information to Clients & Client Consent
- Monitoring, the Rules, and Instructions
- Best Execution for Specific Types of Firms

Approved Persons Regime
- The Basis of the Regime
- Fitness and Propriety
- The Controlled Functions
- Principles for Approved Persons
- The Code of Practice for Approved Persons

Corporate Actions
- Corporate Structure and Finance
- Life Cycle of an Event
- Mandatory Events
- Voluntary Events

Wealth

Client Assets and Client Money
- Protecting Client Assets and Client Money
- Segregation and Holding
- Due Diligence of Custodians and Banks
- Reconciliations
- Records and Accounts
- CASS Oversight

Investment Principles and Risk
- Diversification
- Factfind and Risk Profiling
- Investment Management
- Modern Portfolio Theory and Investing Styles
- Direct and Indirect Investments
- Socially Responsible Investment
- Collective Investments
- Investment Trusts
- Dealing in Debt Securities and Equities

Banking Standards
- Introduction and Background
- Strengthening Individual Accountability
- Reforming Corporate Governance
- Securing Better Outcomes for Consumers
- Enhancing Financial Stability

Suitability of Client Investments
- Assessing Suitability
- Risk Profiling
- Establishing Risk Appetite
- Obtaining Customer Information
- Suitable Questions and Answers
- Making Suitable Investment Selections
- Guidance, Reports and Record Keeping

International

Foreign Account Tax Compliance Act (FATCA)
- Foreign Financial Institutions
- Due Diligence Requirements
- Reporting
- Compliance

MiFID II
- The Organisations Covered by MiFID II
- The Products Subject to MiFID II
- The Origins of MiFID II
- The Impact of MiFID II
- The Products Covered by MiFID II
- Cross-Border Business Under MiFID II

UCITS
- The Original UCITS Directive
- UCITS III
- UCITS IV
- Non-UCITS Funds
- Latest Developments

cisi.org/refresher

Feedback to the CISI

Have you found this workbook to be a valuable aid to your studies? We would like your views, so please email us at learningresources@cisi.org with any thoughts, ideas or comments.

Accredited Training Partners

Support for exam students studying for the Chartered Institute for Securities & Investment (CISI) qualifications is provided by several Accredited Training Partners (ATPs), including Fitch Learning and BPP. The CISI's ATPs offer a range of face-to-face training courses, distance learning programmes, their own learning resources and study packs which have been accredited by the CISI. The CISI works in close collaboration with its ATPs to ensure they are kept informed of changes to CISI exams so they can build them into their own courses and study packs.

CISI Workbook Specialists Wanted

Workbook Authors

Experienced freelance authors with finance experience, and who have published work in their area of specialism, are sought. Responsibilities include:

- Updating workbooks in line with new syllabuses and any industry developments
- Ensuring that the syllabus is fully covered

Workbook Reviewers

Individuals with a high-level knowledge of the subject area are sought. Responsibilities include:

- Highlighting any inconsistencies against the syllabus
- Assessing the author's interpretation of the workbook

Workbook Technical Reviewers

Technical reviewers to provide a detailed review of the workbook and bring the review comments to the panel. Responsibilities include:

- Cross-checking the workbook against the syllabus
- Ensuring sufficient coverage of each learning objective

Workbook Proofreaders

Proofreaders are needed to proof workbooks both grammatically and also in terms of the format and layout. Responsibilities include:

- Checking for spelling and grammar mistakes
- Checking for formatting inconsistencies

If you are interested in becoming a CISI external specialist call:
+44 20 7645 0609

or email:
externalspecialists@cisi.org

For bookings, orders, membership and general enquiries please contact our Customer Support Centre on +44 20 7645 0777, or visit our website at cisi.org